11291480

THE
WANDERING
JEW

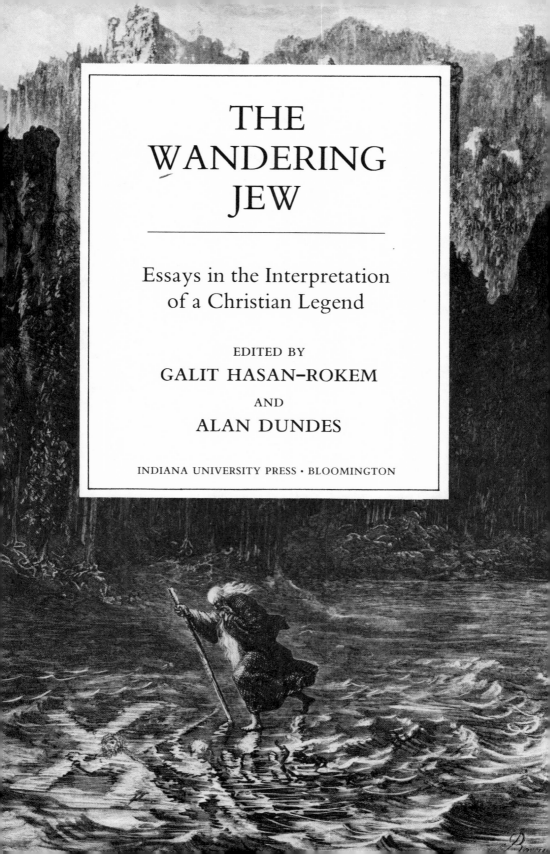

THE WANDERING JEW

Essays in the Interpretation of a Christian Legend

EDITED BY

GALIT HASAN-ROKEM

AND

ALAN DUNDES

INDIANA UNIVERSITY PRESS · BLOOMINGTON

*This volume is dedicated to all the Jews
whom prejudice and intolerance
have forced to wander.*

Library of Congress Cataloging in Publication Data
Main entry under title:
The Wandering Jew.
Bibliography: p.
1. Wandering Jew—Addresses, essays, lectures.
I. Hasan-Rokem, Galit. II. Dundes, Alan.
PN687.W3W36 1985   809'.93351   84-48248
ISBN 0-253-36340-3
1   2   3   4   5   89   88   87   86

CONTENTS

INTRODUCTION

Few traditional stories have appealed to a wider audience of scholars and writers than the legend of the Wandering Jew. One reason for its popularity is almost certainly its pivotal reflection of Jewish-Christian relationships. Strange as it may seem, the well-known saga of the Wandering Jew is not common in Jewish oral tradition. In fact, it is virtually nonexistent. In view of the generally negative depiction of the Jew in the legend, cursed by Jesus himself for a slight (typically the Jew's unwillingness to allow a weary cross-bearing Jesus a moment's temporary respite) to wander the earth forever or until the Second Coming, one can understand why this story would have little appeal for Jews. By the same token, the confrontation of Judaism with the founder of Christianity could account in part for the legend's continued attraction for European Catholics and Protestants.

The temporal frame of the legend spans the period between two major foci in Christianity, the Crucifixion and the Second Coming. It is supposed that with the fulfillment of the promise of the Second Coming Jews will voluntarily embrace the Christian faith. It is as if the Christians yearn for this ultimate validation of their creed. If older Judaism yields to younger Christianity, then we have a veritable metamorphosis of the classic Indo-European and Semitic hero pattern (in which the new son-hero replaces the old father-king).

The plight of the Wandering Jew has formed the basis for innumerable literary plots in both prose and poetry. A host of dramas as well have been inspired by the legend. In some instances, it is only the character or figure of the Jew which is borrowed for literary purposes, without the full-fledged legend plot. This volume is less concerned with the many literary manifestations than with the folkloristic or oral renderings of the story, along with the remarkable range of interpretations which have been proposed over the past century.

The relationship of the Wandering Jew to literature is not more interesting than the relationship of the legend to history. Some regard the events described in the legend as fact; others deem it pure fancy. Literal/historical approaches are in marked contrast to symbolic/psychological ones. Is the Wandering Jew a reflection of reality or of fantasy?

There has traditionally been an air of mystery surrounding the figure of the Wandering Jew. Where does he come from? Where is he going? Is he a villain or is he a victim? The Wandering Jew evokes both sympathy and scorn. Is eternal life a blessing or a curse? Is he a positive symbol of the survival of an ancient people or is he the inevitable scapegoat who shares in the blame for the crucifixion? It is these kinds of fascinating questions which have intrigued scholars from a variety of academic disciplines. The enigmatic character of the Wandering Jew has stimulated endless speculations about the possible meanings of the story.

In selecting essays from the voluminous writings devoted to the Wandering Jew, we have tried to choose a wide but representative sampling of diverse approaches and perspectives. We begin with a lucid survey of the legend and its origins by a Danish scholar, R. Edelmann (1968). Then we follow with an inquiry by König (1907) into the generic nature of the story, a detailed review by Schaffer (1920) of the editions of the central 1602 German chapbook version of the story, and a short onomastic note by Daube (1955) on the possible source of the name Ahasver. A most unusual essay by Bagatti (1949) recounts with some embarrassment the frequent occurrence of the legend in pilgrim's reports of their travels to the Holy Land.

Although our intent is not to present unanalyzed versions of the story, the charming text recorded in the valley of Aosta in northern Italy by Jaccod (1919) deserves a wider audience if only for its documentation of the role of the legend embedded in the ritual context of a village Easter celebration. Then follows a series of essays treating the Wandering Jew as he appears in a variety of places: France (Champfleury, 1869), England (Anderson, 1947), the United States (Glanz, 1961), Finland (Hasan-Rokem, 1982), and Sweden (af Klintberg, 1968). Although the Wandering Jew occurs in other locations, these accounts should serve to demonstrate the general nature of the tradition.

Questions about the meaning or significance of the legend of the Wandering Jew have been raised in a number of provocative interpretative essays. The interpretations proposed are based on different theoretical premises. At the end of the nineteenth century, a form of comparative mythology flourished which depended heavily upon philological and etymological arguments. Often mythological heroes and events were reduced to celestial or meteorological phenomena, e.g., astral, lunar, or solar mythology. These intellectual influences are apparent in Karl Blind's comparison (1880) of the Wandering Jew with the Wild Huntsman.

Some of the more imaginative and original interpretations of the Wandering Jew tend to be those based on a specific psychological theory. One of the earliest, proposed by Meige (1893), claimed to be supported by actual observational data obtained at the famed Charcot clinic (which Freud later visited). A recognizably Freudian analysis of the legend was offered many years later by Isaac-Edersheim (1941). A Jungian interpretation by Hurwitz (1975) completes the selection of psychological readings of the legend.

The volume concludes with philosophical and political considerations of the Wandering Jew and its impact on European cultural history. The essay by Leschnitzer (1971) treats the image through time, up until the nineteenth century, while the ingenious final discussion by Maccoby (1982) reveals the contemporary relevance of the legend for twentieth-century ideology. Five of the essays (Jaccod, Champfleury, Meige, Isaac-Edersheim, and Hurwitz) were translated from French and German and one (Hasan-Rokem) from Hebrew especially for this volume. Finally, a short selected bibliography is appended to direct the interested reader to additional readings on the subject.

AHASUERUS,
THE WANDERING JEW
ORIGIN AND BACKGROUND

R. Edelmann

Those unfamiliar with the Wandering Jew may be surprised to learn that there are literally hundreds of books and articles devoted to the subject. To be sure, the vast majority consist merely of literary renderings of the legend. One of the earliest attempts at a comprehensive study of the legend taking account of the huge number of bibliographical sources available was by Leonhard Neubaur. The first edition of his Die Sage vom ewigen Juden *appeared in 1884. In 1893, he published a useful bibliography: "Bibliographie der Sage vom ewigen Juden,"* Zentralblatt für Bibliothekswesen, *10 (1893): 249–67, 297–316. This was later followed by additional sources in "Zur Bibliographie der Sage vom ewigen Juden,"* Zentralblatt für Bibliothekswesen, *28 (1911): 495–509. Among his numerous essays, one might single out "Zur Geschichte der Sage vom ewigen Juden,"* Zeitschrift des Vereins für Volkskunde, *22 (1912): 33–54. All serious subsequent scholarship has had to refer to Neubaur's painstaking bibliographical surveys.*

Other major treatments of the legend include Gaston Paris, "Le Juif errant," in Légendes du Moyen Age *(Paris, 1903), pp. 149–221; Alice M. Killen, "L'Évolution de la légende du Juif errant,"* Revue de Littérature Comparée, *5 (1925): 5–36; Werner Zirus,* Der ewige Jude in der Dichtung, *Palaestra*

162 (Leipzig, 1928) and Ahasverus, Der ewige Jude *(Berlin, 1930); Josef J.* Gielen, De wandelende Jood in volkskunde en letterkunde *(Amsterdam, 1931);* George K. Anderson, The Legend of the Wandering Jew *(Providence, 1965); and Edgar* Knecht, Le Mythe du Juif errant *(Grenoble, 1977). Anderson's book, the most exhaustive treatment of the legend, its sources, and its appearance in literature, also includes a valuable appendix, "Notes on the Study of the Legend" (pp. 399–413), which gives a chronological summary of the abundant scholarship. Knecht has continued the arduous task of compiling the ever-increasing bibliography. His three-part essay is especially useful insofar as he provides analytic annotations. See "Le Mythe du Juif errant: Esquisse de bibliographie raisonée (1600–1844),"* Romantisme, *8 (1974): 103–16, and its sequel portions in* Romantisme, *12 (1976): 95–102; and* Romantisme, *16 (1977): 101–15.*

In this first essay, Danish scholar R. Edelmann outlines many of the central issues surrounding the legend. Of Christian origin, its dissemination was greatly stimulated by a 1602 German chapbook, whose publication, Edelmann suggests, may be intimately connected with Luther's anti-Semitic diatribes. The legend as related in the chapbook helped to create an image of the Jewish people as a whole. Edelmann tends towards a literal/historical reading of the legend when he mentions actual Jews who wandered and the possibility that these wanderers caused curiosity on the part of Christians, who knew little about Jewish culture. Most of these themes will be discussed at greater length in other essays in this volume. For further consideration of the legend by Edelmann, see his "Ahasverus, Den evige Jøde: Sagnets Oprindelse og Baggrund," Fund og Forskning I Det Kongelige Biblioteks Samlinger, *12 (1965): 42–46.*

When Josef J. Gielen, in 1931, published his comprehensive book on *De wandelende Jood in volkskunde en letterkunde* (The Wandering Jew in folklore and literature) he could list 1,521 items in

Reprinted from *Papers of the Fourth World Congress of Jewish Studies*, Vol. II (Jerusalem: World Union of Jewish Studies, 1968), pp. 111–14.

his bibliography of this subject. The Royal Library of Copenhagen in 1956 acquired Gielen's private copy of the book, where
the author himself had added another 59 items. Since Gielen died
some 10 years ago a great number of further items, novels, poems
and essays have been written, and the present lecturer knows of
scholars now working with the subject in addition to those
hundreds of essays that have appeared already. It is a theme with
a strong and peculiar attraction for Jew and non-Jew alike. However, the object of my lecture here is not to go into an investigation of the psychological and spiritual implications of the
encounter between the Jew and his Christian environment in the
Diaspora, of which our subject is a product, nor will I discuss
theological subtleties in connection with the theme. I find that too
much credit has already been given in this respect to the anonymous author of the pamphlet which is the base and starting point
of the whole discussion, and to those who used the pamphlet
according to the intentions of its author. Much has been written
and much confusion has been brought into the treatment of the
subject. Whether I have succeeded in avoiding bringing more confusion into the theme or not I must leave to you, ladies and gentlemen, to decide.

The figure of the Wandering Jew, which has preoccupied the
Western world to such a degree for more than 350 years in literature as well as in pictorial art, in music and in the popular imagination, is, after all, a concern of Christians. He is a Christian
invention. Ahasuerus, the Wandering Jew, is a Jew by postulate
only, not even by name. It is this postulate that puts him into the
sphere of Jewish interest, because it puts the focus upon the Jew.
This has been the case since the first edition of the pamphlet was
issued in 1602 with the title: *Kurtze Beschreibung und Erzehlung von
einem Juden mit Namen Ahasuerus*. The appearance of this pamphlet
was a turning point in the old traditions that had been known
throughout the Middle Ages.

Another interesting feature of the mediaeval Christian traditions
which is of importance for our investigation is the fact that the
main trait of the principal character was his *longevity* and *not* his
wandering, as in the pamphlet of 1602. His wanderings appeared
as a factor of secondary importance in one or two of the confused

versions of the two main traditions, before they became the chief
trait of the principal character in the pamphlet of 1602.

One of these two traditions goes back to the *NT*, John xxi: 22–
23, where Jesus says to Peter about John: ' "If I will that he tarry
till I come, what is that to thee? . . ." Then went this saying
abroad among the brethren, that that disciple should not die . . .'

The other tradition likewise has its source in the *NT*, John xviii:
22, where the text relates that one of the High Priest's officers
struck Jesus with the palm of his hand. An early tradition identified this officer with the servant of the High Priest, called Malchus
and mentioned in John xviii: 10.

These two traditions can be distinguished from one another.
But mostly they appear in a version that displays a mixture of
both with some additional traits. In neither of them does the Jewish factor come into the foreground, as already mentioned.

Of the two best known versions of the mediaeval traditions one
is that about a certain Johannes (John) Buttadæus, apparently orig-
inating in Italy. This is, in my opinion, the later of the two.

The other version is the legend the principal character of which
is called Cartaphilus. This legend seems to be a popular mixture
of Jesus' saying about an eternal life for a much loved disciple on
the one hand and the Malchus episode on the other. In the first
case eternal life means a gift of mercy and bliss, an idea that can
be found in Jewish sources of the time. (It would take us too far
afield to go into this now.) In the case of Malchus, on the other
hand, longevity is meant to be an eternal *punishment*, a punishment
not after death, but still in this life. This, now, is a Christian
innovation. The offender against Jesus is *punished* by longevity or
eternal life; he is denied salvation. And his condemnation was
attributed to Jesus himself.

The legend we are now going to deal with seems to have its
origin in the Christian Orient. In two different sources Armenia
is mentioned. It appears in Europe for the first time in a Latin
chronicle. The unknown author tells about some pilgrims who in
1223 arrived in Ferraria in southern Italy in the same year when
the Emperor Frederic II had held a meeting there, and these pilgrims related that in Armenia they saw a certain Jew who had
witnessed the sufferings of Jesus and had driven him on with the

words: "Go on, you seducer, that you may receive what you merit." Jesus had answered him: "I will go, but you shall wait till I will come again." According to this version, which is one of the two expressly mentioning the principal character as a Jew, he lives permanently in Armenia, rejuvenating himself every hundred years. This version, however, was not known in Europe before it was published in a learned publication in 1888 and then was read only by a few scholars.

Most important, however, for the history of the pamphlet about the Wandering Jew is the version known from the story told by the monk Roger of Wendover in St. Albans near London in his book *Flores historiorum* and a little later repeated by his younger fellow monk in St. Albans, Matthew of Paris. According to this version, Pontius Pilate's doorkeeper Cartaphilus struck Jesus on the neck when he was on his way from Pilate's palace to Golgotha, and he said to him: "Go, Jesus, why do you tarry?"—whereupon Jesus said to him: "I will go, but you shall wait until I will come again." Since then Cartaphilus can not die. He soon was aware of what he had done and became a repenting Christian, having been baptized by the same Ananias who had also baptized Paul. He was now living a peaceful life somewhere in Armenia under the name of Joseph. All this was related by the Armenian archbishop when he visited the monastery of St. Albans in 1228, and was written down by Roger of Wendover. Matthew of Paris a few years later incorporated this story into his own chronicle. It was printed, in its *Latin* origin, for the first time in 1571 in London, and again in 1586 in Zurich. It seems to have had a wide circulation within learned circles.

This now brings us to the pamphlet about Ahasuerus, the Wandering Jew. In 1602 a small pamphlet of 8 pages was printed *in German*, with the title: *Kurtze Beschreibung und Erzehlung von einem Juden mit Namen Ahasuerus, etc.* Within this single year of 1602 alone, 20 different editions of the pamphlet appeared (with only small variants among them), all of them in Germany. We will soon come back to this striking fact.

It is impossible to establish where most of the editions were printed and by whom. The indications given on the title pages, such as Christof Creuzer in Leyden or Wolfgang Suchnach in

Bautzen, can easily be recognized as forgeries. For certain reasons, however, we can take for granted that of the earliest prints only the statements giving Nicolaus Wegener in Schlesvig, and the heirs of Jacob Roth in Danzig, respectively, are reliable.

The author of the pamphlet is unknown. The name mentioned as the author, Chrysostomus Dudulaeus Westphalus, is a pseudonym the true identity of which has not been discovered. In the pamphlet he mentions as his informant nobody less than Paul von Eitzen, who as a young man had been studying with Martin Luther in Wittenberg and had become bishop in Schlesvig and won a reputation as a learned man. He had died four years before the appearance of the pamphlet, in 1598, and his memory must still have been alive at that time.

In the pamphlet the pseudonymous author relates that Paul von Eitzen had told him that, when he was a student and happened to be on holiday with his parents in Hamburg in 1542, on the first Sunday he attended the service in the church. During the sermon he perceived a man of very strange appearance. This man proved to be born in Jerusalem, was called Ahasuerus and was a shoemaker by profession. He was a contemporary of Jesus and had been present when Jesus was taken to be executed. On his way to Golgotha Jesus had leaned against his house, but he had driven him away, whereupon Jesus said to him: "I will stay and rest, but you shall go." Since then Ahasuerus had had to give up his home and his family and roam the world.

It seems to be clear that we have here a new version of the Cartaphilus legend. In both these versions the principal character struck Jesus when he was on his way from Pilate's palace to Golgotha, and in both versions he was condemned by Jesus himself to longevity. But there are important differences. The Roman heathen Cartaphilus has in the pamphlet become the Jew Ahasuerus. That the author of the pamphlet chose just this name for the Jew does not, in my opinion, mean anything more than so many other more or less artificial and strange sounding names found in the literature of the time. The author found it in one of the many biblical Esther plays performed in churches and schools. (32 German Esther plays are known of from the 70-year period from 1530 till 1601.) The fact that the two names, Cartaphilus and Ahasuerus, have the same rhythm and the same vowels may also have had some influence upon his choice.

But the most important innovation is the fact that, whereas Cartaphilus is doomed to longevity only ("*I am going*, but *you shall wait* till I will come"), and having been baptized lives a tranquil and peaceful life in one place, somewhere in the Orient, far away, unseen, the Jew is punished with eternal *wandering* ("*I will stay* and rest, but *you shall go*"). Although, as is presumed, he repents, there is no question of baptism in connection with him. He *has* to remain a Jew under the doom, eternally. He has become the symbol of the Jew κατ᾽ ἐξοχήν within the frame of the christological concept of life. His continued life serves, as is expressly stated in the pamphlet, as a testimony of Jesus' sufferings and death and as *a warning* for the godless people and the unbelievers, which means that his fate is a punishment. The Jew carries the collective guilt upon his shoulders and consequently also the collective punishment through all ages and all countries.

I think that here we can find the reason why this pamphlet appeared just then and on the authority of a person pointing back to Luther himself. It was the time when princes and worldly authorities in the recently reformed country worked out their policy in worldly matters in accordance with what Luther had taught. Paul von Eitzen had studied with Luther just during the period when he was at the peak of his anti-Semitic stage (in 1542 von Eitzen was on holiday in Hamburg, in 1543 Luther's poisonous book, *Concerning the Jews and their lies*, appeared), and this Paul von Eitzen was an important authority in theological questions.

The great number of editions of the pamphlet based on the authority of such a man, appearing within one single year at different places, now looks like a studied, concentrated action with the purpose of propagating the lore voiced in the pamphlet. This would also account for the author's hiding behind a pseudonym and the use of bogus names for the printers.

There must also have been a special, concrete occasion which made the author write his pamphlet. This occasion we may elaborate by the following consideration.

In the whole of northern Germany there were practically no Jews living at the time. Only in Hamburg had some Marrano families settled down during the second half of the 16th century, and after some time they had openly assumed Judaism, to the consternation of the clergy. There were also Jews living in Danzig with the connivance, but without the permission, of the authorities. And it is just in these two places that the Wandering Jew had been seen, the Jew who had been doomed, allegedly by Jesus himself, to be deprived of a permanent dwelling, and whom it therefore was a good Christian deed to chase away. In this connection we are reminded of the fact that in 1603, that is to say within one year after the appearance of the pamphlet, citizens of Hamburg, backed by the clergy, demanded that the Senate of the city banish the Jews living there. The Sephardim, however, were too much of an asset for Hamburg because of their international connections, and in 1612 they were permitted to stay. From Danzig, however, the Jews were expelled a few years later, in 1616, after they had been prohibited from meeting for religious exercises by an edict of the council in 1605.

The pamphlet dealt with here is usually called a chapbook, whereas, as we have seen, it was written by its author for a certain purpose. But it became a chapbook. Within a few decades after its first appearance in 1602, it had spread all over Europe, and everywhere the theme was taken up and transformed in accordance with local conceptions and spiritual conditions. I want to draw your attention to the fact that, though the legend had been known in one version or the other during the Middle Ages, it did not have the character of a popular legend circulating among the illiterate common people, as became the case with the pamphlet from 1602. We find the various versions in a few Latin sources, only *one* in Italian. It is the *German* pamphlet which makes the legend about the Wandering Jew common property for the broad masses all over Europe and a source of further development within European folklore. And like the Faustus legend and others, it also soon became one of the most oft-treated motives of European art and literature. It is, however, not my intention here to follow the fate of the motif and the paths of its subsequent developments since 1602.

There is one question left that has not been properly answered yet, namely: what was the reason for the astonishing rapidity with which the folk motif of the Wandering Jew spread over Europe and became the common property of the broad masses? Several reasons can be mentioned. But I here beg to draw your attention, ladies and gentlemen, to one fact which might give at least a partial answer to the question.

The Ahasuerus pamphlet was primarily a cunningly camou-flaged statement of the new theology about its attitude towards the Jew and his position in the world, an attitude which in itself was not new but had only to be restated. The statement was brought about by a certain situation. The principal character of the pamphlet, therefore, must be understood as a symbol for the Jewish people as a whole, an abstraction. The broad masses, how-ever, the illiterates, do not think in abstractions. They must have something concrete to fix their imagination on. In the pamphlet they were presented with a figure which they could recognize as a real person, whom they had met and noticed, or they had heard others mention him, or he had lived in the memory of the com-mon people through generations and been spoken about. In no case, however, could they explain the nature of this person, and he was, therefore, shrouded in great mystery in the imagination of the people. Here in the Ahasuerus pamphlet they found an explanation of this figure, one they were ready to accept and to develop further.

What I am thinking of is the Ba'al-Teshuva, the Galut wanderer as he is known in Judaism throughout the ages, starting with Philon and ending with Agnon's writings. This phenomenon was very wide-spread especially during the Middle Ages, but it also seems to have been practiced throughout the centuries up till our own time. There are many indications of this.

Such a wandering, penitent Jew in a European country must have made a deep impression upon the people through his whole appearance. He could not avoid attracting attention in the small places of those days with their few and bad communications. He kept people's imaginations occupied for a long time after he had disappeared, and travellers would bring stories about him to eager listeners in other places. They were not able to form an idea for themselves about such a wanderer and his purpose; they did not know much about the life and doings of the Jews. When, therefore, the Ahasuerus pamphlet appeared with its mythical Jewish figure as an illustration of the place allotted to the Jew by the theology within the Christological world system, the fancy of the people combined this abstract figure with the concrete Ba'al-Teshuva, the pious Jewish Galut wanderer, and the Wandering Jew of the folk literature was clothed in the attire of a real person.

THE WANDERING JEW
LEGEND OR MYTH?

Eduard König

One question which folklorists normally raise with respect to a folk narrative is to what genre does it belong? For the folklorist, a myth is a sacred narrative explaining how the world and man came to be in their present form. To the extent that the story of the Wandering Jew contributes to the formation of Christian notions of the position of the Jew in the world, one might argue that it has a mythical quality. However, in the strict sense of the myth genre, the Wandering Jew is not a myth. A folktale, unlike myth and legend, is a story not believed to be literally true. No one believes that Cinderella and Little Red Riding Hood were historical figures. Since the Wandering Jew is often reported as having been observed in a particular location, his story would not appear to be classifiable as a folktale. However, for reasons which are not altogether clear, the story has been assigned a tale type number (777) in the standard catalog: Antti Aarne and Stith Thompson, The Types of the Folktale: A Classification and Bibliography *(Helsinki, 1961). This would suggest that the plot was fictional rather than historical. A legend is a story told as true and set in the real post-creation world.*

In the following essay by Eduard König, which is essentially a translation of his short book Ahasver, 'der ewige Jude' *(Gutersloh, 1907), the genre issue is raised. For König, legends stem from actual events while myths derive from an impulse to represent an idea in concrete form. However, König's decision to clas-*

sify the story as a legend is not simply a matter of clarifying
generic distinctions. Rather, he has an anti-Semitic axe to grind.
If the Wandering Jew is legend, according to König, it is based on
historical reality. In other words, there are wandering Jews who
are cursed for their alleged role in Christ's Crucifixion. König
also seeks to identify a so-called Jewish spirit in literary renderings
of the Ahasverus theme, which confirms for him the negative
nature of Jews.

König felt strongly enough about the genre issue to criticize
Neubaur for misrepresenting his views on the subject. See König,
"*Zur Idee von Ahasver, dem ewigen Juden,*" Zeitschrift des
Vereins für Volkskunde, *22 (1912): 300–301; and Neubaur's*
response, "*Noch einmal die Sage von Ahasver,*" *ibid., pp. 411–*
12. For more of König's views of the genre question, see also his
shorter German version of the present essay, "*Sage und Mythus*
in bezug auf den 'ewigen Juden', " Nord und Süd, *141 (1912):*
217–21.

At the beginning of the seventeenth century a book appeared
with the following title: "A brief description and tale of a Jew by
name *Ahasuerus*, who was present in person at the Crucifixion of
Christ, who moreover shouted with the rest 'Crucify Him! Crucify Him!' and instead of desiring His acquittal, desired that of
Barabbas, the murderer; but after the Crucifixion was never able
to return to Jerusalem, also never saw his wife and children again,
has remained alive ever since, and came to Hamburg a few years
ago, etc."[1]
The contents of the book, which bears the date 1602, may be
briefly stated thus:

> Paul von Eitzen, Doctor in the Holy Scriptures, and Bishop of
> Schleswig, who is respected by all, and considered to be a teller
> of the truth, told this to me and to other students very often:
> Once, when during my student days in the winter of 1542, I
> went to visit my parents at Hamburg, I saw the next Sunday in
> church during the sermon, a very tall man standing opposite the

Reprinted from *Nineteenth Century*, 61 (1907): 969–79.

pulpit; he was barefoot, and his hair hung down over his shoulders. The man listened to the sermon with such attention that he stood there perfectly still and stiff, but every time the name Jesus Christ was mentioned, he bowed, beat his breast, and gave a deep sigh. In conversations which I had with the man later, he informed me that he had been in Jerusalem at the time of Christ, had helped towards His condemnation, and on His last sorrowful journey had repulsed Him from his house with rough words. Thereupon Jesus had looked hard at him, and said: "I shall stand here and rest, but you shall wander forth and be everlastingly restless." Then he saw Jesus die on the Cross, but could not possibly return to his people in the town of Jerusalem; ever since he had been a wanderer on the face of the earth, and longed for death. The same man was also seen in the town of Danzig shortly before 1602.

Is this to be regarded as a legend or a myth? These two terms have of late been greatly confused. Originally they were quite distinct. A legend denotes a tale connected with an actual event or locality, concerning something of importance which had a real existence. It easily becomes amplified, and possibly later embodies an idea, a tendency, or a warning. The myth, on the contrary, is a tale in which at its very outset an idea is illustrated or personified. It would be well if this distinction was always adhered to, for the question is whether the tale about Ahasuerus was connected with an actual event, or arose from probably an unconscious impulse to give concrete form to an idea.

It is not so easy to answer this question. If the tale is considered a legend, the narrative is supposed to have been made up from other narratives earlier in circulation.

Thus, Roger of Wendover (died 1237), a monk of the English abbey of St. Albans, relates the following in his chronicle, under the year 1228:

In this year a certain Archbishop of Armenia Major came on a pilgrimage to England, to see the relics of the saints and visit the sacred places in this kingdom, as he had done in others; he also produced letters of recommendation from his Holiness the Pope to the religious men and prelates of the churches, in which they were enjoined to receive and entertain him with due reverence and honour. On his arrival he went to St. Albans, where he was received with all respect by the abbot and monks; at this place, being fatigued with his journey, he remained some days to rest himself and his followers, and a conversation was commenced between him and the inhabitants of the convent by means of their interpreters, during which he made many inquiries concerning the religion and religious observances of this country, and related many strange things concerning eastern countries. In the course of conversation he was asked whether he had ever seen or heard anything of Joseph, a man of whom there was much talk in the world, who, when our Lord suffered, was present and spoke to Him, and who is still alive in evidence of the Christian faith; in reply to which a knight in his retinue, who was his interpreter, replied, speaking in French, "My Lord well knows that man, and a little before he took his journey to the western countries, the said Joseph ate at the table of my lord the Archbishop in Armenia, and he had often seen and held converse with him." He was then asked about what had passed between Christ and the same Joseph, to which he replied, "At the time of the suffering of Jesus Christ, he was seized by the Jews and led into the hall of judgment, before Pilate the governor, that he might be judged by him on the accusation of the Jews; and Pilate finding no cause for adjudging him to death, said to them: 'Take him and judge him according to your law'; the shouts of the Jews, however, increasing, he, at their request, released unto them Barabbas, and delivered Jesus to them to be crucified. When, therefore, the Jews were dragging Jesus forth, and had reached the door, Cartaphilus, a porter of the hall in Pilate's service, as Jesus was going out of the door, impiously struck Him on the back with his hand, and said in mockery, 'Go quicker, Jesus, go quicker; why do you loiter?' And Jesus, looking back on him, with a severe countenance said to him, 'I am going, and you will wait till I return.' " And according as our Lord said, this Cartaphilus is still awaiting His return; at the time of our Lord's suffering he was thirty years old, and when he attains the age of a hundred years he always returns to the same age as he was when our Lord suffered. After Christ's death, when the Catholic faith gained ground, this Cartaphilus was baptised by Ananias (who also baptised the Apostle Paul), and was called Joseph. He often dwells in both divisions of Armenia and other eastern countries, passing his time amidst the bishops and other prelates of the church; he is a man of holy conversation and religious, a man of few words and circumspect in his behaviour, for he does not speak at all unless when questioned by the bishops and religious men; and then he tells of the events of old times, and of the events which occurred at the suffering and resurrection of our Lord, etc.

In L. Neubaur's excellent book, *Die Sage vom ewigen Juden* (Leipzig, 1884), p. 6, Cartaphilus is mentioned as "the prototype of the Wandering Jew." But the reader cannot fail to perceive the great differences between the two figures. The first part of the word Cartaphilus, according to Neubaur, resembles the Greek κάρτα "very," so that the name signifies "very much loved," and reminds one of John, the "disciple whom Jesus loved," of whom it was supposed that he will remain alive until the second advent of Christ. But the individual in the other story bore the name Ahasuerus. The one was a doorkeeper, the other a shoemaker.

Of course, the same person could easily combine the post of doorkeeper with the trade of a shoemaker. But the one is represented as a Christian who received the name of Joseph, while the other remained a Jew and was called Ahasuerus. Moreover, it is important to note that no credible testimony of the life of the legend about Cartaphilus-Joseph can be traced in the sixteenth century (Neubaur, p. 12). The narrative of Ahasuerus, printed in 1602, makes no reference to earlier statements. An edition printed at Danzig, however, has a statement on its title-page that the same Jew was named earlier by an Italian author, Johannes Buttadeus. The first part of that name was probably derived from the Italian *buttare*, "to thrust out," and therefore may signify a fighter against God, an aggressor of Christ. In the narrative of 1602, however, there is no mention of a blow given by Ahasuerus to Jesus. The identity of Cartaphilus and Ahasuerus was questioned by Lessing in a letter to his brother, and I am myself of opinion that the absolute independence which clothes the Ahasuerus figure of the 1602 narrative renders it scarcely possible to suppose that it was evolved from earlier fables.

Is, then, the 1602 narrative a myth?

The idea that the Jewish people were, soon after the Crucifixion (and, indeed, as a result of that event), driven from their homes to become wanderers on the face of the earth, may easily have been crystallised into a concrete tale. The significant words of the bearer of the cross to the women of Jerusalem, "Do not lament for Me; lament for yourselves and for your children," might easily be developed into a tale of the miserable fate of one native of Jerusalem, as the representative of the people of Jerusalem. We should then have before us the material husk of a truth equally concerned with the history of religion and of civilization.

If the tale is regarded as a myth, the name 'Ahasuerus' appears, however, at a first glance, to present an insurmountable obstacle. It is so rare that it is unlikely to have been invented. It occurs only twice in the ancient Hebrew Scriptures—as the name of a Median prince (Dan. ix. 1), and as the name of the king of Persia in whose reign the story of Esther takes place (Esther i. ff.). In many of the manuscripts of the Apocryphal supplements to the ancient Hebrew and primitive Christian literature the name is found only in the additions to the Book of Esther. Josephus does not mention the name Ahasuerus, nor does the *Jewish Encyclopædia* (completed by the publication of its twelfth volume in December [1906]) mention any other bearer of that name. In the Greek translation of the ancient Hebrew Scriptures the name is written *Assueros*, and in the Latin version, *Assuerus*.[2]

But the name Ahasuerus, which, at a first glance, seems to offer an obstacle to the mythical significance of the Ahasuerus narrative, affords, on the contrary, a distinct support to that solution. For in reflecting over the question whence in that narrative the name Ahasuerus exactly occurs—a question as yet scarcely propounded—I am inclined to the hypothesis that it arose from the Purim Festival of the Jews. At that festival, especially in earlier times, the dramatic reading aloud of the Book of Esther, and the interruptions and shouts of the assembly, gave an opportunity of cursing all who were of different faith—Persians, Mohammedans, and especially Christians. This is clearly stated in the *Encyclopædia Biblica* (1899–1903), edited by T. K. Cheyne and A. S. Black, col. 3977. During the celebration of the Purim Festival—at least in the seventeenth century—an "Ahasuerus play" was performed which bore a very hostile character. This is proved by the fact that in 1708 its performance was forbidden at Frankfurt a/M. The president of the Frankfurt Jewish community had all the printed copies burnt.[3] It is not unlikely that, in view of this abuse hurled every spring through words and mimicry at the religious standpoint of the Christians, the idea of composing a counterpiece should have suggested itself to one of them. The author might even have created an Ahasuerus who was deeply repentant for his former mocking attitude towards Christ, the Man of Sorrows.

The explanation is rendered plausible by other considerations, but it also has some almost insurmountable difficulties. When an author has formed a plan of this kind, coloured by a strong motive, he generally works it out with clearness, and thus the details employed in the 1602 narrative would have been distinctly comprehensible. The words "Everyone is free to have his own opinion about this man," which are added to the 1602 narrative, can hardly point to the purely invented character of the figure of Ahasuerus; that explanation of the words is contradicted by the continuation: "The works of God are wonderful." Moreover, the pseudonymity of the author which most of the 1602 editions present— namely, the so far unexplained designation, Chrysostomus Dudulæus Westphalus—proves that the tale is not a mere fiction. On the contrary, many passages in the tale correspond with the possibility of the hypothesis that the author wrote in good faith.

I think, however, that I can show such a possibility. A representative, like Ahasuerus, of the people of Israel might occasionally present himself. That many a self-judging soul of the people of Israel should adopt his point of view is by no means incredible. Some quiet thinker among the scattered tribes of Israel might have taken the conduct of the Jews towards Jesus so deeply to heart that at the thought he beat his breast and sighed for a way of reconciling the attitude of his nation with the greatest Son of Israel. A man of that temperament, belonging to the homeless, scattered nation of Israel, who wandered through generations from place to place, might actually feel himself to be the representative of his nation; he might throw himself back into the past so eagerly that he might consider and speak of their former relations to Jesus, the bearer of the cross, and the homelessness which was the immediate consequence, as if they were his own personal conduct and personal fate. The personification of the people of Israel, and the strong bond that unites the later generations of Israel with the earlier, is constantly seen in the liveliest colours in the religious literature of the nation. How often is the nation mentioned as the slave of the Lord (Isaiah xli. 8), and in Psalm xliv. 14, 16, Israel says: "Thou makest us a by-word among our neighbours," and again: "All the day long is my dishonour before me."

In any case, it is quite possible that the conscience of Israel, which in many a silent soul regretted the conduct of the nation towards Jesus, had here and there manifested itself in a wanderer, at least in gesture and attitude. His sighs may have rendered audible the undertone which perhaps vibrated in many a heart during the conventional cursing on the occasion of the Purim Festival. In the same way, in the major key of the loud-toned *Play of Ahasuerus*, a faint echo in the melancholy minor key may have been heard. Such an echo would easily have made itself heard in those times, when people were looking forward with anxiety to a change in the conditions of the world. At the end of the sixteenth century and during the transition of the seventeenth century, men firmly believed—a fact emphatically stated at the end of the 1602 book—that the Day of Judgment and the end of the world were at hand. With that particular time, according to the ancient Christian expectation, a turning-point in the fate of Israel was combined (Rom. xi. 25 ff.). Who can assert that in such times, and in some Israelitish hearts, it was impossible a powerful longing may not have awakened for deliverance from the burdensome oppression of Israel which had lasted through so many centuries? May not the desire have become implanted in the hearts of some that the long-lasting national misfortune might be removed if the jarring relations of Israel to Jesus underwent a change? Who can deny that the thought may have struck this or that wandering Jew that the contemporaries of Jesus had meted out to him too much cruelty and pitilessness?

This cannot be proved impossible. Thus the origin of the Ahasuerus figure of the 1602 book may be found in the history of civilisation, and becomes psychologically comprehensible. I am the more inclined to that view since the recently completed *Jewish Encyclopædia* gives no historical explanation of the figure. In the last volume (vol. xii, p. 462) the Wandering Jew is merely described as an "imaginary figure of a Jerusalem shoemaker," and the very questionable idea is put forward that the upholding of the existence of the Wandering Jew was eagerly favoured by the Reformation because he was regarded as an eyewitness of the death of Jesus Christ. But was fresh testimony to that fact necessary, and were not similar tales spread abroad, both before and after the Reformation, by other Christians?[4]

Having attempted to describe the historical source of the Ahasuerus figure, I will now turn to the second province in which the figure has played a part—the province of literature. Let us see what fate befell the Ahasuerus figure in its literary treatment, after it had gained a place in the history of ideas. But as I am less acquainted with the representations of the figure in English literature, I shall confine myself in this part of my survey to the main points of the direction followed.

Together with such research, it is of interest to inquire how the Jewish intellectual world stands in regard to the theme. It is self-evident that the genesis of the myth—if the above decision be admitted—can scarcely redound to the positive greatness of the Jews. But how has Jewish intellect regarded the subject when it entered into the consciousness of the civilised world?

In order to judge this point, let us look at the one-act play *Ahasver*, which the Dutch author Heijermans wrote in 1893. The setting is a Russian persecution of the Jews. The grandfather of the family in question has already fallen a victim to it. When the storm of persecution bursts forth afresh, the only son of the house turns Christian. The Cossacks inform the father. He hurls violent curses at his son, and, accompanied by his wife, takes to flight, while the son breaks down under the weight of the curses. Here, a Jew who sends his baptised son to hell, and betakes himself to homeless wandering, is termed a modern Ahasuerus. What strong partisanship is revealed in such a presentation! It can only be explained by the justifiable indignation at the violence of a Russian persecution of the Jews. But it cannot thereby be excused. The father who cursed his son because he turned Christian ought not to be called Ahasuerus. For although the Ahasuerus of the old tale practised cruelty towards Jesus, Jesus did not abuse him, but bore His terrible sufferings in silence.

Similarly a purely Jewish spirit permeates *The Wandering Jew* of Robert Buchanan (1893), who has ventured to represent Christ as Ahasuerus. He sets Christ on a mountain confronting humanity, which comes forward as His accuser and judge. And why? He has not given peace to mankind; He has taken peace from them. How does the author come to make such an assertion? Quite simply. The sufferings which have been brought on humanity through the struggles of selfish men against Christ and His religion of self-sacrifice—the author numbers amongst those sufferings the war against the Turks—those sufferings are in Buchanan's poem stated to be Christ's fault. It was not enough that His noble religious and moral work should be once misjudged. He must be condemned and tortured a second time.

A connecting link between works written from the Jewish point of view about Ahasuerus and a second group of representations of the subject may be found in Berthold Auerbach's novel, *Spinoza*. For he puts in the mouth of the wanderer, whose tears had been dried by time, the following reason for his hatred towards Jesus: "We loved the earth, and He showed us the heavens; we wished for a sword, and He taught us to love the foreign yoke; He was not our Messiah." Auerbach shows no trace of comprehension of the aim of Jesus as it appears in the history of religion. He desired to perfect the prophetical perspective according to the inner organic law of its being. Just as the majority of Christ's contemporaries failed to recognize His mission, so did Auerbach. On the other hand, Auerbach causes Spinoza, the Pantheist, with whom God is the Universe, to be thus apostrophised by his Ahasuerus, "Thou art come to be a Saviour to mankind, me too thou wilt save." And then he makes Ahasuerus bend over the sleeping philosopher and kiss him. The caress redeems the wanderer, "who bore on himself the doom of Israel."

This presentment of the Ahasuerus figure is made up of two ingredients—of the dregs of the Jewish ideas of the future, and of the froth of a pantheistic philosophical view of the world. I purposely mention the dregs of the Israelitish ideas of the future. For Judaism itself is not satisfied with Auerbach's description of the Messianic ideal. Materialistic and political blessings cannot, for the spirit of Judaism which desires to remain true to itself, form the only or the highest factors of its strivings toward a future. And Spinoza "led Judaism to philosophical liberty." Thus does Th. Kappstein express himself, who (in his [1906] book, *Ahasver in der Weltpoesie*) sets forth a chronological list of modern works on the subject. It is to be hoped that in the people of Israel there are many souls who eagerly desire to be freed from the burden of the consciousness of guilt through a suffering representative of Israel, in the manner of the lamb who was led to the sacrifice, and whose voice was not uplifted.

Like Auerbach, but without his outspoken inclination to the Jewish point of view, a second group of modern workers of the Ahasuerus theme have seen in it the representative of a new philosophy.

Carmen Sylva (Elizabeth, Queen of Roumania), in her poem *Jehova* (1882), makes her Ahasuerus burst out into the following words at the sight of a pair of lovers:

> I have loved goodness, I have served goodness—throughout
> my wandering!—
> In the desert, in the snowstorm, in the ocean I sought God.—
> I sought him in my own breast: sorrow filled my cup.
> But now my eyes see: God is in 'becoming,' God is an
> eternal 'becoming.'

This is not the place to criticise the particular idea expressed in those words. The tendency to make the Ahasuerus figure the bringer-in of Pantheism, of the apotheosis of the universe, is fairly powerfully bound up with the figure. For even if we merely take into account the long-lasting restless wandering, that characteristic is but a faint reflex of all the alleged vicissitudes of the surviving pantheistic processes of the universe.

It is easier to represent Ahasuerus as the prophet of an inspired pessimistic view of the universe and of life. That has actually been done several times.

In Edgar Quinet's *Ahasvérus* (1833), Ahasuerus is represented as a man who has himself been pursued by misfortune; whithersoever he turned misfortune was always in his train. Death and Love fight for his soul: Death in the form of an old woman who dwells by the Rhine, Love in the form of Rachel, an angel, whose tears of compassion for Ahasuerus had caused the gates of the Holy City to be closed against her, and who now acts as Death's servant. By the side of this woman Ahasuerus continues to fulfil his mission of collecting all the sorrow of the earth; and even the redemption which Quinet permits him to find in the woman's love is only an ephemeral episode in the gloomy world-drama which is to conclude with a general crash. It is, in fact, an image of the barrenness of spirit of the unhappy poet himself, who, after he had lost his belief in religion, wandered over Europe and Asia, but found himself everywhere confronted with hollow-eyed ruins.

Others went even further in the mistaken desire of bringing into the foreground only one side of Ahasuerus's fate. According to Th. Kappstein's book, already referred to, "the kernel of the legend" was revealed when it was developed "into a poem of the blessing of death" (p. 94). But then the fading of a leaf becomes the "kernel" of the tree.

While those who describe Ahasuerus as a pessimist declare his fate to be merely the result of his conduct, others analyse the motive of his acts, in order to represent him from that time forward as the herald of a new philosophy of life. This is what F. Lienhard does in his *Ahasver* (1901). He makes him discard a sort of religious materialism for a natural philosophy of falsely generalising deduction, and so represents Ahasuerus as a powerful, striving fighter for materialism.

A third group of authors imagine they see in Ahasuerus a representative of the idea of evolution, which is either mere formal greatness or mere formal strength. The following offer examples of that point of view.

In the three parts of his *Ahasver* (1865–68), S. Heller describes a spirit which during its wandering and development enters the *clientèle* of its "brother-legend" Faust, and imagines he recognises, in the age of the invention of printing, of the discoveries of new lands, of the Reformation, and of the worship of free humanity, the last and loftiest religion. Yet it is an abuse of the Ahasuerus figure if a chameleon *rôle* is assigned to it. If Heller leads Ahasuerus through the Reformation to the worship of free humanity, the Reformation is then cut off from its positive source; and to those who know history will occur the words of Goethe's *Faust*: "What is called the spirit of the age is your own spirit, in which the age is reflected."

So Ahasuerus has often, and in modern times, been represented as the prototype of an impetuous fighter. He is taken from the sphere of negative opposition and placed in that of positive struggle. He has also been represented as the embodiment of the Prometheus idea, as in J. G. Fischer's *Der ewige Jude* (1854). Fischer regards Ahasuerus as the representative of struggling humanity. Alluding to the Prometheus myth, he ventures to say of himself and his relations with mankind:

> Yes, chain me to the rocky wall—
> I still remain a free man,
> I alone can redeem thy colossal ignorance,
> I, with creative brain and the divine ether beam,
> With the bold brow of thought,
> Stole fire from Heaven.

There is some truth in what J. Prost[5] observes: "The metaphysical ideas of mortality and immortality, of finite and infinite, must challenge the ingenuity of the poet and urge him to descend into the deepest depths, and clothe the history of the Universe and of nations with the imaginative enchantment of poetry." But much of what modern authors have attributed to the Ahasuerus figure is not suited to its nature. Goethe had so much historical sense that he recognised the primitive character of the Ahasuerus figure, and wished to retain it, although in many variations. Prost, on the basis of careful research of some material left by Goethe, comes to the conclusion that "For Goethe, the legend belonged to the region of religion and church, and revolved round the ideas of cursing, repentance, perdition, redemption, round the contrast between Judaism and Christianity" (p. 16). In later times other minds are not to seek which preserve the religious and historical point of view which was formerly comprised in the idea of the Wandering Jew.

To this fourth group of modern authors who have carefully examined the religious origin of the Ahasuerus idea belongs Wilhelm Hauff. He writes in his *Memoiren des Satan*,[6] "The legend contains a deep moral, for the most abandoned of men is evidently he who vents his sorrow over his disappointed hopes on him who raised those hopes." Historical truth is surely disregarded here, if it is meant that Jesus roused expectations of political and material well-being. Many of His contemporaries cherished such expectations, however much Jesus demonstrated the spiritual character of the true salvation of men which His real pioneer in the history of religion had already pointed out.

Schubart, in his well-known poem, *Der ewige Jude* (1783), has treated the Ahasuerus figure from the correct religious and historical point of view. The accuracy of his representation is not to be questioned because he throws his Ahasuerus from Mount Carmel into the sea, and causes him to be put to rest by an angel. For he is only to be regarded as a sleeper who is to be wrapped in unconsciousness until the Day of Judgment.

Among the later authors who have treated Ahasuerus from the correct historical standpoint we may note two, the French author Eugène Sue and the German author Gustav Renner.

The strong contrast between the indescribable suffering of Jesus and the cruel pitilessness practised by Ahasuerus has often of late been the point in his career on which men's judgment of Ahasuerus rests. Eugène Sue brings this out in his voluminous novel, *Le Juif errant*, and attempts to explain his conduct. His idea is that on a certain day the bearer of the cross went past the house of Ahasuerus when he was sitting at his work, filled with anxiety and hatred because, notwithstanding the hardest toil on his part, he could not keep bitter want from his family. Suffering himself, he refused pity to the Sufferer. Such an explanation is unsatisfying. For the two cases of suffering cannot be compared either in kind or measure. The unpleasant taste left by the driving away of the bearer of the cross, who sets down His load for a moment, cannot possibly be removed in that way.

Gustav Renner has shown a specially acute feeling for the delicate contrast between the outward striving on the one side and the inward need on the other, which forms the main point of Christ's life-work. He puts it forward in his striking poem, *Ahasver* (1902), admirable for its skilful form, and even more for its choice imagery. He rightly takes the self-denial of Jesus, who turns aside His eyes from earthly splendour, and draws back His hand from worldly power, as the central point of his production. In those traits of the Master of masters he found the typical guidance for the most valuable achievement of the Man, and therefore announces as the loftiest standard for the Day of Judgment:

Only he who has forsaken himself
Will find himself for ever;
He whom no bond fetters,
He will be bound for ever.
Only he who conquers himself
Will be freed from his own will:
He has conquered the world
And it is his.

And, as Renner's *Ahasver* acknowledges at last:

What offered me hope vanished like froth,
Death became life, and life death;

so should I like, at the conclusion of this critical wandering on
Ahasuerus's track, to express the two following reasons for my
conviction, reasons which I have always found particularly con-
soling. On the one side, an historical and academic judgment on
Christianity will not regard the verdict on the Ahasuerus figure as
the last and only right verdict; and on the other, I should be
greatly in error if I believed that the spirit of Judaism will always
estimate the perfection to be hoped for in the future after this
earthly fashion. Therefore the study of these ideas about Ahasuerus has always inclined me to think that a reconciling influence
may lie in the Ahasuerus figure itself.

NOTES

1. The German title runs: "Kurze Beschreibung und Erzählung von
einem Juden mit Namen *Ahasverus*, welcher bei der Kreuzigung Christi
selbst persönlich dabeigewesen ist, auch das *Kreuzige, kreuzige ihn!* über
Christus mitgeschrieen, und statt seiner Freisprechung die des Mörders
Barrabas gewünscht hat, aber nach Christi Kreuzigung nicht mehr nach
Jerusalem hat kommen können, auch sein Weib und Kinder nicht mehr
gesehen hat und seitdem am Leben geblieben ist, vor etlichen Jahren
nach Hamburg gekommen ist, u.s.w."

2. Thus is explained the form of the name *Asuerus*, which occurs in an
edition of the 1602 book (Neubaur, p. 74), and also in the Dutch edition
(Neubaur, p. 99), where he says: "Myn naam is Azuweer." Yet the true

form of the name had already been established. For, in the fifteenth century, there was an edition of the Book of Esther inscribed with the title, "Concerning (or Regarding) Ahasuerus," as we learn from Johann Gottfried Eichhorn's *Einleitung in das Alte Testament* (vol. iii. p. 635, ed. 1823–24). The name Ahasuerus may have been taken from the German Bible, but not necessarily so. Where then was it created?

3. Gustav Karpeles, in an article, "Das Theater bei den Juden," in the *Nationalzeitung,* 13th of April, 1889.

4. The English expression, 'the wandering Jew,' and the French expression, 'le Juif errant,' are more correct than the German, 'der ewige Jude,' *the eternal Jew*; and it is not employed in the 1602 book. It occurs first in an impression of 1694.

5. *Die Sage vom ewigen Juden in der neuern deutschen Literatur,* 1905.

6. Hempel'sche edition, p. 59.

THE AHASVER-VOLKSBUCH
OF 1602

Aaron Schaffer

Among the appearances of the Wandering Jew in print, perhaps the most influential and persistent is the chapbook version of 1602 as many scholars have remarked. The following discussion of this important source illustrates a classical technique for studying manuscripts and printed materials. True to philological tradition, the evidence adduced consists of names of authors or characters in their various forms as well as attempts to date both earlier and later editions. In such stemma research, the whole set of family tree relationships assumed to exist between different versions or editions is invariably hypothesized. The relationships are usually determined on the basis of detailed line-by-line textual comparisons.

After Schaffer has concluded his reconstruction of the publishing history of the Volksbuch, he proceeds to take issue with König with respect to the notion that there were actual conscience-stricken Jews who inspired the characterization of the Wandering Jew in the chapbook. Schaffer's stemma research is indebted, as he himself notes, to the pioneering work by Leonhard Neubaur, e.g., "Zur Geschichte und Bibliographie des Volksbuchs von Ahasverus," Zeitschrift für Bücherfreunde, 5 *(1914): 211–23. See also his* "Einige Bermerkungen zur Sage von Ewigen Juden," Zeitschrift für Bücherfreunde, 9 *(1917): 310–13.*

Reprinted from *Modern Philology*, 17 (1919–1920): 597–604.

Several very interesting questions, which have, in the past, been only partially, or not at all, answered by scholars, arise in connection with the first appearance of Ahasuerus, the Wandering Jew, in German literature. This occurred in the now celebrated 1602 pamphlet: *Kurtze Beschreibung und Erzehlung von einem Juden mit Namen Ahasverus, welcher bey der Creutzigung Christi selbst Persönlich gewesen: auch das "Crucifige" uber Christum hab helffen schreyen,* etc., which is now regularly counted among the German *Volksbücher*. For the very fullest information on the subject of this four-page *Flugblatt* we are indebted to the excellent and thorough study of Dr. L. Neubaur, *Die Sage vom ewigen Juden* (Leipzig, 1893). Inasmuch as nothing is known of the ostensible Leyden printer of the pamphlet, Christoff Creutzer, Neubaur ingeniously, and, perhaps, correctly, suggests that this name is only a wordplay on some such expression as *Das Leiden des gekreuzigten Christus,* and gives as the likely publisher of the pamphlet the Basel printer, Johannes Schröter. Be that as it may, the pamphlet, immediately upon its appearance, became exceedingly popular. Neubaur gives the titles and the variants on the title-pages of no less than twelve editions published at various places in 1602, of thirty-three editions altogether in the seventeenth century, and of forty editions before the end of the eighteenth century. The title page, in every instance, bears a quotation from the Gospel of Matthew, 16:28, and it is evident that the Ahasuerus theme is a development of the two medieval traditions that the apostle John had been rewarded for his faithfulness by Jesus with immortality, and that Malchus, the servant of the high priest Caiaphas, had been doomed by Jesus to eternal wandering for having struck him while in the synagogue. The first nine editions of the pamphlet are anonymous; the tenth and most of those which follow give the name of an author, Chrysostomus Dudulaeus Westphalus, which is undoubtedly a pseudonym.

The successive editions of the pamphlet are interesting because of the individual touches each adds to the original account. The tenth edition, for example, besides being the first to give an ostensible authorship, is noteworthy because of a poem of sixteen verses which is printed on the reverse side of the title-page. This is perhaps the earliest poem in German, if not in all literature, on the subject of the Wandering Jew, whose name here appears as Aschverus. The poem is in the regular octosyllabic short-rhymed couplets characteristic of sixteenth-century German verse. The fifteenth edition tells us that the "ewiger Jude" had been seen, in addition to the places previously mentioned, in Lübeck in 1601; the sixteenth (dated Refel, 1614) adds Reval, Cracow, and Königsberg. Not until the thirty-first impression, published in 1694, is Ahasuerus referred to as the "ewiger Jude" (the title begins: *Newe Zeitung von dem so genennten ewigen Jud*). Very worthy of note is the fact that the original pamphlet bears two names and places of publication. Toward the end of the text we read: *Datum Schleswig den 9. Junii Anno 1564*, whilst the title page, as we have seen, gives the date as Leyden 1602. The question propounded by Simrock, *Deutsche Volksbücher*, Vol. II, as to whether the pamphlet may not have originally appeared in 1564, must, it seems to me, be answered in the negative, inasmuch as the closest search has apparently revealed no traces of any Ahasuerus pamphlet older than 1602. The fact that the pamphlet went through so many editions in the year 1602, which may seem to be a point in favor of Simrock's theory, can, in my opinion, be explained in some such manner as the following: The legend of the Wandering Jew, growing up out of the Christian oral traditions about John and Malchus, and crystallizing in such stories as that of Cartaphilus Joseph related by Roger of Wendover, in his *Flores Historiarum*, and incorporated by Matthew Paris in his *Chronica Majora*, gained impetus throughout the Middle Ages, until some ingenious ecclesiastic, realizing its value as a weapon for the Protestant church, wrote the pamphlet in 1602, which, because of the inflammable state of mind of the Germany of that time, spread like wildfire through the land, experiencing edition after edition.

A comparison of the early editions of the pamphlet, which has been made possible by Neubaur, who prints the first and tenth editions in full and gives the title pages and variants of all the others, reveals interesting results. We find that the first six editions, the first published ostensibly in Leyden by Christoff Creutzer, the others in Bautzen by Wolfgang Suchnach, are, with the exception of occasional orthographical variants, practically identical from the point of view of the text. The seventh edition, published *erstlich zu Bautzen, zum Anderen zu Schlesswig bey Nico-laus Wegener*, shows an interesting misprint on the title page, where the date appears as 1502 instead of 1602. With the exception of a rather lengthy interpolation toward the end and orthographi-cal differences, the text is precisely that of I and II. The same holds true of VIII and IX, except that the former evidently had IV as its *Vorlage*, as they are identical in make-up, woodcut, and orthog-raphy, and different from the others in these details. It is quite apparent, however, that the authors and printers of the second to the ninth editions (inclusive) had I as their direct *Vorlage*.

When we examine the tenth edition, however, we encounter an entirely different set of conditions. Aside from the title, which bears only a slight resemblance to that of I, and begins: *Wunder-barlicher Bericht von einem Juden aus Jerusalem bürtig und Ahasverus genennet*, etc., the text shows numerous variations. The introduc-tory paragraph of I tells us that, inasmuch as the author had noth-ing new to relate, he was going to recount something old which was so surprising that it would be considered by many as new; the tenth edition begins with a bare announcement that what fol-lows is a piece of news written to a friend in Danzig. The succes-sive episodes of the story which Paulus von Eitzen, later bishop of Schleswig, is made to relate to his pupils, follow in precisely the same order and, very frequently, in identical phraseology. However, in addition to the interpolations and omissions in X, its style is generally so different from I that the careful reader is compelled to pause and take notice. A close comparison of the two editions yields the following result: The account in I is told in a simple, straightforward manner, with few stylistic adorn-ments; that in X is, as far as can be expected, elaborate, drawn out, and adorned with frequent epithets and allusions. A few ex-amples will serve to corroborate this statement. Two parallel pas-sages showing the stylistic contrast in the two editions are given:

> I: Als nun Paulus von Eitzen solches gehoret, hat er sich noch mehr darab verwundert, und gelegenheit gesucht / selbsten mit im zu reden.
> X: Als nun der Doctor Paulus von Eitzen von ihme nach not-turfft und lust / ja mit grosser verwunderung wegen der nie vor-hin erhöreten und auch ungleublichen Zeitungen alles gehöret /

hat er in ferner gebeten / domit er besser und gründlicher wissenschaft dieser dinge uberkmmen möchte / das er in solches nach allen umbstenden fleissiger erzehlen wolte.

And again, an instance in which the author of X elaborates on I:

> I: Was nun Gott mit ime für habe / das er ihm so lang in disem elenden Leben herumb führe / ob er in vielleicht biss am Jüngsten Tag / als ein lebendiger zeugen des Leyden Christi zu mehrer uberzeigung de Gottlosen und ungleubigen also erhalten wolle / sey im unwissent.
>
> X: Was nun Gott mit im vorhabe / das er in diesem elenden Leben so herumb gewandert / und so elendiglichen ihn auschawen lesset / könne er nicht anders gedencken Gott wolle an im vielleicht biss an den jüngsten Tag wieder die Juden [this is a significant interpolation] einen lebendigen Zeugen haben / dadurch die ungleubigen und Gottlosen des sterbens Christi erinnert und zur Busse bekehret werden sollen.

One example will suffice to show how close the parallelism in phraseology often is:

> I: Alsbald hab er sein Kind nidergesetzt uund im Hauss nicht bleiben können: Sondern mit nach gefolget und zugesehen / wie er ist hingerichtet worden.
>
> X: Hierauff habe er alsbald sein Kind nidergesetzt / und gar nit lenger daselbst bleiben konnen / sonder Christo immer nachgefolget / und also gesehē / wie er elendiglichen gecreutziget / gemartert / und getödtet wurden.

A few of the more interesting variants are these. The date of Eitzen's encounter with Ahasuerus in Hamburg is given in I as 1542, in X as 1547; the former date conforms more closely to the facts of Eitzen's career. Again, almost every time that Hamburg is mentioned in I, it is coupled with Danzig in X. Furthermore, the crucial sentence of the *Flugblatt*, the curse inflicted by Christ upon Ahasuerus, reads in I: *Ich will sitzen und ruhen / du aber solt gehen;* in X: *Ich will alhie stehen und ruhen / aber du solt gehen biss an den Jüngsten Tag,* which is in entire agreement with the trait of elaboration peculiar to X already noted above. The Spanish city in which the two German ecclesiastical secretaries claimed to have met Ahasuerus is given in I as "Malduit," in X as "Madriel," which latter form makes it clear that the city of Madrid is meant. The name of the first of the two secretaries occurs in I as Christoph Ehringer, in X as Christoph Krause. The date, *Schlesswig den 9. Junii Anno 1564,* found in I, is lacking in X. I closes with the statement that the soles of the Jew were said to have been two fingers' breadth in thickness and to have been as hard as horn, because of his ceaseless wanderings. X omits this entirely, and concludes with an enlargement of the bare assertion in I that Ahasuerus was said to have been seen in Danzig in 1599 into a statement that the *Wundermann* had been seen in Vienna, whence he intended to journey to Poland, and farther on from Poland to Moscow.

These numerous differences and the fact that X is written in a much more polished and rounded style than is I have led me to a conclusion which seems to have been generally overlooked. I cannot help feeling that the author of X, the self-styled Chrysostomus Dudulaeus Westphalus, had nothing at all to do with the composition of the anonymous first edition; what he did was, by recasting phrases, reversing the order of words, elaborations, interpolations, and omissions, to attempt, as far as possible, to conceal the fact that he was using I directly as a *Vorlage.* Apparently, he succeeded in his attempt, for practically all the later editions of the seventeenth century are ascribed to him. Moreover, it is this tenth edition which seems to be in the minds of most modern writers who refer to the *Ahasver-Volksbuch.* It seems clear, however, that X is but a plagiarized version of I, the plagiarization being but crudely disguised.

Lack of time prevents my devoting any attention here to such questions as the actual relationship of Paulus von Eitzen to the *Volksbuch,* and the connection of the *Volksbuch* with earlier versions of the story such as that of Roger of Wendover and Matthew Paris. A far more important question, one that arises immediately in the mind of the reader of the 1602 *Volksbuch,* is: How does the name of the Jew of Jerusalem happen to be Ahasuerus? Does it not seem to be a trick of fate to give to the Jewish shoemaker the name of that Persian king who was willing to see all the Jews in his mighty empire annihilated? Students of the phenomenon of the

Wandering Jew have maintained an almost unanimous silence on
this point. The sole explanation I have seen offered, and one which
I have not the slightest doubt is correct, is given by König, in his
brief essay, "The Wandering Jew," Gutersläh, 1907, a translation
of which appeared in *The Nineteenth Century and After*, Vol. LXI
(1907), 969 ff. He believes that the author of the *Volksbuch*, when
casting about for a name to give to his central figure, conceived
the idea of using a name which was very prominent in a whole
group of productions common at the time—the so-called "Purim-
Spiele." The facts about these Purim plays, which König only
barely touches upon, and for which I am indebted to Israel Abra-
hams' chapter on the subject in his *Jewish Life in the Middle Ages*,
pp. 260–72, are very instructive. The biblical festival of Purim,
which celebrates the deliverance of the Jewish nation by Esther
and Mordecai from the machinations of Haman, has, since as far
back as the Talmudic period, been a season of great joy and mer-
rymaking. Crude dramatizations of the story are as old as Gaonic
times (i.e., the ninth and tenth centuries). In medieval and early
modern Germany, inasmuch as the festival of Purim occurs during the period of Lent, it came to be celebrated, in accordance
with the Christian fashion, by a sort of *Fastnachtspiele*, the Purim
plays. The exact date of the oldest of these plays cannot be ascer-
tained; the earliest extant instance is that known as the *Ahaschwer-
osch-Spiel*, which dates from 1708. It is written in the Judeo-
German jargon, and abounds in the crude slapstick which marks
all the Purim plays of the period. There can be no doubt that
numerous Purim plays were produced in Germany before the year
1708. Henry Malter, writing on the subject in the *Jewish Encyclopaedia*, X, 279, informs us that, from a satirical Judeo-German
poem of the year 1598, we learn that a play, entitled *Das Spiel von
Tab Jäklein mit seim Weib*, was enacted every Purim, during the
sixteenth century, at the town of Tannhausen. There is no trace
of this play to be found, and it may never even have been published. It is quite probable, however, that the German Purim plays
date from the early sixteenth century, so that the author of the
Volksbuch might well have had considerable opportunity to see or
hear of such a play.

Whether the author of the *Volksbuch* intentionally gave his hero

the name not, as might have been expected, of Mordecai, but of
Ahasuerus, because of the polemical value the name of such a
royal personage might carry with it, is problematical. König's
assertion that the author of the 1602 pamphlet wrote in good faith
may, or may not, hold water; but his labored attempt to prove
that, in the sixteenth century, there may have been many Jews
who were weary of their century-old dispersion (this much is, of
course, perfectly true) and who felt somewhat conscience-stricken
because of the attitude of their people toward Christ, falls, in my
opinion, entirely flat. In the first place, it overlooks the fact that
this is no reason why the *Volksbuch* author should not have chosen
Mordecai or even Haman as the name of his hero; and, in the
second place, it ignores, and, indeed, König scoffs at, what seems
to me to be the very correct assumption of Joseph Jacobs, *Jewish
Encyclopaedia*, XII, 462, that the discovery of a living eyewitness
of the life and crucifixion of Jesus was believed by devout Protestants to be an incontrovertible proof of the reliability of the New
Testament accounts and of the truth of the doctrines of Christianity.

My own explanation of the choice of the name of Ahasuerus by
the author of the *Volksbuch*, a pure conjecture, of course, would
be somewhat as follows: The *Volksbuch* author was, undoubtedly,
familiar with the Purim plays. In them he had seen Mordecai
praised to the skies, Haman reviled and hissed, and Ahasuerus,
the vacillating monarch, first cursed and then lauded. In preparing
to make a polemical use of the joint New Testament traditions of
John and Malchus, which were already current among the people,
zu mehrer Uberzeigung der Gottlosen und ungleubigen, as he himself
tells us, he conceived the notion of making his hero a Jew who
was willing to defend Christ and Christianity and thus prove a
powerful missionary agent. Having the choice of hundreds of
biblical names before him, he went to the already popularized
Book of Esther. Haman, a personage actually loathed by the Jews,
was out of the question; to give the hero the name of so faithful a
Jew as Mordecai would raise the story above the bounds of the
probable. Ahasuerus, however, who, as a powerful Persian poten-
tate and, in the end, the friend of the Jewish people, was a name
to conjure with, and had the added advantage of being exceed-

ingly unusual. That the pamphlet was understood to be a polemical instrument, even in the year of its publication, is evident from the above-cited interpolation in X, *wieder die Juden*, and from the fact that all the editions, including and following the twenty-second (Refel, 1634), contain, as a sort of appendix or commentary to the *Volksbuch*, a *Bericht von den zwölff Jüdischen Stämmen*, in which the Jews are taken to account for the sufferings they had supposedly brought upon Jesus by their false and malicious testimony.

I cannot bring this brief study to a close without hinting that, although much has been written regarding the Wandering Jew, there still remain a number of questions in this connection to be answered. One of these, particularly, and one which I should have liked to take up here, involves the study and comparison of all the legends centering about an "eternal wanderer" for the purpose of ascertaining which one possesses the priority in point of time. Among these wanderers are the "Fliegender Holländer," to whom Heine, in his *Aus den Memorien des Herrn von Schnabelewopski*, refers as the "ewiger Jude des Ozeans"; the "wilder Jäger," and perhaps even Tannhäuser and Faust. This phase of the subject has not, to my knowledge, been probed at all; moreover, Goethe's fragmentary *Der ewige Jude* has by no means been exhausted in the researches of such scholars as Minor,[1] Hoffman,[2] and Düntzer.[3] The theme of the Wandering Jew is well-nigh inexhaustible, and offers the student rich as well as fascinating material.

NOTES

1. Jakob Minor, *Goethes Fragmente vom ewigen Juden und vom wiederkehrenden Heiland* (Stuttgart und Berlin, 1904).
2. Paul Hoffmann, "Untersuchungen über Goethes ewigen Juden," *Vierteljahrschrift für Literaturgeschichte,* IV(1891), 116–52 ff.
3. Heinrich Düntzer, "Ueber Goethes Bruchstück des Gedichtes, *Der ewige Jude,*" *Zeitschrift für deutsche Philologie,* XXV (1893), 289–303.

AHASVER

David Daube

One of the puzzles which has perplexed scholars studying the Wandering Jew is the name Ahasver, which seems to have first appeared in the 1602 Volksbuch. There is a consensus (cf. Edelmann, König, Schaffer) that the name was probably borrowed from the Book of Esther in the Old Testament. But why this particular name was selected for the Wandering Jew is not so clear. The choice of a nonJewish name emphasizes that a knowledge of authentic Jewish tradition was probably not available to the creators and transmitters of this Christian legend. But that would not explain why the specific name of Ahasver was employed. David Daube in a brief note proposes a novel variation on the Purim-play theory. For a somewhat popular overview of the variety of names attributed to the Wandering Jew, see Livia Bitton, "The Names of the Wandering Jew," Literary Onomastics Studies, 2 (1975): 169–80.

At least from the early 17th century the Wandering Jew is called Ahasver. Why? At first glance a less suitable name could hardly be imagined. The biblical Ahasverus was a pagan; and, owing to the role assigned to him in post-biblical Jewish legend, no Jew was ever named after him. Even supposing (what is really impossible) that there was an eccentric Jewish couple who called their son Ahasverus, the problem remains unanswered. Had we to de-

Reprinted from *Jewish Quarterly Review*, 45 (1955): 243–44.

36

pict a typical German we should not introduce him as Ibrahim, even if we did know of an exceptional case of a German bearing this name. To be sure, the Wandering Jew in most versions of the story figures as a convert to Christianity. But this does not help as far as the difficulty outlined is concerned.

No satisfactory solution has so far been offered. That Ahasverus ended by being friendly to the Jews, that part of his name may sound to a German ear a little like *Hass*, "hatred"—these and similar suggestions are clearly counsels of despair.

Yet, the explanation appears to be comparatively simple. Since the story of the Wandering Jew began to spread through Europe in the 13th century, he received many different names. One of them was Koutondes—Simpleton, Idiot. Now in medieval Jewish legend Ahasverus is represented as very stupid. The precise reasons need not here be investigated. It may suffice to point out that according to the Talmud (Meg. 11 ff.) already Gamaliel II, about 100 CE, remarked that first he got rid of a wife (Vashti) to please his friend (Memucan, identified by the Rabbis with Haman), and then of his friend (Haman) to please a wife (Esther); and Samuel, of the first half of the 3rd century, spoke of him as a silly king. At any rate, in the Middle Ages, as today, Jews might say of an imbecile that he is "an Ahasverus." In the traditional plays acted by Jews on the Feast of Esther, Esther and Mordecai are the heroine and hero, Haman the villain, and Ahasverus the fool. When the Wandering Jew is called Ahasver, therefore, this is nothing but a translation into Jewish idiom of one of his epithets.

If this view is correct, it may point to the translation having originated in a Greek-speaking region, since it is mostly there that we find the Wandering Jew called Fool—Koutondes or the like. Let us note that in Belgium, too, his surname, though Hebrew, is not a name any Jew would ever bear but a designation of his nature, i.e., Laquedem, To the East or To Olden Times. (His first name in Belgium is Isaac—natural enough.) More generally, there are quite a few versions of the story adorned by Jewish ideas or ideas that counted as such among those who used them.

The earliest extant evidence of the Wandering Jew being called Ahasver is in a book of 1602. Here we are told that some fifty years before, a bishop met him in a church at Hamburg, penitent,

ill-clothed and distracted at the thought of having to move on
again in a few weeks. One cannot help feeling that this particular
tale is related to the attempts, made at that period by Jews expelled
from Spain and Portugal, to be allowed to settle in Hamburg—if
only temporarily; and to the fact that a number had lived there for
some time, outwardly professing to be Christians but at heart
keeping to their old religion. Occasionally, indeed, it is a crypto-
Jew, a Marrano, who is given the part of the Wandering Jew, or
that of an author of his story. For this point we may refer to a
note by Malone to Dr. Johnson's comment on *The Turkish Spy*,
recorded by Boswell as of April 10, 1783.

THE LEGEND OF THE WANDERING JEW

A FRANCISCAN HEADACHE

P. B. Bagatti

The Wandering Jew was reported well before 1602, and among the places where he supposedly appeared is the Holy Land, which is of interest inasmuch as, according to all of the versions of the story, this was the site of the original incident. The accounts of the Wandering Jew's appearance in Jerusalem were a source of continued annoyance to the Franciscans residing there. First, the legend itself presents an image of an impatient, vengeful Jesus who rather than turning His other cheek lashes out with a powerful curse, an image in conflict with the more traditional one of infinite love and forgiveness. Second, the Franciscans were evidently plagued by constant requests from pilgrims to be shown the place where the alleged incident occurred. In the following unusual essay written from the Franciscan perspective, we gain insight into the sincere but inevitably unsuccessful struggle to ban a legend. Legends, of course, like all folklore, have a life of their own and cannot be stopped by official decrees.

This story, in one form or another, circulated throughout Palestine and was fairly well established many years before the arrival

Reprinted from *Franciscan Studies*, 9 (1949): 1–9.

of the Franciscans (1335) but had not as yet been definitely connected with any of the Holy Places. In later times, however, it acquired local coloring to such an extent that the Franciscans, as custodians of the Holy Places, were obliged to take a firm stand. To trace this legend through the old chronicles is to recover a completely forgotten tale—one with its full quota of adventure, duplicity, gullibility, and humor.

Its first appearance was in the Byzantine period (4th–7th century) in this general form: A stranger, usually an Ethiopian, addresses himself to a worthy villager and says: "I am the man who struck the Creator of the world in the time of His suffering. And, therefore, I must never cease to weep." This account was popular among the monks and in the seventh century; Moschus related it in his *Lemonarium*.[1] Eventually he was identified as Malchus.

In medieval times there was also known in Palestine a similar legend coupled with the name "Cartaphilus." When Jesus was carrying His cross to Calvary, this man Cartaphilus jeered: "Go on! Faster!" To which the Savior quietly replied, "I go, but thou shalt wait till I come." This anecdote originated in Armenia during the thirteenth century; later it found its way into Europe.[2]

So far the legend has a twofold aspect: (a) As Malchus, who struck the blow; (b) as Cartaphilus, who taunted Christ. And so far, neither has been assigned as yet to a particular spot in Jerusalem.

In the fourteenth century, the legend acquired "local habitation and a name." The name was "John Buttadeus" (Buttadeus— "strike God"). In the *Libellus de Locis Ultramarinis* written by the Dominican Father Peter of Penna (c. 1350) we read: "Here [where Simon of Cyrene helped Jesus carry the cross] is shown the place where John Buttadeus derided Christ when He was going to die. . . . A few simple-minded people assured us that he had been seen by many, but this is not accepted by learned men, for the person to whom they were referring was known as John Devout-of-God, an equerry of Charlemagne, who lived 210 years."[3]

Not long afterwards, the Franciscans were accompanying pilgrims around the "Holy Circle," i.e., in and around Jerusalem.[4] Naturally, some pilgrims would bring up the story, but the Franciscans endeavored to give it no importance. In fact, when the record of indulgences for the Holy Places was published, all mention of Buttadeus was omitted. No indulgence meant no veneration, and since the great majority of the pilgrims depended entirely on the Franciscans for their information about the Holy Places, we can readily understand that this omission had inflicted a mortal wound. The following two chronicles bear out this point.

In 1431, the Italian priest, Ser Mariano de Siena, was visiting the shrines for the third time, under the direction of the Guardian or Custos, Fr. Luigi de Bologna. In the Via Dolorosa, they came upon this same spot and passed it by, for as Ser Mariano wrote, "There was no indulgence."[5]

In 1480–83, the Dominican Father Felix Fabri of Wurttemberg related that when he was visiting the house of Annas on Mt. Sion, he slyly asked the Friar who accompanied him, to show him where the Wandering Jew stood when he struck Christ. The Friar conducted him out of the house to an old olive tree and said, "According to the tradition of the Oriental peoples, which they claim to have in an old book, Christ was tied to this olive tree while His judges dined." Apparently the Friar had never heard of the Wandering Jew and merely recounted his stock of tales, hoping that one or the other would answer his guest's query.[6] Moreover, Fr. Fabri wrote it as his personal opinion that the legend clashed with the Holy Scriptures and was against the Christian Tradition, "because Christ in His Passion would give a perfect example of patience, but never of vengeance."[7]

The legend seemed to be dying when it received new life with charming effect. At the end of the sixteenth century, Peter Brantius Pennalius paid a visit to the Holy Places and on one occasion, years after his return to his native country, during a sumptuous banquet, related the following experience:

> One day I was in the piazza of Jerusalem [in front of the Holy Sepulcher] when a Turk approached me and asked, "Do you know me?"
> I looked at him carefully but had to admit that I did not know him. He replied: "But I know you! For I was a slave in your uncle's house in Turin and I received many favors from you and from your parents." He gave my parents' names correctly and

also those of many prominent people in Turin. "When I was released," the stranger continued, "I went to Venice and soon gained the friendship of some Turkish merchants. They brought me in their ship to Constantinople. There I sought out my old master whom I had served in the naval forces in 1571. He received me kindly and took me again into his service. A few months later he was appointed Sangiak, or Governor, of Jerusalem. Four months later, his Police Captain died, and my master selected me for the post. Now, as a token of my gratitude for your kindness and courtesy, I hope you will do me the favor to sup with me this night. We shall be alone." He described his house and advised me to come at four in the evening, so as not to be seen. But if I were seen by any police, I was not to worry for he was their chief.

I accepted the invitation and at the appointed time I went to his house, where I was received with much display of friendship. After a splendid meal, he told me he would show me something which no other living man knew, except the Captain *pro tempore* of the city of Jerusalem. He mentioned, too, that there was a penalty of impalement if he revealed it to any other person. He took a bunch of keys from an iron box, prepared a piece of wood for a torch, and lit a lantern which he then carefully covered. He led me out of the room, shut the door and gave me his hand to walk with him a good distance in the darkness. In a short time, we came to a large drawbridge which led to another room. He shut the door from the inside and uncovered the lantern. Then he trudged an equally good distance to an iron door. He opened it and we walked low in a corridor all worked in mosaic. Near the end we passed five iron doors and entered a large hall ornamented with very fine marble and mosaic work in the vault. At the left end of the hall there was a man, well-armed in the old fashion, with a halberd on his shoulder and a sword at his side. The man was continually marching from one side of the hall to the other without rest. The Turk said to me: "See if you can stop him." I tried two or three times with all my strength, but it was impossible for me to hold him. He lighted the torch and gave it to me so I could see the man more clearly. I observed that he was of middle stature, thin and emaciated, with hollow eyes, black beard and black hair. I asked the Turk who this man was and he answered, "I will tell you only if you swear by your Christ not to reveal it for ten years." This, I knew, was the extreme limit of office for a Captain of Police. Curious to know, I gave my solemn pledge.

"This man," he said to me, "is the servant who struck your Christ before the High Priest Annas. For punishment of his grievous crime he was condemned by your Christ to remain here. We too believe in the old traditions. In this place he stays, never eating nor drinking; never sleeping nor taking rest; but always walking as you see him, and always,—look, my friend,—always the arm that struck, twitches!''

We left and returned to the room where we had dined. At my departure he tactfully reminded me of my oath, and said that if I met any Turk on my way back to my lodgings, I was not to salute him for such was the custom in this quarter. He begged me to remember him to his friends in Turin and offered me money if I had need. I told him I lacked nothing and thanked him warmly for his kindness, and following his instructions, found my way to the inn. I came back to my native country, spent some fifteen years in Candia, Corfu and Zara, and now I can tell what I saw without scruple, having observed the oath.

This much we *do* know: that the tale appeared in several works and was transmitted by many writers in substantially the same form. There were some important differences. According to Fr. Quaresmi,[8] it all happened to a certain nobleman of Vercelli, one Charles de Rancis. According to D. Laffi,[9] it happened to a Charles Carini. We have good reason also to think it was at one time connected with the name of the well-known musician and author John Francis Alcarotto, Canon of the Cathedral of Novara.[10] In Fr. Quaresmi's book, the Turk was from Vicentia; in Laffi's, from Turin. These differences, taken together, imply at least some fabrication—but this may be accounted for by the wiles of publishers seeking to acquire printing rights. Moreover, the name "Pennalius" is not found in the *Navis Peregrinorum*,[11] a collection of the names of pilgrims from 1561 till 1695. Still, it is also true that these lists are not absolutely complete, having been based mostly on the guest-registers of the Franciscans. Practically all pilgrims availed themselves of Franciscan hospitality, but not necessarily all. In fact, Pennalius himself related that he stayed at an inn, i.e., an arab khan.

So much for the objections. On the other hand, only a man who was reasonably familiar with the precincts of the Dome of the Rock, could have described so well the mosaic work, the iron doors, the finest marble, etc. And also it is well to note that the prohibition against Christians entering the mosque area was not such an iron-clad rule that there were never any exceptions. With the use of bribes in the right places, access was quite possible. One who had this experience in 1514 was the Venetian merchant (later consul at Damascus) Barbone Morosini. He wrote a very interesting redaction, unedited till now, in the Marciana of Venice.[12] For July 28–29, he writes: "I was in the house of the Cadi Ambely. This house is situated in Solomon's Temple area. From his quarters, he showed me a great part of it." For August 15, he has this to say:

> On the invitation of the Cadi of Al Aqsa Mosque, I went to his home one day at the noon hour. At this time no one else is walking around because of the great heat. His house was inside the old wall of the temple. There I remained incognito for the rest of the day, being refreshed by my host with excellent fruits and good waters. At sunset when the Moors go into the mosque for prayers, I went with the Cadi into the Temple of Our Lady (Al Aqsa Mosque), dressed exactly as the others. In external actions I followed them closely; internally, I experienced great devotion in this Holy Place. . . . When the prayers of the Moors were ended and the people went out, I explored the interior with the Cadi. It was as bright as day inside, for, as the Cadi told me, there were more than seven hundred lamps. . . . Afterwards, we went to Solomon's Temple (Dome of the Rock) and saw everything inside and out. Then I returned to Our Lady's Temple (Al Aqsa), for I could not see enough of it. I remained there till the second time of prayer, i.e., around 2:30 A.M. and later. At last, going out the Golden Gate, I arrived at Mt. Sion, accompanied by the Cadi's slaves. To the Cadi, I left a generous offering, for it is impossible otherwise to receive such a favor."

From this account and from his interesting descriptions elsewhere, there comes to our mind the possibility that the correctness of detail we noted above in the record of Pennalius might have been due to these narrations of Morosini, or of some similar visitor. But granting that Pennalius saw all that he claimed to have seen, it is still possible that his friend the Turk might have had an agreement with the guard to play upon the pilgrim's gullibility. Remembering that access to a mosque was prohibited to Christians under penalty of death, we shall find that the elaborate precautions taken by the Turk were by no means unreasonable. We might justly be accused of too much skepticism, were it not for the fact that the history of the times records other instances of similar skulduggery.

In 1573, the Franciscan, Father Bonifatius Stefani of Ragusa, Bishop of Stagno, published his book, *Liber de Perenni Cultu Terrae Sanctae*,[13] composed in Jerusalem during his years of guardianship (1552–1564). Describing the Flagellation Chapel, then in Moslem hands, he writes: "Only in 1558, my seventh year as Guardian, was I able to enter and see and adore in the place where such abundant Blood was shed. An old woman took me there one day when the bad man [the Governor] was away worshipping in Hebron. Shortly after we arrived at the place, I heard a noise as if Christ were again being scourged. I asked the old woman and the other Friars, and they too heard it. The old woman said she had heard it day and night for 60 years—the whole time she had been with this family. I asked her what caused it and she said, 'The Jews! They are confined in that dark prison over there and after the final judgment they will be flung headlong into hell, for they flogged your Christ.' I remarked that it was the Roman soldiers who scourged Christ. But she replied with animation: 'Those soldiers are the accursed Jews!' Nor could we persuade her otherwise, so I gave her the promised money and we left."

Obviously Fr. Bonifatius had little faith in the old woman's story, but in his book he failed to make that fact perfectly clear. As his book soon became famous throughout the Christian world, everyone heard the tale. When the story of Malchus as told by Pennalius appeared a score of years later, it was to simple-minded people a confirmation.

Pilgrims began arriving with the added hope of seeing "the strange man" and of hearing "the miraculous noise." Franciscans who accompanied all pilgrims soon found themselves at a loss for argument. The best proof was to pay a visit to the place. However, it was the house of the Sangiak (Governor) and this individual proved himself unfavorable to the idea of having an endless stream of pilgrims roaming through his apartments. But the Friars did whatever they could. In 1616, the well-known explorer of Rome, Peter Della Valle, visited Jerusalem and the Franciscans were his guides. Probably at their suggestion, he wrote in a letter: "The story printed in Naples, which our Signor Andrea sent to me in Constantinople, makes mention of a place with a miraculous noise of scourging. This is a lie. Also the story of the man who struck the blow is a fable. I have the story here with me, have investigated and have found there was nothing to it. If there were, the Turks would gladly show for money."[14]

During these years from 1616 to 1626, Fr. Francis Quaresmi was composing his monumental work, *Elucidatio Terrae Sanctae*, which was first published in 1637. He devoted many pages to a refutation of the old woman's story and of the story of Malchus, although he did admit the possibility of the latter.[15] This work had great influence on later writers.

A similar denial was voiced by Fr. Antony Del Castillo in a guide for Spanish pilgrims.[16] But the tale was so attractive that pilgrims ignored or speedily forgot all repudiations and through their influence it continued. What was needed was a new and stronger argument against it, something much more decisive.

For this reason, Fr. Mariano Morone da Maleo, Custos of the Holy Land (1652–1658) availed himself of the friendship of the Emir of Gaza, as he tells in his valuable work,[17] while the Emir's son—Governor of Jerusalem—was absent from the city. He begged the Emir to reveal to them whether or not there was something of great interest to Christians to be found in his house in Jerusalem. The Emir, who probably knew the story of Malchus, roared with laughter, but did them the favor of showing them every part of his house. Fr. Mariano was attended by his Vicar, by the Procurator and by a dragoman. Together they made a thorough search but failed to find any sign of Malchus. Following this, he wrote a blistering denial of the whole story of the supposed Jew and added the following points: "(1) No one ever heard of his existence before Pennalius wrote of it; (2) Christ was struck when He was in the house of Annas on Mt. Sion, not when He was in the Pretorium (then the palace of the Emir); (3) The Turks always have an eye peeled for ready cash and are likely to see or hear or show anything the market will bear. And furthermore this name, "Pennalius," was not found on any of the Franciscan guest-lists and so I, Fr. Mariano, personally believe that Pennalius never saw the Holy Land."

Despite his wrath, perhaps fomented by poorly suppressed

Moslem mirth, Fr. Mariano did not reject the absolute possibility of the story, for, as he said, "Elias and Henoch remain alive and the Seven Holy Sleepers miraculously existed for centuries."

Nevertheless there still appeared writers, some of them Franciscans, who loved to report the myth and who casually neglected to identify it as such—a circumstance which probably made many weary writers turn over in their graves.

The German Franciscan, Fr. Francis Ferdinand of Trolio, describing his voyage in 1666–70[18] dedicated some pages to this and to similar stories. About 1670, the French Franciscan, Fr. Leonard of Clou, who had been a Councilor of the Holy Land, likewise repeated it, omitting any judgments against it.[19] In 1679, the Italian priest, Ser Dominicus Laffi, related it, leaving all responsibility for it to other authors. He hastened to say, however, that he thought the Jew "had not been punished as much as he deserved." (!!)[20] In 1700 another Italian priest, Ser Didacus Angeli, told how he visited the places but had heard no scourging and had seen no strange man pacing the floor. But he did observe that "the writer [of the story of Malchus] described details so well as easily to deceive the unwary."[21]

In 1704, the Franciscan, Fr. Peter of Vicentia, wrote a guide to the Holy Places in which he mentioned all the arguments of Fr. Mariano and suggested that Rome prohibit any further publication of the fable.[22] In 1713, a noted Latin poet, the Franciscan Fr. Conrad Heitling, at one time Guardian at Bethlehem, condemned it again.[23]

More than any prohibiting laws or vehement denials, the one thing that contributed most to its collapse was simply opening the door of the place in question and letting everyone see for themselves.

By the middle of the nineteenth century the local coloring of the legend was quite dead, when the renowned architect, Hermes Pierotti, who lived in Palestine from 1854 till 1862, in his work on ancient and modern Jerusalem,[24] noted a Jewish house (really of crusader time) near the VIIth station and identified it as "the house of the Wandering Jew."(!) Perhaps he was unduly influenced by the itinerary of Ser Mariano da Siena. However, in his great work, *Jerusalem Explored*[25] he wrote: "Farther on [after Veronica's house] the street is arched over, and in the side-walls are remains of ancient masonry. Here, some place the house of the Wandering Jew. This tradition, however, (or rather legend) is not accepted by the Christians of Jerusalem." In the mind of Pierotti, it is safe to say, the "Christians" are the Franciscans. When the fable was entirely excluded from the *Guide to the Holy Places* of Brother Lavinus of Hamme (Ghent 1875) the deathblow was finally given. Today, no one connects the Wandering Jew with any specific remains in Palestine. To which we add a fervent, Amen.[26]

NOTES

1. *Patrologia Latina*, Migne, V. 74, c. 133. See also *Catholic Encyclopedia*, "An old Italian legend knows of . . . punishment inflicted on the soldier who struck Christ before the High Priest, and later this soldier was identified with Malchus whose ear was cut off by Peter." (John xviii.10).—Arthur F. J. Remy.

2. See for example, *The Jewish Encyclopedia* under "Wandering Jew"; or the *Enciclopedia Italiana* I. Treccani: "Ebreo errante." Here we find a good resumé of the legend but without any mention of Palestine.

3. In *Revue de l'Orient Latin* 1902, p. 358.

4. See Introduction to *A Voyage Beyond the Seas* by Fr. Niccolo of Poggibonsi (Jerusalem, 1945), pp. xvii ff., and also the Introduction to *A Visit to the Holy Places of Egypt, Sinai, Palestine and Syria* by Frescobaldi, Gucci and Sigoli (Jerusalem, 1949), pp. 15 ff.

5. *Del Viaggio in Terra Santa* (Firenze, 1822), p. 29.

6. If he *had* heard the story of the Wandering Jew, he could have pointed out a spot *in the house* of Annas, not outside, for it is clear from John XVIII.22 that it was in the house that the servant struck the blow and said, "Answerest thou the High Priest so?" Afterwards Christ was sent "bound to Caiphas the High Priest" (v.24).

7. *The Wanderings*. Palestine Pilgrims' Text (London, 1897), VII, p. 317.

8. *Terrae Sanctae Elucidatio* (Venetiis, 1881), II, p. 142.

9. *Viaggio in Levante* (Bologna, 1683), p. 161.

10. Alcarotti in his book *Del Viaggio in Terra Santa* (Novara, 1595) says nothing about Malchus, but Quaresmi and Laffi testified independently that the tale was published in this work. Probably they found it in some pamphlets.

11. Zimolong Bert. *Navis Peregrinorum, Ein Pilgerverzeichnis aus Jeru-*

salem von 1561 bis 1695 (Köln, 1938) and Lemmens' *Collectanea Terrae Sanctae* (Quaracchi, 1933), p. 254.

12. Fr. G. Guzzo, Commissary of the Holy Land in Venice, sent me a faithful copy of this MS.

13. (Venetiis, 1875) p. 223. Fr. E. Roger in *Terre Sainte* (Paris, 1664), p. 123, relates the same things, but as heard by Mustafa Bey, son of Muhamed Bascia of Jerusalem, after the year 1623.

14. *Viaggi* (Roma, 1660), I, p. 509.

15. *Elucidatio*, II, p. 142 ff.

16. *El Devoto Peregrino, Viage de Tierra Santa* (Madrid, 1705), p. 163.

17. *Terra Santa Nuovamente Illustrata* (Piacenza, 1669), I, p. 88.

18. *Orientalische Reisebeschreibung* (Dresden, 1676), pp. 174–178.

19. *Itinerarium breve Terrae Sanctae* (Florentiae, 1891), p. 161.

20. *Viaggio in Levante*, p. 161.

21. *Viaggio in Terra Santa* (Venezia, 1737), p. 84.

22. *Guide fedele alla Santa Città di Gierusalemme* (Venezia, 1704), pp. 80–81.

23. *Peregrinus affectuosus per Terram Sanctam et Jerusalem* (Graecii, 1713), I, p. 107.

24. *Plan de Jerusalem ancienne et moderne* par le Docteur Ermete Pierotti, Architecte, Ingénieur, Ancien Commandant du Génie Sarde, (Paris chez Kaeppelin).

25. *Jerusalem Explored*, being a Description of the Ancient and Modern City, translated by Thomas George Bonney (London, 1864), p. 199.

26. Appreciation is hereby expressed for the work of Fr. Peter Eichelberger, O.F.M., in helping to prepare the MS. for publication in English.

THE THREE APPLES
OF EASTER
A LEGEND OF THE VALLEY
OF AOSTA

Louis Jaccod

*Despite the efforts of some clerics to disavow the legend, the
Wandering Jew has managed to remain localized in many areas,
sometimes even in conjunction with the official Christian calendar. In a small village in northern Italy very near the French and
Swiss borders, the Wandering Jew surfaces as a figure in the
celebration of Good Friday. His original association with the
Passion story is reenacted through his appearance on that holy
day. The following narrative, although evidently bearing traces
of literary embellishment, is invoked to explain a custom of plac-
ing apples on Easter branches. The author does remark that the
legend was known to him from oral sources.*

*Jaccod provides a charming account of the legend, but he offers
no interpretation of it. Yet, one cannot help but associate the apple
with the original sin of Adam in the Garden of Eden, for which
Christ's Crucifixion was intended to redeem mankind. The three
apples might symbolize the three days of the Passion. The ritual
of hanging apples on Easter boughs would thus be a celebration of
the triumph over Original Sin. This interpretation is supported
by the folk belief mentioned at the very end of the essay, which
claims that the ritual might be responsible for the fact that the*

inhabitants of that region are immune from being bitten by little vipers.

While this is not really a typical version of the legend of the Wandering Jew, it is representative of the vast majority of written reports of the Jew's appearance insofar as it describes how he was seen at a particular place and time.

The memories of the legend of the Wandering Jew are few in the Valley of Aosta, through which the Wandering Jew was believed to have passed on his way to the Canavais, where his presence is thought to have been reported in several localities. At Châtillon, we know only one version of this passage, and that one is filled with anachronisms and improbabilities. It mixes customs which disappeared centuries ago with things belonging to a time fairly close to ours. For example, the tradition mentions potatoes, which were offered to the Wandering Jew. In fact, this tuber was introduced here only around 1770, probably by emigrants from Germany or Switzerland where this precious vegetable was introduced from Peru at the beginning of the sixteenth century. This allowed us to trace the name which our patois gave to this plant to the German dialectal form (kartoffel—tartifla—trüffel—trifola),[1] the latter perhaps influenced by the Piedmont dialect. It is noteworthy that the first form, in certain parts of the country, also designates a stupid woman, probably for reasons which have nothing to do with the memory of the classic meaning of *Tartuffe*.

The legend of the Wandering Jew does not go back beyond the twelfth century, and the famous lament must belong to the second half of the seventeenth century. The basic oral tradition must go back rather far, probably to the sixteenth century. Some minstrel may have brought it to us, singing it while accompanying himself on the hurdy-gurdy, under the carved ceilings of our manors, near the vast fireplace of black stone, before the beguiled chatelaine. This legend, transmitted orally from age to age, was doubtless

Reprinted from *Augusta Praetoria (Aosta) Revue Valdotaine*, 1 (1919): 165–77. We are greatly indebted to folklorist Lee Benzinger for translating this essay from French into English.

enriched with the details, usages, and customs of each succeeding generation, which thus contributed its particular mode of life and thought.

The story which we collected is not without faults. It lacks unity; many details are trivial; incongruous traits are not rare; and everything points to the conclusion that two or three versions were juxtaposed in order to arrive at the present form. Since I did not believe it possible to reproduce the exact translation of the patois text with its lacunae and incongruities, I felt it necessary to adapt it by trimming the useless parts and adding some traits which are characteristic of the period, while respecting that which appeared to be the true essence of the legend. The story which follows, although an original contribution to the local folklore, includes some elaboration of the traditional element and paints, in its descriptive passages, an old picture of customs forever gone.

We can give only a conjectural date to the period when the passage of the Wandering Jew was supposed to have taken place. This, incidentally, is confirmed by the text itself which mentions the passage of troops. We believe that this particular event occurred toward the end of the seventeenth century, during the invasion by the Marquis de la Hoguette.

The scene takes place at Domianaz, a hamlet situated on a small plateau to the east of Châtillon, on the road which climbs to the pastures of Nissod. It is a tiny village of around eighty inhabitants, whose chapel is dedicated to Our Lady of Lorette. Perched on a mountain promontory and connected to the main town by a parish road, it is located almost at the extreme limit of the region which, in the local speech, is called *Lë Clabaüdin*. This name serves to designate the inhabitants and, by extension, all the territory which stretches from the tower of Grange to the limits of the township above the highway near Saint-Vincent. Perhaps it is attached to *clabaud* in memory of an insurrection attempted by the peasants against their lord. What allows us to advance this hypothesis is the existence of an old saying which characterizes the inhabitants of this area as *briseurs de cloches* [breakers of bells]. We know nothing more.

Perhaps the reader wonders why the Wandering Jew decided to leave the highway and climb up to this isolated village. No one knows the answer, just as one cannot explain the presence of the Wandering Jew at Pollein, a rarely visited place on the right bank of the Doire. As to the name Brunet, several families with the names de Brunod and de Brunet still live throughout this region. We see a Bruna on a fifteenth century charter, and it is probably to one of its branches that the Brunet family of the tradition attaches itself.

The almost illiterate servant from whose mouth I have collected this popular account, although a native of Chambaye, was a long-time servant of the Domaine family about fifty years ago at Crêta d'Honda, in the very heart of the Claboudins. She often heard it told by the old people there, and it is this version which she repeated for me.

This legend has survived very clearly in my memory since childhood. I heard it again, after thirty years, from the same person, not without feeling the old yeast of the simple joys of my native village swelling within me. The sonorous speech of my forefathers still sounded as sweet and familiar to my enchanted ear. Therefore I asked the old servant to repeat for me the naïve lament in 24 couplets which she knows entirely by heart:

> Est-il rien sur terre
> Qui soit plus surprenant
> Que la grande misère
> Du pauvre Juif errant?

> Is there nothing on earth
> Which is more astonishing
> Than the great misery
> Of the poor wandering Jew?

And in my mind's eye, I saw again the little village square of long ago, where a hooded pilgrim would sing the old couplets to the villagers, gathered in their Sunday finery in front of the sign of the Three Kings on a festival day. He would chant the verses in his languid voice while the sun clothed in purple the same horizon and the same beloved landscape toward which the inexorable wave of old memories carried me.

It was the year of our Lord 1696.

The clear rays of the young April sun caressed all the tender leaves of the vine whose fine tendrils traced pale green ribbons on the posts of the arbor. Beneath it, our good Aostan earth prepared itself with joy to fertilize the vigorous vine stocks. The willows swayed their velvety catkins in the soft breeze all along the streams which were flowing at full crest. Around the hamlet of Domianaz, in the barony of Châtillon, the young grass, flecked with golden daisies, spread a sash of greenery on the clearings of the wooded slopes. The grey stone cottages, with their rustic wooden balconies, clung to the hillside, under the high canopies of the century-old chestnut trees.

The small black hens with crinkled feet stretched their stiff legs on the crooked perch to the rhythm of a discreet chirping. They pecked at reddish worms while strutting along the stony path where ventured the first lizards in their black spotted robes. Along the vast soothing horizon could be heard the crisp sounds of pruning shears in the vineyards and of woodsmen's axes as they split wood for heating the communal oven, where the village women would bake the bread for the holy day of Easter.

It was Good Friday.

The sun had already passed the summit of Mont Roux.[2] It was almost noon. The Angelus of eleven o'clock had not rung in the Romanesque bell tower of Bourg because the bell clappers had been fastened until the ten o'clock Gloria of Holy Saturday, when all hurry to wash their faces in the waters of the stream while petitioning Saint Lucy to preserve them from eye disease. The few goats who were browsing among the young birch shoots were also without bells. These had been removed during the church mourning, just as the custom of removing the bells of herds belonging to families in mourning is observed today.

It was time to bake the rye bread which the women had kneaded in the ancient redwood trough near the high fireplace, for in olden days the kneading trough was next to the hearth. These two essential elements, fire and bread, had their place in the largest room of the house. Easter bread had to be savory, and the dough prepared with great care. It had been well salted, thanks to the salt bought from the smugglers of Verrayes,[3] and it also contained a measure of wheat from the fields at Nissod.

On a very white, thoroughly-washed board, Julienne Brunet, wife of the trustee of the Claboudins quarter, arranged the dough into shapes, some round, some large with a hole in the center, some *fiantse*,[4] some like tarts, and some like roosters with notched combs for the children. A servant came and took the bread to the nearby oven whose small triangular mouth crackled noisily.

It was a large household. Three generations lived under the absolute and respected authority of Jérôme Brunet, a handsome old man of eighty-seven, who wore a *brestou*[5] of green cloth with copper buttons. He was a former member of the canton's board of arbitration, a former deputy of the Administrative Council for the Third Estate, an honest and austere man who wore on his virile face the enduring honor of his lineage, rooted for centuries to the same soil.

Thus, a "hémine" of the finest rye and a "quartaine"[6] of wheat had been kneaded, because it was customary to eat fresh bread from the eve of Easter Sunday until Octave Sunday.

During the long Lenten period, strict fasting had been observed by the Brunets, as by all the families of the parish. The men made do with a few pieces of dry bread chopped on the butcher block, a handful of roasted chestnuts, a little *sérac*, and a sip of *piquette*.[7] The women had a sauce of dried beans boiled with some rye flour seasoned with sage, and some dairy products. Each evening at nightfall the villagers met in the chapel, where, by the flickering light of a lamp burning the golden walnut oil of our vales, the elder Brunet recited the psalms of penitence in his capacity as prior of the brotherhood of the Holy Sacrament.

That is why everyone—noble, bourgeois, and peasant—now prepared to celebrate the feast of Easter, the most solemn feast of the year, after Christmas. They would eat lard and meat, and drink a "quarteron" of wine from the little barrel which was not touched more than four or five times a year. In the evening after vespers, they would eat the tart-shaped breads filled with honey, and the men would play a game of *tsan*[8] in the large meadows near Barral.

Suddenly, the air was pierced by sharp cries from the feathered inhabitants and by the yelping voice of Griset, the little dog with the pointed snout. There was a confusion of screeching hens, of flapping wings, and tumbling latticed barriers—a crescendo of unusual uproar.

"Aunt Philomène," said Julienne Brunet to the little old shriveled woman sitting near the door where she was peeling large chestnuts into a flat reed basket, "Won't you go see what the trouble is? Perhaps it's that accursed fox who is after our hens. It's very possible that he managed to get here, especially if the trap was not set."

The old woman raised her head and answered in a broken voice: "The problem is that it is Good Friday, the day of the venerable Passion, and also the day of the dreaded *tempore*.[9] Young people don't believe in it, but I have often heard the sorcerers whistling to each other while they attend the synagogue."[10]

Then she added: "I also hear mewing. It must be the Jeanin's cat who is coming to see if our pullets have eaten up all the mash. He certainly doesn't feast every day, that ugly cat, skinny as a lizard."

As the uproar increased, and the sound of footsteps could be clearly perceived, Julienne Brunet quickly went to the wide open door, then ran down the road, which went through the village, to see if the children were throwing stones at the rooster with the long yellow spurs, ill-natured and jealous lord of the poultry yard.

Only the women were at home. The children were making little houses out of the still humid sand of the *bouëil*,[11] and the men were all outside, some in the vineyards, others at the Nissod farm, yet others at the village where they had delivered two loads of wine to squire Jehan Carrel, ducal attorney. Old Brunet was enjoying the sun at the back of the orchard, near the buzzing beehives in front of which one could still see the small reed troughs where, during the very cold season, the bees came to suck the warm nectar carefully prepared for the little workers by the grandfather.

Valiant woman that she was, Julienne Brunet left the front of the house, turned in the direction of the hubbub, and saw a man coming slowly toward her, a boxwood cane attached to his right hand by a slim strap.

"It's another beggar, a vagabond, a stranger," she thought. "What does he want here? Could he be a thief or a *barbet*?[12] You never know what kind of people you're dealing with after the passage of all those troops."[13]

He was a tall, vigorous man. The skin on his face resembled the parchment of the ancient scribes. A pointed hat rested on his very white hair. He wore a small leather apron. A haversack hung at his side, and a gourd was suspended from his neck by a strap with a yellow buckle. He looked very old yet robust. A silken beard, long as that of the emperor Charles, hung down to his worn apron. He was a strange being, mysterious and attractive at the same time; his eyes, very black and mobile, were marked by great sadness. He seemed very weary.

"Good day, honorable lady," said he when he was close to the threshold, doffing his hat in a comfortable and natural manner. "If only you would permit me to rest for a moment on your stone bench. I shan't stay long; *I cannot stay long.*"

"As you please," answered the woman, who was not yet reassured about this foreigner, a disquieting personage before whom she felt a strange uneasiness. "Sir," she continued, "if you are a pilgrim on the way to Our Lady of Lorette or to the most holy city of Rome, you are welcome and be seated. Presently, I shall bring you a crusty bread, fresh from the oven, and you will drink a cup of our wine in the name of God and for the repose of our good deceased."

"Alas!" continued the stranger, taking a few more steps, "but I am not a pilgrim who is going to kneel at the tomb of Saint Peter or Saint James of Compostela! By misfortune, I am a wretched one who is not worthy to sit before this door where I see with terror the venerable sign of the cross at which I scoffed. I am a great sinner, a publican, a creature cursed by God."

"By our Lady who protects us, who are you then?" asked Julienne Brunet, having been joined by aunt Philomène and Sandrine, the youngest servant-maid. "Where do you come from? What have you done? Which crime have you committed? Are you by chance possessed, a "pascatin"? Do you have the *pépi?*[14] Do speak."

And the three trembling women crossed themselves while invoking the glorious archangel Saint Michael, slayer of the Dragon.

"Fear naught, my good ladies," continued the stranger, "I harm neither persons nor animals. And since you seem to have pity on me, I shall tell you, in few words, the terrible story of my destiny."

Having said these words, he seated himself on the bench of disjointed stones and began: "Today is a very sad anniversary for me. Soon, it will be one thousand seven hundred years since I committed the crime which I am still expiating to this day and the reason for which you see me here.

"I was born near Jerusalem in Judea, where my ancestors had built a magnificent temple of marble and precious wood. I had a shop for repairing old shoes in a street near the synagogue. There I earned a good living with my wife and my little daughter Myrra, the apple of my eye, gentle as a dove, to whom I would tell at sunset the story of Judith and Holophernes.

"Well, one day, toward the noon hour, there passed before my shop a procession of three criminals condemned to the torments of the cross, a death reserved for slaves. One of the criminals was named Jesus, son of a carpenter from Nazareth. I had heard him spoken of as an exalted one, a rebel who proclaimed the greatest disdain for the law, and preached revolt against the emperor. He called himself king of the Jews and exerted over the crowds the most pernicious influence. Others said that he was the Messiah, that he worked miracles, that through his ministrations the blind saw and the lame carried off their pallets, that he even spoke words of forgiveness to courtesans. Well, I must tell you that it was not easy to know what to make of all this or where to stand.

"But at that moment, I saw in him nothing but a common criminal. Because he had been condemned to such a torture, one could not doubt that he had committed a deplorable crime. Alas! My eyes were open but I could not see the abyss into which I was to plunge.

"The procession, which was to end outside the city at a height named Golgotha, was large and noisy: legionnaires with iron helmets, carrying thin brown lances, scribes dressed in white woolen robes, disheveled women, ragged children, all crying, shouting, jostling each other, and pushing before them the three condemned prisoners, prey to the taunts and mockery of the populace.

"When the procession had arrived at the level of my shop, where I was beating the leather with great blows, the Nazarene stopped, out of breath and weak under the heavy burden of his torment. He was covered with blood. A branch of brambles surrounded his bare head with its luminous hair. A scarlet robe enveloped his bruised body and nearly hid his bare finely-shaped feet. He was a handsome man of thirty odd years, with a beard the color of gold, and with large, most gentle eyes. He stopped and sank down under the weight of the cross which he was dragging.

"Then a simple woman of the people, Veronica, if I remember correctly, approached him and, kneeling beside him, wiped his bleeding face with a cloth upon which his features remained imprinted to the great astonishment of everyone. Some cried out 'Master, you are truly the Son of man; we believe in you and want to follow you.'

"But I, alas! Seeing in him but a guilty man being drawn to his punishment, and the persecutor of my religion, I shouted at him: 'Walk to your death which you have justly deserved; do not stop here, for my threshold would be soiled by your presence. Go away.' Jesus cast upon me a look of infinite tenderness and said: 'Grant me leave to rest an instant before I drain my chalice to the dregs.' Irritated by these mysterious words, I retorted, 'Walk, gallows bird,' and I got up from my stool to strike him with a thong which I used to put stray dogs to flight.

"Then the Nazarene, in a tone of great sadness, added, 'You yourself will walk until the end of time. Arise and walk, you who have dared to drive away the Son of man from the threshold of your dwelling. You will be a father without children, a husband without a wife, a traveller who knows not the destination of his voyage, an eternal pilgrim among men, themselves pilgrims for only a day. You will always have five farthings in your purse, and no water clock will measure your sleep, for your rest will not exceed a quarter of an hour. You will invoke death, the enemy of men, but death will flee from you.'

"At once, compelled by a mysterious force, without even saying adieu to my wife and adored Myrra, who was playing at the Temple square, I left my bench, dressed as I was, left the city, and walked toward the East. Since then, I have never stopped to rest for more than a few moments. I have seen murderous combats, plagues, and famines. Earthquakes have felled me. Lightning has struck at my feet. I have crossed deserts without water and oceans in the midst of storms, immense rivers and high mountains covered with ice—"

"Higher than the Derbion?"[15] interrupted aunt Philomène, who was drinking in the words of the stranger.

"Yes, much higher and much more dangerous, good woman," he continued, "but nowhere has death wanted me, in accordance with the words of the divine Master.

"I passed through this region a long time ago. In those days, the inhabitants spoke a strange language which resembled that of the people of Latium where Rome is situated. Vast forests covered the land, and at night the bear and the lynx were my traveling companions. At that time, the houses of Châtillon were massed lower down, near the donkey-back bridge of Tournefol, on the plateau which you still call the *Bor viei*.[16] There passed the old paved Roman road, and that is the road which I followed from Chambaye par Briel,[17] where a peasant offered me some whey in a bowl of gleaming pewter.

"Alas! Everything changes, everything is transformed, everything ages, everything dies; only I remain the same, carrying with me my eternal punishment, until the earth is reduced to ashes at the sound of the four avenging trumpets, when the dead shall arise from the open tombs, and when we shall all meet in the Valley of Josaphat, where Saint Peter will hold the scales of justice."

"Shall I be there as well?" asked Sandrine timidly.

"Keep quiet, *tôca*,"[18] scolded her mistress in a severe tone.

"What more is there to say?" continued the stranger. "I insulted and disowned my Savior, who was about to die on a cross. It is just that I expiate my sin. I am the Wandering Jew, that unfortunate Jew who drove away the divine Master as one drives away a dog." And some tears fell slowly onto his hollow cheeks and formed, on his long wavy beard, a rosary of thick pearls, the pearls of sincere repentance.

"It is true that you are a very great sinner," said Julienne Brunet with emotion, when the man had fallen silent, "but our Savior God will take pity on you, and our Lady will intercede for you, because you have suffered much. Before resuming your journey, would you accept, sire, this crisp bread, and drink this pitcher of our Glireyaz[19] wine. Then, may your good angel keep you in his holy care!" And the servant presented him with a large golden loaf of bread and a tall wooden tankard[20] with handles whose carved lid she lifted.

After he had placed the bread in his haversack and emptied the tankard, the old man stood up, preparing to take his leave of the three women. With a long bony hand, he fumbled in his bag and extracted from it three small red apples of an oblong shape, which he presented to Julienne Brunet saying:

"Most honored woman, since you have been so merciful toward me, and since you have kindly offered me a taste of your bread and a drink of your wine, accept in turn these three apples. A saintly anchorite gave them to me. They have the virtue of protecting one from the bite of serpents.

"On Easter Sunday at sunrise, have each one of your family eat a little bit of them before breaking fast. The vipers will be powerless against them. Plant the seeds of the largest apple at the right angle of your orchard toward the East, and you will always have fruit similar to these, thanks to God's sunshine. This is the only remembrance that the poor Wandering Jew can leave you."

Having given the three apples, the stranger took the winding path which descends toward the village of Torrensec, above Saint-Vincent. The three women watched him depart and remained immobile and mute until the shadow of the traveler had disappeared behind the striated trunks of the chestnut trees.

The sun touched the peak of the Barbeston,[21] and the sundial of the square *mistral* house,[22] above the black mass of the church of Bourg, marked one o'clock.

Two days later was the feast of Easter.

At three o'clock in the morning, the large procession[23] was to take place. Since the previous day, the villagers had been arriving at the small market town from the twenty hamlets of the parish. All night one could see in the distance, on the tortuous mountain trails, some flickering lights which appeared here and there. They were cast by the resin torches carried by latecomers, who were hurrying down toward the plain. The fine, vigorous mules, with their multicolored pompons, paraded in the darkness of the stony paths to the joyous fanfare of their small bells. Young voices, calls, religious refrains, repeated words, a confused clamor mounted toward the church, glowing with light, from which a flood of faithful would soon burst forth.

At the stroke of three, it was first the Bourgeoise, the bell with a deep timbre, which, from the height of the Romanesque arches, sent out her metallic greeting in the vast transparent sky, awakening the echoes of the vales. No harmonies, no babbling carillons, her royal voice alone reverberated in the still air: one stroke, then two, then three, then the regular majestic tolling filled the white space of the moon. The sonorous wave seemed to descend from the sky alive with stars to envelop the living soul of the plain. Then came the flutelike voice of the Capuchin monastery's bell answering the call, then the bell of the chapel of the bridge which crosses the Marmore, then the tiny bell of the château, then those of Barral, Albard, Domianaz, and still others, some massive and sonorous, others light and muffled. And all these voices, near and distant, escaping like a flock of swallows from the invisible steeples, intermingled, melted together, disappeared, and reappeared on the first breeze of dawn, acclaiming at the same time the glory of the resurrection of Christ and the joy of the immortal regeneration of nature in this marvelous basin stretching from Chambaye to Saint-Vincent and crowned by the harmonious serrated peaks of the neighboring mountains.

Soon a little bell, rung with two hands by a brother in a white cloak, added its slightly sour note to the immense concert. The man who carried it walked three times around the church, crossing the cemetery which surrounded it, and started to descend the steep road which ended in the market town by way of the rue des Moulins. The bell ringer was accompanied by two staff-bearers, each with a tall painted staff topped by a royal crown bearing the monogram of Christ, the emblem of their order. Next came the yellow penitents, the brotherhood of Mount Carmel, and the brotherhood of the Holy Rosary preceded by their banners. Then came the crowd of faithful. First the men alone, in two columns, reciting the rosary aloud, then the married and widowed women, then the young girls answering in even voices the invocations of the priors. Next came the large red gonfalon of the brotherhood of the Holy Sacrament, whose members had the honor of preceding the canopy. All these people were directed without too much ceremony by other staff-bearers who presided over the procession, uniting the scattered ranks, hurrying the latecomers, shouting, and giving orders. Then came the choristers, those famous choristers of Châtillon, renowned in the whole region, singing the *Te Deum* in plainsong, slowly, measured, in full supple voices as resonant as organ pipes. Finally, there was the bearer of the cross of embossed silver, then the white silk canopy which sheltered the priest dressed in the red and gold cape with the coat of arms of Challant, bearing the sacred host in a magnificent silver monstrance with four little steeples. Next came the baron of Châtillon and the knights of Challant in silk stockings and carrying engraved swords, then the notables of Bourg, the trustees of the neighborhoods with large lighted tapers, and the judge of the barony preceded by the baton of justice.

From the rue des Moulins, the procession went along the main street and reentered the church via the street which climbed from the place de la Commune, after the clergy had stopped for a moment of prayer before the oratory of the Souls. Here, between two burning tapers, a copper tray received offerings for the funeral service celebrated each year on the second of November for the solace of all the deceased of the parish. This mass was followed by an abundant *donna*.[24]

Julienne Brunet mingled with the contemplative crowd. She wore a black woolen dress, a large floral scarf on her shoulders, and a little barrette with silk ribbons to hold back her thick auburn hair, which was barely turning grey at the temples. Her gloved hands, on which shone the thin circle of nuptial gold, held before her, like a relic, a branch of laurel on which she had fastened the three apples of the Wandering Jew so that the resurrected Christ would bless the gift of the unhappy sinner.

A truly strong and discreet woman, like those in the Scriptures, she humbly followed the procession, preceded by her daughters, her sisters-in-law, and her servants. She prayed for her large generation, living and dead, for her husband, who had the honor of following the canopy, a taper in his hand, and for the stranger, terrifying example of divine justice, so that the Lord would take pity on him. She invoked heavenly blessings on the great Brunet vineyards, on their fields, on their orchards, on their meadows, on their houses, and on their beasts, so that peace would be with her own, that the bread would be abundant, and the chestnuts nicely plump. She prayed for the health of her beloved sovereign, Duke Victor Amédée, and for the faithful people of Châtillon.

When Julienne Brunet returned to her large farm after the first low Mass, she cut two apples into very small pieces and distributed them to the household, with the hot cinnamon-flavored wine and the good bread exuding the fragrance of fennel. She stuck the third apple onto the blessed branch of rosemary from Palm Sunday and placed it beside the large oak bed with the carved posts where all the Brunets had been born for more than two hundred years.

The following day, Easter Monday, after returning from the procession of Saint-Clair,[25] the venerable grandfather, in the presence of the whole family assembled up to the fourth degree, put the seeds of the largest apple into the earth in the right angle of the enclosure toward the East, in accordance with the stranger's instruction.

That is why, says the legend, we place apples in the branches on Palm Sunday. First, three were used in memory of the Wandering Jew, then five, then a larger number. Only a few years ago, one could still see, at the procession of Palm Sunday, some pretty little larches all covered with beautiful red apples. And it was not one of our lesser joys of childhood to have many apples to stick onto the laurel branch which we paraded like a trophy in the streets of the town, without suspecting the origin of this characteristic tradition.

In several families, the blessed apples are displayed with the candle of Saint Barbe during storms and hail showers to appease the unleashed elements. Others, with whom the primitive memory persists, eat some before breakfast on the morning of Easter Sunday and on Ascension Day, for the seeds of the Brunet family produced a beautiful tree and, in time, pretty little red apples.

As news of the marvel spread, many villagers took cuttings from the tree. That is why the whole canton is covered with vast orchards—the most beautiful of the lower valley—where ripen the delicious *martins-secs*[26] in their golden robes and the oblong apples with the fragrant flesh.

They also say that, since that time, no inhabitant of the Claboudins—provided that he was at peace with God—has been bitten by the small black vipers which are not rare in our sunny vineyards, between the Grange tower and Silliod, and beyond the bridge of Saint-Valentin.

NOTES

1. It is also possible that the theme of the Franco-Provençal dialects was borrowed, through an analogy of form, from the term *Trifoula*, "truffle," in Provençal, *Tartifle*, a mushroom (fungus) which was certainly known here long before the potato.

2. The Mont-Ljane (2059 meters) spur which separates the Vale of Champdepraz from the principal valley.

3. An old saying refers to the inhabitants of Verrayes as dealers in contraband salt. The patois states: *Verrayon, voler de sa.* [Trans. note: Since this is patois, the *sa* may have any number of meanings besides the feminine possessive pronoun, which leaves the sentence incomplete.] Perhaps it alludes to the pillage of some loads of salt from the ducal gabelle (salt duty), which was introduced here in 1540.

4. Oblong bread, prepared with the finest white flour, much thinner than ordinary bread. The word seems to attach to the French *flan* and the German *flaven*, "cake," "tart." These kinds of cakes were primarily in favor at Christmas, Epiphany, and Easter. On Twelfth Night, bakers

presented them as gifts to their customers. As a child, I saw very lovely
fiantse, golden and sweet, which measured almost two feet in length
(more than half a meter).

5. A kind of vest with a double flap; same word in Savoyan dialect.

6. Old measure of volume for solids and liquids.

7. [Trans. Note: *Serac* is a white Alpine cheese; *piquette* is sour wine.]

8. Popular game, well-known especially between Châtillon and
Nus—from the low Latin *campum* meaning "enclosed field."

9. Deformation of dialect, from the Latin *tempora*, a series of three
days during which one fasts at the beginning of each of the four seasons.
In French, "les quatre temps." Popular imagination attributes sorcery,
bad omens, black masses, etc. to these periods fixed by Catholic liturgy.

10. This word designates the meeting of nocturnal sorcerers, who
called to each other by whistling and who danced in certain deserted
places. The common people placed heretics and sorcerers on the same
level. Also known as *synagogue* was the high-kicking dance performed
on the night of the Thursday before Lent by the light of resin torches.
This custom is disappearing.

11. A hollowed-out tree trunk serving as drinking and laundry trough.

12. The inhabitants of the Vaudois valleys of the Piedmont region
called the doctors and ministers of their church by the collective name
barbes out of respect. From the low Latin *barba, barbanus,* "uncle," that
is, an old and wise man. The inhabitants of these valleys thus received
the name *barbets*. In our area, this word took the meaning of an excommunicated person, one who must be refused bread and lodging, in the
same way that the word heretic passed from the original meaning to
magician or sorcerer. *Haereticus* gave the French *erège*, from which came
the patois *eriedzo*, "sorcerer." In the same pejorative sense, *pascatin* was
a person who did not carry out the paschal precepts and whom everyone
avoided like a scabby sheep.

13. As we have already said, this probably refers to the movement of
troops, which has been documented since 1691.

14. The *pépi*, "familiar devil," which certain persons carried in their
pockets.

15. Point to the northeast of Châtillon from which one enjoys a beautiful panorama of the valley of the Pennine Alps. The word is probably
of Celtic origin meaning "height," "summit"; altitude 2721 meters.

16. The old Bourg. [Trans. note: Bourg is the name of the town; the
word means "borough" or "market town."]

17. This is the name of two hamlets between the suburb of Chameran
and Chambaye. The etymology seems to attach to a Celtic root indicating an elevated wooded place.

18. *Tôca*, "fool," probably from the French *toqué*. I prefer to discard
the hypothesis that this word is related to the Piedmontese *tucchini*, indicating the peasants who revolted against their lords at the end of the

14th century. The term *tôca*, incidentally, is common to all the Franco-Provençal dialects.

19. Small village between Châtillon and Saint-Vincent with beautiful terraced vineyards, above the highway. One can connect this word to the Latin *glarea*, "sandy ground."

20. The wooden drinking vessel from which our ancestors drank is called *grolla*, which must be a dialectal form of the low Latin *gradalis*, a kind of urn without brim. See the French *graal*, the famous mystical urn.

21. Peak to the south of Châtillon, above Valmeriana, altitude 2,483 meters.

22. Old house with pointed windows of which some have been walled in. Today, it is the school house, having been arranged for this purpose.

23. This procession, instituted in 1536 in memory of Calvin's flight, only takes place at Aosta, Châtillon, and Bard. At Châtillon, it followed the limits of the former feudal market town—from the Romanesque bridge to the hospital, very near the Capuchin monastery (whose limits had been fixed by the franchise accorded to the inhabitants of Bourg by the noble Pierre, lord of Châtillon, on July 14, 1238 and renewed by Count François de Challant on May 21, 1430). According to tradition, the noon Angelus is rung at eleven o'clock throughout the region, also in memory of Calvin, who was supposed to have crossed the Durand Pass, or the Fenêtre Pass, around eleven o'clock in the morning.

After the departure of the reformer, who had a number of partisans in the duchy, the Val d'Aosta kept its Catholic religion and remained faithful to the dukes of Savoy. Since that time, one can see on the stone lintels of doorways the monograms of Christ with two hearts and the date. At Châtillon, there are several very well preserved examples.

24. Alms which are still distributed to the poor, on the day of the funeral or the seventh day service, at the door of the deceased's house. Only bread or money is distributed today. The patois word corresponds to the low Latin *dona*. The French verb *donnée* has the same meaning.

25. Hillock which is isolated due to erosion of the Marmore and the Doire, very near their confluence. In the 12th and 13th centuries, some charters mention a fortified house and a *Bourg des Rives* [Trans. note: a town whose name means town or market place at the river banks], of which a section of ancient walls still remain at the crest of the little hill. A chapel was built there and dedicated to Saint Clair. This is the destination of the Easter Monday procession.

26. [Trans. note: *Martin-sec* is a kind of pear.]

FRENCH IMAGES
OF THE WANDERING JEW

Champfleury

*The Wandering Jew has inspired not only countless literary
accounts but also numerous visual representations. Probably the
first attempts to depict the Wandering Jew came in the form of
illustrations accompanying narrative texts. These illustrations
often display standard stereotypic features associated with Jews.
The features are part of the traditional anti-Semitic caricature
found in Europe and elsewhere. As the Wandering Jew story
became an increasingly popular subject of romantic prose and poetry, the image changed in similar fashion, perhaps culminating
with the dramatic and striking series of etchings by Gustave Doré.*

*The first and really only serious study of the imagery of the
Wandering Jew was written by Champfleury (Jules Fleury). He
devoted a substantial portion of his book* Histoire de l'imagerie
populaire *(1869), pp. 1–104, to the subject. The small section of
that essay reprinted here treats the image in France. For an earlier
essay by Champfleury in which he surveys the Wandering Jew in
legend, ballad, and iconography, see "D'Une Nouvelle Interpretation de la légende gothique du Juif-errant,"* Revue Germanique et Francaise, *30 (1864): 299–325.*

Reprinted from *Histoire de l'imagerie populaire* (Paris, 1869), pp. 63–75. We are
indebted once again to folklorist Lee Benzinger for translating the essay from
the original French.

The picture of *Ahasvérus* has been the most popular of all those which have made the presses of Epinal, Metz, and Nancy groan. Since the beginning of the century, the Wandering Jew has decorated every poor hovel, balanced by a picture of Napoleon. It seems that the common man gave an equal place in his imagination to these two great *marcheurs*.[1] Today, when the progress of scholarship relies on engraved monuments, it would be useful to know the origin of this print.

Why did the scholars of preceding centuries fail to understand the importance of popular images and, for a long time, hold prejudices against them? These images were precious teaching tools, addressing people who were not able to read. Even today, how many French peasants can only become acquainted with the legend by means of the engraving?

It is a barbaric art, according to some. But do we not make troublesome journeys abroad in order to bring back traces of ancient peoples' barbaric art?

These prints, which we scorn for having them too often in view, have a function. Who knows if Kaulbach, when introducing the Wandering Jew into his great composition of the Destruction of Jerusalem, was not remembering the naïve images which struck him during his childhood?

After the German prints reproduced in this study, the oldest in France, to my knowledge, is the portrait of the Wandering Jew engraved by Le Blond, and that one was intended for the bourgeois rather than the common people. The engraving is not bad, but the seventeenth-century draftsman hardly understood the legendary mask any better than the composer of the royal ballets who used the same theme. It is a figure of an old man, without any particular character, underneath which one reads this verse:

> I am wandering for ever and ever,
> My elsewhere is continually changing.
> I shall have neither rest nor peace
> Until that great day
> When the Redeemer of humans
> Judges the work of His hands.
> At Zion I was given birth,
> I have seen the Savior in torment,

> From him have I received my sentence
> Which filled me with astonishment,
> When he ordered me to wander
> Without being able to limit my journey.

In this classical engraving, the popular sentiment did not guide the draftsman's graving tool.

There is another old plate which was printed until the end of the Restoration by Bonnet at the rue Saint-Jacques. The first woodcarvers did not produce more naïve work. As with the primitive German masters, the subject is divided into three compartments, containing the Wandering Jew and two scenes depicting the principal features of the drama. The Wandering Jew is shown shod in sandals as he wanders across the deserts. The prologue of the drama in which he is involved unfolds in the first compartment, where Jesus, fallen under the weight of his cross, receives the harsh words of the cobbler; while the second depicts some bourgeois in Louis XV costumes conversing with Ahasvérus. This print is the one I am reproducing on the frontispiece for the pleasure of iconophiles, for there is no other old monument extant in Paris, painted or engraved, which deals with the Wandering Jew.[2]

At the museum of the Antiquarian Society of Caen, one can see a wood carving riddled with worm holes, from which escapes a yellowish dust similar to that which lies within the trunks of old willows. This engraving, of an extreme crudeness and on whose cutting connoisseurs would cast a disdainful look, has been religiously preserved by the archaeologists of Normandy, and, for this, one cannot praise them enough. Nevertheless, this xylographic monument would be nothing special if the subject did not show how the people of Normandy understood the legend.[3]

The drama is divided into four parts, in the manner of old prints. The first picture shows Ahasvérus leaving his cobbler's shop in order to watch Jesus walking to his torment. The Jew is holding the hammer of his profession, and a large leather apron covers him from his chest to his knees. Without pity, the man insults Christ. At a second floor window, a woman watches with a contrite air as the unfortunate one succumbs under the burden

The Wandering Jew
According to an old engraving
from Paris.

of the cross while climbing to Calvary escorted by soldiers. The second section of the plate represents Christ crucified between the two thieves. No spectator is present at this drama.

In the third picture, Ahasvérus is standing. Four men seated at a table facing him are offering him a glass of wine. Their invitation is the approximate translation of the citizens of Brussels.

> . . . Enter into this inn,
> Venerable old man;
> Of a pot of fresh beer
> You will take your part, etc.

To this the Wandering Jew replies:

> . . . I would agree to have
> A couple of drinks with you,
> But I cannot sit down,
> I must remain standing, etc.

While the popular artists have all consistently placed this scene at the door of the tavern, the Caen print is the only one I have seen whose engraver felt obliged to place the Wandering Jew inside the tavern. This is contrary to the popular tradition of the eternal wanderer in the open air. With the help of such details, I seek the interpretations of the various regions.

The draftsman in Normandy once more displayed his free interpretation of the legend through the manner in which he treated the fourth image. The Wandering Jew finds himself caught in the cross-fire of four soldiers, divided into two groups, symbols of the two armies involved. From each side, the rifles are aimed at him. At his feet lies a dead man, victim of the frightful volleys. Only Ahasvérus remains, impassive, defying the fire of men as he defied that of lightning and volcanoes.

Paris, Rennes, Orleans, Metz, Nancy, Montbéliard, Epinal, have all engraved Isaac Laquedem,[4] and, with some difficulty, I have been able to gather these diverse representations of the Wandering Jew, with the sole aim of showing the peculiarities of costume which the common people attributed to him.

> Large breeches he wears in the naval fashion,
> And a skirt in the Florentine,
> A coat so long it trails on the ground;
> As for the rest, he is like any other man.

In the beginning, some of the Epinal print-makers followed this text quite closely, but the modern spirit has done away with all the character of the traditional costume. I point out for the public indignation the procedure of the printers at Monbéliard who, in order to modernize a Wandering Jew wearing a three-cornered hat in the 1828 fashion, replaced it in 1829 with a kind of *gateau de Savoie* edged in fur.[5]

One of the strangest images, insofar as costume is concerned, is

The Wandering Jew
According to 17th-century engraved poster from the
Museum of Caen.

the one printed in 1816 by Desfeuilles, an engraver at Nancy. The Wandering Jew, wrapped in a greatcoat trimmed with fur, is wearing an old wide-brimmed felt hat and is shod in boots into which his trousers disappear. A strange coloring principle embellishes this print. Apparently, only two colors, bright yellow and violet, composed the artist's palette. The Jew's trousers are yellow, the greatcoat violet, his hands yellow, and the fur yellow. Two palm trees, placed like candelabra next to Ahasvérus, are treated with the same simplicity: violet trunks and yellow foliage.

This picture improves with age like bottled wine. Is it because it was made fifty years ago that it charms me? I do not think so. At that time, a particular feeling, which was not at all related to the art of the capital, circulated in the provinces.

Today, an Epinal sculptor saw the drawings by Gavarni.[6] One can imagine what strange elegance his pencils convey. It seems incredible that, around 1842, a draftsman in Lorraine would feel the need to dress Ahasvérus as a bandit with feather in his hat, producing a kind of variant of Fra Diavolo.[7] Naïveté has taken flight. The melodramas of Ambigu[8] find an echo in the villages of the Vosges Mountains. And down to the two-penny pictures, the successors of Pellerin of Epinal use *gold* (oh disastrous influence of the elder Mr. Dumas!) to enhance the embroideries of the Musketeers, with whom the Wandering Jew converses.

Onto this scene has come the Wandering Jew of Gustave Doré, some of whose traits reappear in the work of the engravers of Metz and Nancy. (One can imagine what the figure of the Wandering Jew becomes in these imitations!) Doré places particular stress on the setting. He sacrifices Ahasvérus to the old houses of Brabant, to the tempests, the deluges, the pine forests, and the crocodiles. Unfortunately, these are but bothersome Roman candles which the artist lights during the presentation of the drama at each act, at each scene, at each couplet, with the result that the spectator witnesses the punishment of a man condemned to watch a week-long fireworks display. A certain effect is always sought and sometimes attained, but it vanishes amidst the phantom visions of a Ruggieri of the pencil.

The first popular draftsmen were simpler, less diffuse, and saner. But Doré gladly listens to his collaborator, Pierre Dupont, who sings the praises of his "genius" a bit too fawningly. If the young and prolific producer would deign to glance at the modest pictures which illustrate the old German and French chapbook editions, he would see that he does not possess the secret of the figure of the Wandering Jew.

NOTES

1. [Trans. note: The French *marcheur* has a double meaning: "one who walks," that is, the Wandering Jew, and "one who marches," that is, Napoleon.]

2. The print room of the imperial library does not own this precious picture which must be of the same period as the lament. [Ed. note: We have taken the liberty of reproducing Champfleury's frontispiece in this essay.]

3. I say "the people of Normandy" since the wood, in all probability, comes from the factories of Caen, where *Imagerie* [print makers] and *Bibliothèque Bleue* supported one another in former times. No text accompanies the picture, and the worm-eaten wood has disintegrated at

the place where the name of the printer is normally found. I wish to thank particularly Mr. Charma, Dean of the School of Letters of Caen, and vice-president of the Association of Antiquarians of Normandy, who informed me of the existence of the old woodcut of the Wandering Jew of which Mr. Le Bland-Hardel, a printer, was kind enough to make me a copy.

4. [Trans. note: *Isaac Laquedem* is the name often given to the Wandering Jew in Belgium. This ties in with the reference to the good people of Brussels who invite the Wandering Jew to have a drink with them. For a convenient reprinting of the text of this standard Belgium lament, see Roland Auguet, *Le Juif errant* (Paris, 1977), pp. 124–28.]

5. Nissard, *Histoire des livres populaires*, I, p. 494, cites a brochure printed by Buffet, at Charmes, which "felt impelled to give the Wandering Jew a sort of coat in the fashion of Talma and a dog-ear hairstyle." [Trans. note: *Talma* was Napoleon's favorite actor.]

6. [Trans. note: Paul Gavarni (1804–1866) was a French artist who depicted, with intelligence and wit, the customs of the bourgeoisie, according to the *Petit Larousse*, 1972, p. 1364.]

7. [Trans. note: Fra Diavolo (1771–1806) was the leader of a group of Italian outlaws. He fought against the French at Naples.]

8. [Trans. note: *Ambigu-Comique* was a Parisian theater founded by the comedian Audinot in 1770. In the beginning of the nineteenth century, it tended to specialize in melodramas.]

POPULAR SURVIVALS
OF THE WANDERING JEW
IN ENGLAND

G. K. Anderson

Among the handful of scholars who have devoted themselves to the study of the Wandering Jew, G. K. Anderson stands out. His comprehensive volume, The Legend of the Wandering Jew, *published in 1965, is probably the best single survey of the subject, especially of its literary ramifications. In the essay presented here, Anderson reviews in detail reports of the appearance of the Wandering Jew in Britain.*

The majority of treatments of the legend tend to be purely descriptive, offering little or nothing in the way of analysis or interpretation. Such accounts are typically limited to one particular region or country without even mentioning the comparative aspects of the legend. Anderson is the exception, since he controlled much of the enormous bibliography of Wandering Jew scholarship.

I

Based on a combination of older legends which were current in many regions of the eastern Mediterranean and the Near East, the

Reprinted from the *Journal of English and Germanic Philology*, 46 (1947): 367–82.

legend of the Wandering Jew, as an independent saga, took definite shape in the later Middle Ages. The place of its origin was probably Italy; the date of its origin probably the time of the later Crusades; and the purpose of the legend as a whole was the glorification of God through an example of the miraculous nature of his wondrous works.[1]

Scattered allusions to the Wandering Jew have survived from the thirteenth century through the sixteenth. Most of these come either from Italy or from the Iberian peninsula; there are also a few from France, but only a few.[2] It is a curious fact that the first reference to the Wandering Jew in extant literature actually appears in England,[3] but this can hardly establish any great interest in the legend on the part of the English, for the two or three subsequent English allusions from the Middle Ages have a decided French flavor and are comparatively trivial. Virtually all of these references in the Middle Ages are from men of letters or of science; but it is to be assumed that the legend was building up among the people throughout the period.

Medieval Germany seems to have had no appreciable knowledge of the legend. But in the later sixteenth century, an Italian religious and political refugee, Giovanni Bernardini Bonifacio, Marquis d'Oria (1517–1597) took up residence in Danzig, where he became the leader of a literary coterie which included the most prominent printer of Danzig, Jakob Rhode.[4] Shortly after the death of the Marquis, Rhode printed a pamphlet, *Kurtze Beschreibung und Erzehlung von einem Juden mit Namen Ahasverus* (1602), which stands as a landmark in the history of the legend of the Wandering Jew, because it establishes the Jew as a contrite sinner, with patriarchal appearance, ragged and unkempt, super-solemn, with a distinctive name not previously used.[5] The author of the pamphlet is not known; but he was presumably a member of the circle of the Marquis d'Oria, who thus emerges as a likely link between the legend in Italy and in darkest Germany, for it seems altogether probable that he brought the legend, which was native to Italy, and transplanted it in fresh soil. Be that as it may, the *Kurtze Beschreibung*, under its several imprints and including also revisions and adaptations of it[6] which continued until about 1650, constitutes the Ahasuerus-Book, comparable in nature and in im-

portance of influence on the legend it celebrates to the famous
Faust-Book of only a few years earlier.[7] And from the Ahasuerus-
Book spring both the anti-Semitism (which is not at all a feature
of the medieval treatment of the protagonist) and the varied sym-
bolisms of the Jew as a representative of sin, omniscience, political
liberty, social unconventionality, and Jewish nationalism, which
characterize the art-form of the legend of the Wandering Jew in
later years.

II

Perhaps there was a prose translation of the *Kurtze Beschreibung*
into English as early as 1612;[8] certainly there was one ultimately
derived from it by the year 1620.[9] In 1620 also there appeared a
ballad on the same subject and probably from the same source.[10]
These extant works have already been described. There are
enough allusions to the Wandering Jew in English letters of the
seventeenth century to warrant the assumption that the legend
had some popular currency in England at that time,[11] although
the English never seem to have cared for the story as did the
Germans, Italians, or French. In 1640 there was printed a brilliant
satirical pamphlet, *The Wandering Jew Telling Fortunes to Englishmen*, in the manner of Ben Jonson, possibly by one E. Malone(?).[12]
This we may call the first in line of the English examples of the
art-form of the legend, which swelled to enormous proportions
in Continental literature after 1750.[13] It is not, however, the purpose of the present article to deal with these, but rather to give
attention to what is left in the way of popular traces of the legend
in modern England.

   1. That inveterate gossip and collector of curious lore, John
Aubrey, gives us the following in his *Miscellanies* (1696):

> *Anno* 165-. At . . . in the Moorlands, in Staffordshire, lived a
> poor old man, who had been a long time lame. One Sunday, in
> the afternoon, he being alone, one knocked at his door; he bade
> him open it, and come in. The Stranger desired a cup of beer; the
> lame man desired him to take a dish and draw some, for he was
> not able to do it himself. The Stranger asked the poor old man,

how long he had been ill? The poor man told him. Said the Stranger, 'I can cure you. Take two or three balm leaves steeped in your beer for a fortnight or three weeks, and you will be restored to your health; but constantly and zealously serve God.' The poor man did so, and became perfectly well. This Stranger was in a purple-shag gown, such as was not seen or known in those parts. And no body in the street after even song did see any one in such a coloured habit. Doctor Gilbert Sheldon, since Archbishop of Canterbury, was then in the Moorlands, and justified the truth of this to Elias Ashmole, Esq., from whom I had this account, and he hath inserted it in some of his memoirs, which are in the Museum at Oxford.

2. Francis Peck (1692–1743), in his history of Stamford,[14] gives virtually the same story in more circumstantial detail:

Upon Whitsunday, in the year of our Lord 1658, about six of the clock, just after even song, one Samuel Wallis, of Stamford, who had been long wasted with a lingering consumption, was sitting by the fire, reading in that delectable book called *Abraham's Suit for Sodom*.[15] He heard a knock at the door; and as his nurse was absent, he crawled to open it himself. What he saw there, Samuel shall say in his own style:

"I beheld a proper, tall, grave old man. Thus he said: 'Friend, I pray thee, give an old pilgrim a cup of small beere!' And I said: 'Sir, I pray you, come in and welcome.' And he said, 'I am no Sir, therefore call me not Sir; but come in I must, for I cannot pass by thy door.'

"After finishing the beer: 'Friend,' he said, 'thou art not well.' I said, 'No truly, Sir, I have not been well this many years.' He said, 'What is thy disease?' I said, 'A deep consumption, Sir; our doctors say, past cure; for, truly, I am a very poor man, and not able to follow doctor's counsel.' 'Then,' said he, 'I will tell thee what thou shalt do; and, by the help and power of Almighty God above, thou shalt be well. Tomorrow, when thou risest up, go into thy garden, and get there two leaves of red sage, and one of bloodworts, and put them into a cup of thy small beere. Drink as often as need require, and when the cup is empty fill it again, and put in fresh leaves every fourth day, and before twelve days shall be past, thy disease shall be cured and thy body altered.' " After this simple prescription, Wallis pressed him to eat. "But he said: 'No, friend, I will not eat; the Lord Jesus is sufficient for me. Very seldom do I drink any beer neither, but that which comes from the rock. So, friend, the Lord God be with thee.' "

So saying he departed, and was never more heard of; but the
patient got well within the given time, and for many a long day
there was war hot and fierce among the divines of Stamford, as
to whether the stranger was an angel or a devil. His dress has
been minutely described by honest Sam. His coat was purple, and
buttoned down to the waist: "his britches of white, but whether
linen or jersey, deponent knoweth not; his beard and head were
white, and he had a white stick in his hand. The day was rainy
from morning to night, but he had not one spot of dirt upon his
clothes."

The Wandering Jew is usually, in respect to his habits of imbib-
ing, a moderate if not actually abstemious figure.[16] In fact, the
English tales just recounted make something of a contribution to
the popular legend of the Wandering Jew as a whole in that they
allow the protagonist to ask for a drink, although Peck's version
has the Wanderer profess a moderation in the matter of beer. Most
unusual, also, is the white raiment, the symbolism of which,
as indicating immortality, is obvious but rarely encountered in
the saga.

For the rest, Peck's account is a remarkably fine example of
"sophistication" in the development of a popular tale; the added
details are ornament and no more.

3. On many occasions the Wanderer's thirst was intense, if we
are to judge by the words of a nineteenth century reporter:

. . . Sometimes, during the cold winter nights, the lonely cot-
tager would be awoke [sic] by a plaintive demand for 'Water,
good Christians! Water, for the love of God!' And if he looks out
into the moonlight, he will see a venerable old man in antique
raiment, with gray flowing beard and a tall staff, who beseeches
his charity with the most earnest gesture. Woe to the churl who
refuses him water or shelter. My old nurse, who was a Warwick-
shire woman, knew a man who boldly cried out, 'All very fine,
Mr. Ferguson, but you can't lodge here.' And it was decidedly
the worst thing he ever did in all his life, for his best mare fell
dead lame, and corn went down, I am afraid to say how much,
per quarter. If, on the contrary, you treat him well, and refrain
from indelicate inquiries respecting his age—on which point he is
very touchy—his visit is sure to bring good luck. Perhaps years
afterwards, when you are on your deathbed, he may happen to
be passing; and if he should, you are safe; for three knocks with

his staff will make you hale, and he never forgets any kindnesses. Many stories are current of his wonderful cures. . . . [17]

But if there are such stories, they seem to have evaporated before they ever got into print.

The thirst of Ahasuerus in these tales is appropriate enough in a land fond of its ale and tea. There may also be in this case, however, a transference of the thirst of Christ to the man who traditionally insulted him.[18] It still remains a remarkable point of fact, nevertheless, that except in England the Wandering Jew is not afflicted with a thirst so overwhelming as to lead him to a stranger's door to seek relief. That this detail crops up later in the art-form of the legend is only to be expected, inasmuch as this art-form drew upon any and all aspects of the popular tale and even of cognate tales, such as those of the Wild Huntsman, the Flying Dutchman, the Ancient Mariner, Fortunatus, and Faust. Sternberg's account is the only one, moreover, to make the Wanderer sensitive about his apparently advanced age.

In the seventeenth century tales told in Aubrey and Peck, the function of the stranger is benevolent; he seems to be devoting his indefinite stay on earth to the accomplishment of good deeds. This praiseworthy existence brings him into the "Cartaphilus" phase of the legend of the Wandering Jew[19]—that phase to which the Jew belongs when he first breaks into the pages of written literature in Roger of Wendover's chronicle.[20] But in Sternberg's account the Wanderer will, when crossed, bring down disaster upon the man or men who rebuffed him, as he does in many surviving German, Swiss, and French tales.[21]

Sternberg's comments, then, are tantalizing[22] in what they infer but do not tell of the legend in England, where, unlike the countries on the continent, the antiquarians have allowed the legend to trickle away in the desert, so that now true references to the legend in English folklore have become virtually non-existent.[23]

4. Some indications of the furtive survival of the legend in out-of-the-way English oral tradition are clear from the following incident told by Moncure Conway,[24] yet this particular manifestation of the Wandering Jew in England is more worthy of the Celt, with his feeling for what Matthew Arnold called the "magic

of nature," than of the hard-headed Sassenach.[25] According to
Conway, one James Pearson reported from the Lancashire moors
that one evening in 1866 he was in the company of an "intelligent
old man" when they suddenly heard above their heads the cry of
the dotterel, a bird of the plover family. The old man observed
that in his youth the old people considered such a happening a bad
omen, for the person who heard the "Wandering Jew," as he
called the dotterel, would certainly be overtaken by some misfortune. In reference to the name which had been given the birds, he
explained that there was a tradition according to which they were
the souls of those Jews who had participated in the crucifixion of
Christ, and as a consequence had been condemned to fly about
forever in the air.[26] This represents an obvious deviation from the
norm of the legend,[27] which has it, of course, that the Wandering
Jew was the man who taunted Christ in the *Via Crucis* (according
to some, the man who actually struck the Savior with a shoe-
last[28]), and who therefore participated in the Crucifixion only indirectly.

5. And as a certain bird or species of birds may be associated
with the Wandering Jew, so with the flora as well as the fauna. A
few plants are known as the "Wandering Jew," particularly *ze-
brina pandula*, a fast-growing leafy plant of special hardiness,
which will grow in either sun or shade. The name is applied also
to a type of spiderwort (*tradescentia fluminensis*), to the "beefsteak"
or strawberry geranium (*saxifraga sarmentosa*), and to the Kenil-
worth ivy (*linaria cymbalaria*). I can find no record of such a name
applied to any of the four plants mentioned, however, before the
middle of the nineteenth century. The creeping habits of the ivy
and the quasi-perennial nature of all four evidently appealed to
some imaginative popular naturalists whose fortune it was to give
them names which stuck. When it comes to tracing the individual
christener of the plants, of course, it is always a case of the oldest
inhabitant who remembers his grandfather's having said something once about his own grandfather's friend who had heard
somewhere why this plant or that bird was called a "Wandering
Jew"; and so the real facts are never forthcoming. But it is most
likely that the "Wandering Jew" was applied to these plants and
birds as a product of the romanticism which pervaded the science

of the early nineteenth century, when the protagonist of the legend flourished in literally hundreds of European literary creations.[29]

III

Impostors, or at least what the skeptical twentieth century must consider such, have played their part all over Europe in fostering the legend of the Wandering Jew. The Italians had one as early as 1416, when one Giovanni Servo di Dio (a traditional name for the Wandering Jew in early Renaissance literature) discussed politics and the dismal future of mankind with Salvestro di Giovanni Mannini of Florence, in whose diary the impressive event is recorded.[30] In 1547 one Antonio Ruiz was sentenced to a public flogging in Toledo, Spain, for deceiving the credulous mountaineers of the vicinity into believing that he was Juan Espera en Dios, the hero of the Spanish version of the legend of the Wandering Jew.[31] Renaissance Europe has many allusions to such impostors; [32] the wonder is only that there were not more of whom there is record, for the legend offered unusual opportunities to fleece a credulous countryside. As it is, we can be certain that there were more swindlers parading about as the Wandering Jew than ever appeared in print. On at least one occasion, in fact, the Wandering Jew came in a pair.[33]

6. In England the classical instance is that told in John Brand's *Observations on Popular Antiquities*:

> I remember to have seen one of these impostors some years ago in the North of England, who made a very hermit-like appearance and went up and down the streets of Newcastle with a long train of boys at his heels, muttering: "Poor John, alone, alone!" I thought he pronounced his name in a manner singularly plaintive.[34]

Brand further notes that "Poor John!" was otherwise known as "Poor Joe!" *John* is, of course, the traditional name of many a legendary immortal in Christian times and lands, no doubt because of the revered tradition that St. John the Evangelist had never died.[35] The Cartaphilus of Roger of Wendover and Matthew Paris[36] was named Joseph; but this name is on the whole uncommon. Brand's *Poor Joe!* seems rather to be an amusing corruption of *Poor Jew!*

7. Newcastle, indeed, seems to have harbored another "Wandering Jew" at about the same time as when Brand saw his impostor; perhaps this is the same one. At any rate, he had a son. A correspondent from the *Newcastle Weekly Chronicle* described to Conway in 1881 an unappetizing picture:

> He is very eccentric, is known as 'Topper, the Newcastle Fossil,' and attracts a deal of attention on account of his appearance and the condition of his house. He is a very peculiar looking man with features of a decided Jewish cast. His clothes appear to be as old as himself. He has never been known to be clean; and old people in Hull do not remember the counter or floor of his house to have been washed.[37]

So much for the unclean, obscure, and apparently altogether passive son of an illustrious father, a drab and filthy publican who never wandered but took his place instead among the undistinguished gallery of a town's eccentrics.

8. For that matter, Hull gives another account of the Wandering Jew, an account which has just come to light in a hitherto unprinted eighteenth century chap-book bearing the completely unoriginal title, *The Wandering Jew, or the Shoemaker of Jerusalem* and printed without date (but probably in 1769) by one J. Pitts.

> This Jew was born at Jerusalem, and was by trade a shoemaker, when our Saviour was going to the place of crucifixion, being weary and faint, he would have sat down to rest at the shoe-maker's stall, but the shoe-maker came to the door and spitting in our Lord's face buffeted him from the door, saying, that was no place of abode for him. On which Christ said, for this thing, thou shalt never rest, but wander till I come again upon the earth.
>
> From this he is called the Wandering Jew of Jerusalem.
>
> Now according to this saying, of [our] Saviour who was crucified, this man has no power to return home, but went abroad wandering from place to place ever since, even unto this day.

After travelling through Asia, and Africa, he roamed to America, and is now on his journey to visit every town in Europe.

Some time since he landed at Hull, in Yorkshire, where Dr. Hall, taking him for a cheat, caused him to be locked up in a room all night, but next morning they found the door opened though their prisoner had not attempted to escape. Dr. Hall sent for Dr. Harrison, in order to assist in the examination of so remarkable a personage, that they might be sure whether he was impostor or not.

They asked him concerning the breaking of the locks in the room in which he had been shut up. He told them if they would attempt to confine him with chains, it would avail nothing—human force cannot confine him whom the Almighty had sentenced to want a resting place.

They being like Thomas a Dindimus, hard of belief, sent for a smith to put strong chains on him, but they instantly burst asunder to the surprise of a thousand spectators. Not being able to doubt any longer, they sent for a painter, and had his picture drawn, in which he looked neither old nor young, but just as he did seventeen hundred and sixty-nine years ago, when he first began his journey.[38]

The King of France hearing of this, wrote for his picture, which Dr. Hall accordingly sent him.

If he hears any one curse or swear, or take the name of God in vain, he tells them that they crucify their God again. If any one offers him money, though it were the richest Lord or Lady in all the land, he will take no more than one groat and that he says he takes for Christ's sake, and gives it to the next poor person he meets. He is always crying and praying, and wishing to see death, but that ease from his labouring pilgrimage, he says, that can never happen until Christ comes again upon the earth. . . .

These first half-dozen paragraphs of the pamphlet give a fair enough account of the Wandering Jew of tradition. But the assembled ministers then proceed to ask the stranger a series of knotty questions, some of which have a Talmudic and even Cabbalistic aroma. How long, according to Moses and the prophets, will the world last? In six thousand years, comes the answer, the world will be destroyed twice—once by water and once by fire. According to the visitor's calculations, this sinful world has hardly more than two hundred years left after 1769. What was the mark which God set upon Cain's head? The mark was black; from Cain sprang the race of blacks.[39] Why did God hide the body of Moses? To keep the Devil from persuading the children of Israel that there was no God. Why do men and women live a shorter time now than in the days of the Biblical characters? Because they eat too much meat and drink not enough water.

And so the inquisitive ministers who signed the account—Dr. Hall, Dr. Harrison, Mr. Reubens, and Mr. Crouch—were convinced. Theirs were good Yorkshire names all; but not names which can be connected with any church in Hull in the 1760's and 1770's. Nor is it likely that the aged and ailing Louis XV of France would bother to send after the picture of a mysterious stranger in Hull. The whole tale smacks of pure fiction.

9. This impression is confirmed by the appearance of another pamphlet of a little less than a dozen years later:

> The Surprizing / History of the / Wandering JEW of Jerusalem with his / arrival at Dover this year 1780, attest- / ed: And his removal in order to visit / the Holy Island near Berwick, confirm- / ed by three Ministers and an Attorney. / etc.

The first portion of this pamphlet is virtually identical in substance and language with the Hull pamphlet of 1769. The indefatigable Dr. Hall, accompanied this time by Dr. Harris (instead of Harrison), interviewed the stranger. The stranger submitted to chains, which he promptly broke, observed this time by *thousands* of spectators. His portrait was painted and sent off to the King of France. The questioning to which he was subjected was the same as it had been at Hull. When it comes to the interrogation concerning Cain's head, there is a break in the sense of the proceedings, as if the author of the pamphlet, reading off from the Hull chap-book—and some other work or works—had inadvertently included some strange stuff, possibly Cabbalistic, of which he was unaware:

> Now you have resolved this, Can you tell us, said they, what was the mark that God set upon Cain's head? Now explain the third chapter of Genesis, and tell us why Cain should be afraid that he should be slain by any angel, man, or beast, as they were at that time become exceeding fruitful each female woman, at two, three, and four years old, bearing one, two, three, and four

children almost at a time, and other creatures were also amazingly fruitful, which caused the inhabitants of the world in the [s]pace of a hundred years, to be as the sand on the sea-shore for multitude: not as some silly ignorant people vainly imagine that GOD made at the same time, many more persons along with Adam and Eve; for, it is evident without all peradventure, that Eve was the mother of all that lived on the earth then as well as now; and God's words must abide true though every man should turn a liar! the land of Nod, where his heart trembled with horror, and chose him a wife, where were many of the descendants daughters of Adam and Eve—and the mark which God set upon Cain's head was black, etc.

Having returned to coherence, the author of the pamphlet carries the Jew successfully through the rest of his examination. After the attestation by the Ministers, Hall, Harris, Gough, and Davis, comes the following addition:

> This Wandering Jew left Dover the last month, after wandering above forty-two miles up the country: his stay is always short and is possessed of many different languages, when learned men put questions to him, he desires them to go the sacred records, and there they will be fully satisfied; as to his pilgrimage in this world, when he receives fourpence (which he calls a groat) he will have no more until he distribute what he has got to a pious use. He is still in a mourning and praying posture, he sleeps little in any bed, chusing rather more hardships than Christian people can give him. He drinks water and eats sparingly; and has a great delight in little children, because, says he, his great master loved them.
>
> He arrived in a fishing smack at Blyth, on the southward of Berwick; and is on his way to the Holy Island, within a few miles of the town of Berwick. If he returns northward, or southward, or goes to sea, it is not yet known.
>
> Three ministers near Blyth was with him, and several men of repute, who all agree, that he makes the tears fall from their eyes that hears him talk, which is attested by
>
>
>
> Mr. Jos. Burton,
> Mr. Geo. Naperlin, Ministers
> Mr. Chris. Ewbank
> Mr. Jo. Stanton, Attorney
>
>
>
> Overtown[40]
> Jan. 25, 1780

The general impression left is that the Dover pamphlet is a crude, inferior reworking of the Hull pamphlet, to which has been added some fresh material relating to the trip northward, and the touching detail of the stranger's love of children. Not often, it must be remarked, does Ahasuerus say, "Suffer little children to come unto me!"

The narrative elements in these two pamphlets are apparently direct from the English ballad, *The Wandering Jew: or the shoemaker of Jerusalem*, already referred to;[41] from this ballad also comes the itinerary of the Wanderer. Another interesting traditional detail is the inability of any one, whether in or out of authority, to confine the Wandering Jew in prison, for chains, locks, and bolts all yield to him. This detail is found in a variety of earlier versions, but first and most brilliantly in the Italian account of Francesco di Giovanni di Andrea, probably written near 1500.[42] Also to be noted once more is the refusal of Ahasuerus to accept alms higher than one groat, which he then gives to the poor—a detail which goes back, *via* the English ballad and the prose account of Shann[43] through a French translation[44] to the German Ahasuerus-Book sired by the *Kurtze Beschreibung*.

10. Nor did the great Age of Enlightenment have a monopoly on the impostor, in spite of the credulities which enabled it to accept on a disconcerting scale such men as Cagliostro, Casanova, St. Germain, and the querulous visitor to Hull and Dover. The nineteenth century, being romantic, absorbed the legend of the Wandering Jew with fascination. Thus the staid London *Athenaeum*, under the date of November 3, 1866, records one more folktale, not this time from the rustic moorlands or the provincial city, but from the heart of teeming London:

> From the year 1818 (perhaps earlier) to about 1830, a handsomely featured Jew, in semi-eastern costume, fair-haired, bareheaded, his eyes intently fixed on a little ancient book he held in both hands, might be seen gliding through the streets of London, but was never seen to issue from or to enter a house, or to pause upon his way. He was popularly known as 'the Wandering Jew,' but there was something so dignified and anxious in his look that he was never known to suffer the slightest molestation. Young

and old looked silently on him as he passed, and shook their heads pitifully when he had gone by. He disappeared, was seen again in London some ten years later, still young, fair-haired, bare-headed, his eyes bent on his book, his feet going steadily forward as he went straight on; and men again whispered as he glided through our streets for the last time, 'the Wandering Jew!' There were many who believed that he was the very man to whom had been uttered the awful words, 'Tarry thou till I come!'

Certainly the picture of a young, studious, peripatetic Ahasuerus is novel; but in his dignity, his gliding manner, his ability to enter and leave a house undetected, a few shreds of the old legend still cling to him in the comparatively modern streets of the London of the Regency. Thus he flits, shadow-like, through the City; none molests him; none addresses him; he speaks to no one— nothing more than the furtive ghost of the hero of a great legend. And the nineteenth-century sentimentalism that clothes this account of his visitation savors too much of the art-form of the legend. In some ways it is more authentic, from the folklorist point of view, to hear merely that there was for a long time around Boston in Lincolnshire "a belief concerning the existence of a person called the Wandering Jew."[45]

Even more closely allied to the romantic art-form of the legend are the two tales of the Wandering Jew from Pembrokeshire and Glamorganshire.[46] That from Glamorganshire in particular is material for a bad Gothic novel:

A Glamorgan farmer said his grandfather had three sons and two daughters. Of the latter, one was married and the other was single. The unmarried girl was very handsome and spirited. One day a strange man came to the farm, and asked if they could accommodate him with apartments. He wanted to be in the heart of the country, to have quiet for studies. As he offered generous terms, they let him two rooms for an indefinite period. It was late in the autumn, and after the stranger had been there two months the farmer and his family felt quite at home with him. Soon the stranger made friends everywhere in the neighborhood. The Vicar, the Squire, and the Doctor invited him to their houses, for he was not only a man of intellectual attainments, but "good company" in conversation. Spring came, and the stranger still

remained. 'Towards the summer,' said my informant, 'Mr. W—
went away for a few days and came back again. While he was
away my Aunt Winifred was not the same girl—at least, so the
neighbors said. She seemed spiritless. Rumor was about that Mr.
W— had been paying attention to the Squire's daughter. At the
same time, my uncles knew that he had been equally attentive to
their sister. This displeased them, and when Mr. W— came home
they were determined to speak to him about it, 'lodger or no
lodger,' they said, and he paid them handsomely. So they told
him it was not honorable to pay court to two girls at the same
time. Mr. W— expressed surprise and sorrow, which my uncles
knew was genuine, for he spoke so kindly and sadly. "It is my
fate," he said, "to win love; it is my doom never to marry." Very
soon after that he went away. The Squire's daughter and my Aunt
Winifred soon came to know that they had been in love with the
same man, and became fast friends. Mr. W— was remarkably
handsome. In two years time my Aunt Winifred died, having
gradually pined away from the moment Mr. W— left. Twenty
years afterwards, when the roses were blooming over Aunt Winifred's grave, the Squire's daughter, who married a neighboring
baronet in less than two years after her early love-affair, went
with my father to the churchyard. They stood together at the
graveside of one who died too early. "He was a mysterious man,"
said Lady L—. "He was," said my father. "The Squire declared he
was the Wandering Jew," remarked the lady: and they left the
grave. A moment later they were face to face with the very man,
who passed on quickly to my aunt's grave. Lady L— touched my
father's arm. "There he is," she said; and as the stranger stood
bareheaded, they both whispered, "There is a mystery about
him." He was never seen again, and both Lady L— and my father
always declared the mysterious stranger to be the Wandering Jew.

Besides this sickly romantic yarn, the following is much more
effective as narrative and is far closer to a true folk-tale. Although
referred by Trevelyan to Pembrokeshire, it is told from the lips of
a Carmarthenshire squire:

It seems that when his father was a youth, he met a remarkably
clever stranger, who appeared to have studied all that was possible
in the world. Languages, art, science, music, and a host of other
things, were at his fingers' ends. He had travelled all over the
world, and was a most interesting companion. For six months
they travelled together, and then parted. Before parting the
stranger told his companion that they would meet and be together

on three separate occasions of their lives. 'After our third meeting and parting,' said the stranger, 'you will die, but I will continue to wander until the day of doom.' The younger man in due course became squire, was married, and had children. When he was about fifty, the stranger reappeared again in Carmarthenshire, and was as interesting as ever. The Squire invited him to his seat, and when alone, laughingly reminded the stranger of his prophecy. 'It will be verified to the letter,' said his guest. Later on the visitor took his leave. The squire lived until he was eighty-six, and then revealed his story to his son. The latter thought it was an old man's fancy, and humored it but little. A year later, the stranger reappeared, and visited the old squire, who was delighted to see his former friend. Two days he stayed, and when taking his leave of the Squire he said: 'Good-bye, my dear old friend. You will never see me again.' The next night the Squire died, murmuring as he peacefully passed away: 'The Wandering Jew! Poor man! He is the Wandering Jew!'

The virtual omniscience of the Wandering Jew is clearly illustrated in this story; on the other hand, his prophetic powers are not traditionally too impressive in the saga, and when they are shown, they rarely prove to be foreshadowings of death or disaster, although, for that matter, it can be pointed out that the old squire died peacefully at eighty-six, when most people have lived their lives for what they may be. Still, as already observed, this is a more respectable "folk-tale" than the Glamorganshire drama.

The unfortunate fact remains that none of the English popular versions of the story has the same vitality as characterizes the legend on the Continent. It is obvious that the saga had currency in England, and even some degree of popularity; but this currency and this popularity alike seem to spend themselves under the surface, so to speak. Perhaps they once existed to a greater degree than we now realize, but rarely do they emerge into the light of day. And when they do, they assume often mean and trivial forms—the absurd beggar of Newcastle, fathering the unlovely publican in Hull; the cry of the dotterel, a mournful squawk; the arrogant traveler who came to Dover; the studious *Spaziergänger* in the Strand; the breaker of a village maiden's heart. Only the Stamford visitant has the dimensions of the Wandering Jew of the Continent, and even he is unwontedly thirsty.

Why this rather stunted growth of the legend among English-

speaking peoples? It cannot be said that the legend does not take
root in England; it does, although not to the same depth as in
Italy, Germany, and France. Perhaps the difficulty lies in the matter-of-fact temperament of the English yeoman, who would of all
Englishmen be most likely to accept such a legend; perhaps the
Puritan tradition is too discouraging for the dissemination, on any
broad scale, of such fantastic tales as that of the Wandering Jew;
perhaps the smaller proportion of Jews in the British population
than elsewhere renders the legend somewhat remote from the
yeoman's experience—perhaps, in other words, the English regard the legend as a second-hand kind of legend. Yet other nations
have matter-of-fact temperaments among their common people;
they have had the equivalent of Puritan traditions; they have seen
relatively few Jews; and yet the legend has flourished among
them. Evidently the English Puritan and the Scottish Covenanter
drew a sharper line than most between the didactically imaginative
and the fantastically incredible—they could create a *Pilgrim's Progress*, but they would frown upon an Ahasuerus-Book.

IV

Ahasuerus was reported to have made a notable journey to
England late in the seventeenth century, although the English
themselves appear to have known nothing about it. Augustin Calmet, author of the *Dictionnaire du Sainte Bible* (1732), included in
this encyclopedic work a "Dissertation sur le juif errant," from
which we have the following:

> I have a letter . . . written from London by Madame de Mazarin
> to Madame de Bouillon, in which we read that in that country
> there was a man who pretended to have lived more than seventeen
> hundred years. He claimed to be an officer of the Divan of Jeru-
> salem at the time that Jesus Christ was sentenced by Pontius
> Pilate; that he harshly pushed the Savior outside the Praetorium,
> saying to him: 'Go, get out; why are you staying here?' And Jesus
> Christ answered him: 'I shall go, but you will walk until my
> return.' He remembers having seen the Apostles, the features of
> their countenances, their hair, their clothing. He has travelled
> through all the countries of the world, and must wander until the
> end of time; he boasts of having cured the sick by touching them;

he speaks many languages; he has given an account of all that has happened during the ages, so accurate that those who hear him do not know what to think of it. The two universities have sent their learned men to converse with him; but with all their learning they have not been able to surprise or confute him.[47]

After quoting a little more of the letter, in which Madame de Mazarin insists that the individual referred to is believed in only by the stupid, Calmet dismisses the Wandering Jew as "un personnage de théâtre." Indeed, his sensible remarks are a fitting requiem to be chanted over all impostors:

> Those who have appeared at different times and in different regions of the world, were swindlers who, exploiting the credulity of ignorant and gullible people, were anxious to make a spectacle of themselves before the world, to gather in alms or to bask in the inane flatteries of a beguiled community. . . . Certainly, nothing seems more opposed to the spirit of mercy, patience, kindness, or grace, which the Savior showed throughout His Passion, than this vengeance which they say He showed against this Wandering Jew; He prayed for those who blasphemed Him on the Cross; He let Himself be led to agony as a sheep before his shearers; would He have struck with such a curse this shoemaker who refused to let Him rest before his shop? All the circumstances and the fitness of things should suffice to have these fables rejected as utterly false.

That, in short, is the moral weakness of the whole legend. Yet it continues to roll on its unchristian way.

No date is given by Calmet to the letter of Madame de Mazarin, but the lady is known to have lived in London during the last quarter of the seventeenth century. As it happens, another account of the same "incident" is forthcoming in the *Theatrum Europaeum* (1702), which specifies the year 1694 as the year when Ahasuerus appeared in London. Otherwise the account is virtually the same as that in Calmet's *Dictionnaire*; it is stated, however, that Oxford and Cambridge sent down a delegation of scholars.[48] But such brilliant academic victories as the Wandering Jew won over them are commonplaces which go clear back to the *Kurtze Beschreibung*. Unfortunately Oxford and Cambridge never heard of the matter,[49] and no popular English account of a visit in 1694 has been discovered.

Both the Calmet and *Theatrum Europaeum* versions are derived directly from the *Turkish Spy Letters*,[50] but the visit to England is not to be found in the source.[51] It is evidently an increment that seems to have sprung up on the Continent and been given an impetus by the success of the *Turkish Spy Letters*, which was evidently considerable.[52]

A somewhat similar story turns up in an extremely rare German pamphlet of the early eighteenth century (*ca.* 1710-1720?), *Nachdenkliche Prophezeyungen, Visionen, und Träume.* Here the "prophet" stopped in London; the date, however, is not told us. He did not know what to say about his parents and boasted that his kin had been famous even before the days of Adam and Eve (!). He wore on his head a bloody crown; his clothing was neither sewn nor patched, neither of linen, wool, silk, or net; he drank no wine, only water; he satisfied himself with little food, cared nothing for money, wore neither girdle nor sword, but went about boldly under the very noses of his enemies. He argued with no one, left a man's religion to himself, complained about the Protestants, preferring the Catholics because of their fasting; rested little day or night; found fault with various Roman bishops who had expressed no faith in him; cared nothing for beds, rather slept on hard wood; called out with loud voice and outstretched arms against this naughty world, keeping doors and windows open as if he were announcing the Latter Day of the Lord. He was expert in all tongues, so that he could be understood everywhere. He was a particular lover of beautiful gardens; the most distinguished people often had him in to visit them; he greeted no one of his own accord and conversed with very few. Many believed that his tribe would endure until the end of the world. He said that he had been in the Ark with Noah; he prophesied concerning himself that he would die no natural death, rather that this wicked world would try unsuccessfully to destroy him. He had been present at the Crucifixion, yet he believed in no resurrection of the flesh nor in eternal life. It is reported that a similar visionary was later seen in Newcastle (*sic*); perhaps he was the same as the gentleman described in the *Newcastle Weekly Chronicle*; perhaps he was the one mentioned by John Brand. Perhaps he was both of these; perhaps he was neither.

At any rate, it is almost superfluous to point out how this prophet of *Nachdenkliche Prophezeyungen* differs from the accepted picture of the Wandering Jew. Indeed, this individual is distinctive, if only because he lived with Noah. On the other hand, he seems to be ignorant of his parentage;[53] his clothing is miraculous; and his bent toward the Catholics, even if he did not care for some of their bishops (however tenuous his reasons), puts him from the Protestant viewpoint on the side of Antichrist. It is just as well to remember the attitude of early eighteenth century Germany and England towards the Catholics. Would a social climber like this particular "prophet" have risen far with a pro-Catholic, anti-Protestant bias? Admittedly, his love of gardens—not elsewhere a feature of the legend—is English. Obviously, however, he is far removed from the class of John Brand's Wanderer who went about with "Poor John" (or "Joe") on his lips, or the seedy individual in Hull whose dirtiness was remarkable even for his time.

In general, then, this particular Wandering Jew of the *Nachdenkliche Prophezyungen*, assuming the validity of his existence, was an impostor with a certain original proclivity, for he makes the Jew different from his run-of-the-mill colleagues. As to the success of the impostor, one knows not. If, as is most likely, this tale as well as the Calmet, *Theatrum Europaeum*, and Joseph Krantz versions are merely folktales slapped onto England because she was a defenceless foreign country, there is nothing more to be said.

V

The tremendous growth of the legend of the Wandering Jew in the art-form, under the careful nurturing of the English Gothicists and Byronic romanticists,[54] drove the popular tales of the Wanderer in England more and more into the background. Lewis, Shelley, Croly, Caroline Norton, and others contributed large shares to the building up of the Wandering Jew into a universal European romantic creature. It is not possible to concern ourselves here with what *belle-lettres* in the nineteenth century, particularly in Germany, managed to accomplish for the cult of Ahasuerus.

We may assume, however, that the legend of the Wandering Jew persisted in certain localities in England well through the nineteenth century, although, as Wright points out,

> The roll of English traditional stories is a beggarly one, if compared with that of other nations, both those within and those without the British Isles. It is to be feared that few more ears can now be gleaned of what might have been the golden sheaves, for there is no reason to suppose that in early days our forefathers were less fond of a story or less imaginative than other peoples. Some of our tales have been kept alive, and spoilt, by guidebooks. Probably a few short stories, and especially humorous stories or drolls, could still be gathered by the diligent before the wireless fills every winter evening by the fireside.[55]

At least no new folktales concerning the Wandering Jew have come to light in England, although nearly every writer of importance in English literature of the past century and a half not only has known Ahasuerus but has often seen fit to celebrate him in his work, if only as a passing reference.

It is possibly significant that, while the Wandering Jew was known in London and vaguely in the South of England, most of the surviving folktales about him come from the Midlands and from the northeastern coastal section of England. He has never made headway in Celtic territory. At least it is in those particular regions just named that his presence has been acknowledged in such a way that antiquarians can recognize him. This is as it should be, for those northerly regions are the "wide open spaces" of England where legends can most effectively while away the long winter nights. After all, however, the legend of the Wandering Jew is a Continental legend; Ahasuerus came to England as a foreigner; and as a foreigner he did not manage to cover the whole country until the practitioners of the art-form provided him with special transportation.[56]

NOTES

1. These conclusions are my own and are based entirely upon the available evidence, which, however, is not easily accessible in any one

place or in any one work. For the fundamental bibliography, see George K. Anderson, "The Wandering Jew Returns to England" in *Journal of English and Germanic Philology*, xlv, 237–250, particularly p. 237, note 1.

2. For the Italian allusions, see especially S. Morpurgo, *L'ebreo errante in Italia* (Florence, 1891), and R. Renier, "La leggenda dell' Ebreo errante" in *Svaghi critici* (Bari, 1910); for the Portuguese, C. M. de Vasconcellos, "O Judeu errante em Portugal" in *Revista Lusitana*, i, 34–45 and ii, 74–76; for the Spanish, Joseph Gillet, "Traces of the Wandering Jew in Spain" in *Romanic Review*, xxii, 16–27 and Marcel Bataillon, "Peregrinations espagnoles du Juif Errant" in *Bulletin Hispanique*, xliii, 81–122; for the French, Alice M. Killen, "L'Évolution de la légende du Juif Errant" in *Revue de Littérature Comparée*, v, 5–36. The article by de Vasconcellos should be read only in the light of Bataillon's brilliant study.

3. In Roger of Wendover's *Flores Historiarum*, as part of the entry for the year 1228 (cf. H. G. Hewlett's edition, *Rogeri de Wendover liber qui dicitur flores historiarum*, vol. 84 of the *Rolls Series*, II, 352 ff., London, 1886–1889). There is a translation by J. A. Giles in the Bohn Antiquarian Library (London, 1849). Roger's account is repeated with some increments in Matthew Paris's *Chronica Majora* (cf. H. R. Luard's edition, vol. 57 of the *Rolls Series*, III, 161 ff., London, 1872–1873).

4. Arno Schmidt, *Das Volksbuch vom ewigen Juden* (Danzig, 1927) gives a complete account of the genesis of the pamphlet, including a biographical sketch of the Marquis d'Oria and the story of the Rhode family of Danzig. His efforts to establish the exact identity of the author of the pamphlet in question, however, seem to me unsuccessful.

5. I.e., *Ahasuerus*, a generalized name derived from the celebration of the Purim festival in medieval Germany.

6. These have been exhaustively studied by L. Neubaur in his *Die Sage vom ewigen Juden* (rev. ed., Leipzig, 1893), 14 ff. and especially 53 ff. Neubaur, not having the results of Schmidt's researches (see note 4 above) at hand, was led to believe that the pamphlet was issued at Leyden; Schmidt makes it virtually certain that the original was printed at Danzig, with the Leyden and Bautzen imprints fictitious. There seems to have been at this time a common practice of forging imprints in order to create the impression that a pamphlet had wide circulation and was therefore a worthwhile investment. See Anderson (note 1 above), p. 238, note 9.

7. The important component parts of the Ahasuerus-Book are 1) the *Kurtze Beschreibung* (1602); 2) the 'Dudulaeus' version of the same, which bears the date 1602 but was probably printed in 1613 or 1614; 3) the *Relation von einem Juden* (1634). See Neubaur (note 6), 14 ff.

8. William C. Hazlitt, *Bibliographical Collections*, series ii, 247, 316.

9. This is the tale told by Richard Shann (1561–1627) of Methley, Yorkshire, in his family commonplace-book; see Anderson (note 1), 243 ff.

10. "A Ballad called '*Wonderful strange newes out of Germanye of a Jewe that hath lyued wandering ever since our Saviour Christ.*' " See Anderson (note 1), 242. Under the title *The Wandering Jew, or the shoemaker of Jerusalem* it has been printed in *The Roxburghe Ballads* (Hertford, 1889), vi, 687 ff.; with a few variations in Percy's *Reliques of Ancient English Poetry* (1765), ii, 292; and in the 1861 edition of F. J. Child's *English and Scottish Popular Ballads*. It appears also in the mss. of the Bagford and Pepys collections.

11. For example, see John Taylor, *The Old, Old, Very Old Man* (London, 1635), p. 19; William Lithgow, *Travels* (London, 1632), viii, 345; Joseph Hall, *Satyres* (London, 1646), 202; and V. Alsop, *The Mischief of Impositions* (London, 1680), viii, 83.

12. The ascription to Malone, who is otherwise entirely unknown, is made by J. O. Halliwell-Phillips in his rather inaccessible edition of *The Wandering Jew Telling Fortunes to Englishmen*, printed in *Books of Characters* (London, 1857), Part I.

13. It is not practicable to give here any special bibliography of the art-form of the legend; but to get an idea of the tremendous extent of this literature, see A. Soergel, *Ahasver-Dichtungen seit Goethe* (Leipzig, 1905), which specializes on the German art-form, and J. Gielen, *De wandelende Jood in Volkskunde en Letterkunde* (Amsterdam, 1931), which is a more generalized study. Both books have impressive bibliographies.

14. Francis Peck, *Academia Tertia Anglicana, or the Antiquarian Annals of Stamford in Lincoln, Rutland, and Northampton Shires* (London, 1727).

15. Not as yet identified.

16. In the account of the Wandering Jew by Antonio di Francesco di Andrea (early sixteenth century)—see S. Morpurgo, *L'Ebreo errante in Italia* (Florence, 1891), section II—the protagonist is something of a *bon vivant*. Here and there in German folk-tales he may permit himself a drink of *schnapps* or wine for the sake of camaraderie; but he usually never touches liquor. Only when the art-form of the romantic age (and later) endowed him with various habits of debauchery did Ahasuerus appear on special occasions, as a complete worldling.

17. V. T. Sternberg, "The Wandering Jew in England" in *Notes and Queries*, xii, #322 (December 29, 1855), 503–504. The picture of the Jew is traditional.

18. See John, xix, 28. One old legend has it that Christ, on His way to the Cross, stopped and asked a passerby for a drink. He was contemptuously referred to a puddle of water lying in the road and was told that that was good enough for an enemy of Moses. The railing passerby subsequently became, in punishment, the Wild Huntsman.

19. The name "Cartaphilus" seems to signify "dearly beloved," and links this aspect of the Wandering Jew to the legend of St. John, which is summarized briefly but well in L. Neubaur, *Die Sage vom ewigen Juden* (rev. ed., Leipzig, 1893), 2 ff. For the name *Cartaphilus*, see Neubaur,

11; Charles Schoebel, *La légende du Juif-Errant* (Paris, 1877), 24; and Gaston Paris, "Le Juif Errant" in *Encyclopédie des sciences réligieuses*, VII, 498–514 (Paris, 1880), which has also been published as a separate pamphlet (1881).

20. See note 3 above.

21. See T. Vernaleken, *Alpensagen* (Vienna, 1858), 82–83; Jules Fleury ("Champfleury"), *Histoire de l'imagerie populaire* (Paris, 1869), 1–104; and especially Killen (note 2 above).

22. It is also an amusing touch to have a stranger, behind whom lies the dignified majesty of centuries, referred to as "Mr. Ferguson"—a unique name for the Wandering Jew certainly, but one which reminds the reader irresistibly and irrelevantly of the fictitious name imposed upon the unfortunate guide for the unregenerate Mark Twain and his doctor-friend in *Innocents Abroad*.

23. In France, for example, there are the works of Champfleury (note 21) and Paris (note 19) already mentioned; in Italy the researches of d'Ancona (see particularly "La leggenda dell' Ebreo Errante" in *Nuova Antologia rivista di scienze, lettere e arti* (Rome, 1880), 413–427), Morpurgo (note 2) and Giuseppe Pitré (*Fiabe, Novelle e Racconti Populari Siciliani* [Palermo, 1875], section 6, cxxxi–cxxxviii); in Germany the magnificent studies of Neubaur (note 19).

24. Moncure D. Conway, *The Wandering Jew* (London, 1881), 159 ff. The story of Pearson, however, appeared first in *Notes and Queries* for September 30, 1871.

25. Paradoxically, however, Celtic popular literature has put up an unusually successful resistance against the encroachments of the legend of the Wandering Jew, a legend which in its terror and its implications of untold mystery, might have been expected to appeal to the Celtic mind. See Ethel B. Parsons, "The Wandering Jew of Celtic Legend" in *English Journal* (College Edition), xxii, 676–678, for a feeble parallel.

26. The *Gabriel-Hounds* (cf. N. E. D. *GABRIEL*) may be, as usually explained, a flock of wild geese, or they may represent a further survival of the legend of the Wandering Jew. Certainly they are associated in the popular mind with the sinister or demoniac. Cf. Wordsworth's *Though Narrow Be That Old Man's Cares*, 12–14:

> For overhead are sweeping Gabriel's Hounds
> Doomed with their impious Lord the flying Hart
> To chase for ever on aerial Grounds.

But these are shadowings forth of the Wild Huntsman, not the Wandering Jew.

27. Another, which takes us far from the original story, is that in William Henderson, *Folklore of the Northern Counties* (The Folklore Society, 1879), 82:

"An old woman of the North Riding once asked a friend of mine whether it was wrong to wash on Good Friday. 'I used to do so,' she said, 'and thought no harm of it, till once, when I was hanging out my clothes, a young woman passed by (a dressmaker she was, and a Methodist); and she reproved me, and told me this story. . . . "While our Lord Jesus was being led to Calvary, they took him past a woman who was washing, and the woman blirted the thing she was washing in His face, on which He said, 'Cursed be everyone who hereafter shall wash on this day!' " 'And never again,' added the old woman, 'have I washed on Good Friday!' "

Just why the Wandering Jew has usually been portrayed as a former shoemaker has never been explained, except for the reasons a) that shoemakers are by tradition independent, lazy, improvident, defiant, and atheistical; and b) that there would be a fine irony in having a shoemaker wander forever and so wear out shoes with no possibility of repairing them—a professional torture, as it were. But at least one shoemaker used the Wandering Jew as an excuse for his own shortcomings. Henderson (note 27) reports an old shoemaker of Devonshire, who, when reproved for his shiftlessness, observed: "Don't 'ee be hard on me. We shoemakers are a poor slobbering race, and so have been ever since the curse that Jesus Christ laid on us." "And what was that?" asked his wife. "Why," he replied, "when they were carrying Him to the Cross, they passed a shoemaker's bench and the man looked up and spat at Him; and the Lord turned and said, 'A poor slobbering fellow shalt thou be and all shoemakers after thee, for what thou hast done to me.' "

28. As in the version told by Nikolaus Heldvader, *Sylva Chronologica circuli Baltici* (Hamburg, 1625), 271.

29. See the bibliographies in the books by Soergel and Gielen (note 13 above).

30. See Morpurgo (note 2), 45 ff., particularly his comment (p. 47): "Certo i suoi brevi erano uguali a tutti gli altri, cui bisognava credere, non aprire," etc.

31. See Bataillon (note 2), 103 ff. The Spanish legend of Juan Espera en Dios and the Portuguese equivalent of João Espera em Dios were probably based originally on a legend derived ultimately from the legend of St. John, but in their best expression, that to be found in the pages of Fernan Caballero's novel, *La estrella de Vandalia* (Madrid, 1862), 61–63, they have assumed most of the basis of the story of the Wandering Jew. I quote from the 1906 edition in *Coleccion de Escritores Castellanos*, #131, 98 ff.:

—Ese judío—contestó la abuela—es un zapatero que vivía en Jerusalén en la calle de la Amargura, y cuando el Señor pasó por ella con la cruz á cuestas, al llegar á la puerta de su casa, iba tan destrozado y exhausto, que quiso descandar en ella, y le dijo al dueño:

—¡Juan, sufro mucho!

Y Juan contestó:

—¡Anda, anda, que más sufro yo, que estoy aquí cosido al remo del trabajo!

Entonces el Señor, viéndose tan cruelmente despedido, le dijo al zapatero:

—¡Pues anda tú, anda . . . hasta la consumación de los siglos!

Al punto aquel hombre sintio que andaban sus pies sin él moverlos ni poderlos retener, y desde entonces empezó á andar, á andar . . . y desde entonces anda sin nunca pararse, y andará hasta la consumación de los siglos, para que se cumpla la maldición de Dios que se atrajo.

Viendo aquello, conoció aquel despiadado que era un castigo del cielo por su dureza, y por aquella palabra cruel, de "Anda, anda!" que le echara á la cara al maltraído que le pidió descanso, y se arrepintió con el alma de lo que había hecho, y empezó á llorar su culpa y á desesperarse. Y así anduvo, hasta que el año, un Viernes Santo á las tres de la tarde, se le apareció en lo más lejano de los horizontes, y entre los elementos y celajes, un Calvario con tres cruces. Al pie de la más alta, que era la de en medio, estaba una Señora tan hermosa como afligida, tan afligida como mansa. Esta Señora volvió su cara descolorida y llena de lágrimas hacia él, y le dijo:

—¡Juan, espera en Dios!

"This Jew," replied the Grandmother, "is a shoemaker who dwelt in Jerusalem in the Street of Bitterness; and when the Savior passed by bearing His cross, He was in so desperate a state, so exhausted, when he came to the door of the house, that he wished to rest and said to the owner: 'Juan, I am suffering much.' And Juan answered: 'Go, go—I am suffering even more, I who labor here like a galley-slave bound to his oar.'

"Then the Savior, seeing Himself so cruelly rejected said, to the shoemaker, 'Very well! Go yourself, walk . . . until the consummation of Time.'

"Immediately this man felt his feet moving involuntarily, without his being able to stop them, and from that time he walked and walked. . . . And he has been walking ever since without ever stopping, and he will walk until the consummation of Time, that the curse of God, which he drew upon himself, may be fulfilled!

"Seeing what had happened, this man recognized that it was a punishment from Heaven for his hard-heartedness and his cruel words, 'Go! Go!' which he had hurled in the face of the unfortunate one who had asked to rest; and he repented with all his soul for what he had done, and he fell to weeping his offense and to despairing. Thus he walked until, at the end of a year, on Good Friday, at three o'clock in the afternoon, he saw appearing on the dim and distant horizon, mingled with the clouds of Heaven, a Calvary with three crosses. At the foot of the highest of these—the one in the middle— there was a Lady, as beautiful as she was sad, as sad as she was sweet. This Lady turned her face toward him and said to him, her face pale and tear-stained, 'Juan, espera en Dios!' "

The God-baiting usually associated with the legend of the Wandering Jew here amounts to no more than verbal insolence. Moreover, the legend allows the victim hope. Otherwise the outlines of the traditional legend are clear.

32. See Neubaur (note 6), *Neue Mitteilungen*, 20 ff.

33. Martin Dröscher, *Dissertatio theologica de duobus testibus vivis passionis dominicae* (Jena, 1668). This variation had some tenacity of life; in such cases, one Wanderer was a Jew, the other a "heathen"—but see note 52 below.

34. John Brand, *Observations on Popular Antiquities* (rev. ed., London, 1888, in Bohn's Antiquarian Library), iii, 360–361.

35. Apart from the Wandering Jew himself, two striking examples would be Juan de los Tiempos (Jan van den Tyden), who was allegedly *scutifer* in Charlemagne's army and then lived on indefinitely; and the famous Don Juan of amoristic perfection. But the Wandering Jew bears this name only in medieval tradition.

36. See note 3 above.

37. Quoted in Moncure D. Conway, *The Wandering Jew* (London, 1881), 143.

38. This would imply that the pamphlet was printed some thirty years or so after 1769; but later on it is stated specifically that the time from the birth of Christ to the pamphlet came to 1769 years. In other words, the Jew is supposed to have started his wandering at the time of the birth of Christ instead of the Crucifixion, which is an obvious error.

39. The mark of Cain seems to be the source of the mark which was later fixed on the brow of the Wandering Jew; the first writer to make prominent use of this detail, however, is M. G. Lewis in *The Monk*, written (1794–95) a quarter of a century after this pamphlet. The mark on the brow of the Wandering Jew, of course, is traditionally a flaming red. We may call it a detail of the art-form of the legend.

40. This might be Overton, Hampshire; it is more likely a fictitious detail.

41. See note 10 above.

42. Printed in S. Morpurgo, *L'ebreo errante in Italia* (Florence, 1891), 15–40; for a summary, see L. Neubaur (note 6), *Neue Mitteilungen*, 3 ff.

43. See Anderson (note 6), 243 ff.

44. Either the *Discours veritable d'un juif errant* (Bordeaux, 1609) or the version in P. V. P. Cayet, *Chronologie Septenaire* (Paris, 1607), 440 ff.

Both are close translations of the *Kurtze Beschreibung*; and Shann in his account mentions the Cayet material specifically.

45. Cf. Gutch and Peacock's *Examples of Printed Folk-Lore concerning Lincolnshire* (London, 1908).

46. Recorded in Marie Trevelyan, *Folk-Lore and Folk-Stories of Wales* (London, 1909), 337–339. The author prefaces her accounts with the exasperating though understandable remark: "Stories of the Wandering Jew have been heard and chronicled in Pembrokeshire and Glamorgan, and both were connected with county families, whose names, for obvious reasons, were suppressed." It might be added that neither of these stories alters in any way the statement that the legend is virtually nonexistent on Celtic ground.

47. This and the following passage from Calmet are to be found in the 1732 edition of the *Dictionnaire*, II, 472. I quote from the English translation by Charles Taylor (1829).

48. *Theatrum Europaeum* (Frankfurt, 1702), XIV, 723.

49. Johann Jacob Schudt, in his *Judische Merkwürdigkeiten* (Frankfurt and Leipzig, 1714), Book V, Chap. 13, 488–512 and especially paragraph 21, sketches the career of Ahasuerus and refers to the London visit. But he also cites the statement of the Frankfurt jurist Konrad von Uffenbach, who visited England in 1710, that at Cambridge he interviewed the famous scholars Bentley and Baker and learned from their ignorance of the affair that the whole story was a fabrication.

50. Giovanni Marana, *L'espion du grand-seigneur dans le cour des princes chrétiens* (Paris, 1684), II, 176–181. Marana was a Genoese; his work was probably originally in Italian, but if so it has been lost in that form. The first English translation is dated 1686; the last of which I have record was in 1748. The work is a typical series of essays in epistolary form, criticizing the *mores* of Europeans.

51. The theory is suggested by Neubaur (note 6), 42, that the material in Marana was transferred in locale to England by some nameless contributor to the legend.

52. At about the same time, perhaps in 1694 itself, there appeared a German broadside tract, *Wahre Eigentliche Abildung des Unsterblichen Heydens, Joseph Krantz* (undated, and no place of publication given), which seems to draw upon the *Turkish Spy Letters*, and mentions the new increment which placed the Jew in England in 1694. A transcription and discussion of this tract will appear in a forthcoming issue of *The Germanic Review*. It has two or three peculiar points of interest. First, it picks up a twist in the legend which appeared in a 1660 edition of the *Relation* (the third and latest section of the German Ahasuerus Book, for which see Neubaur, 82 ff.)—namely, that there were in actuality *two* wanderers, a heathen and a Jew. (See also M. Dröscher, note 33.) The Jew is, of course, Ahasuerus. The *Wahre Eigentliche Abildung*, however, gives the "heathen" the unique name of Joseph Krantz. Second, it places the

"heathen" Joseph Krantz in the *north* of England and explains that the
report that *Ahasuerus* was in England in 1694 was false. Nay more, it
attempts to differentiate carefully between Ahasuerus and Joseph Krantz.
But in attempting this task, the author of the broadside was sidetracked
into the story as told by Matthew Paris (note 3); as a result he comes up
with the conclusion that the Joseph Cartaphilus of Matthew Paris is in
fact the "heathen" Joseph Krantz, whereas Ahasuerus is—Ahasuerus.
His conclusion, and, indeed, his main character, Joseph Krantz, have not
been perpetuated further, although the author has a case. For Cartaphilus, who represents the earliest known medieval aspect of the protagonist
of the legend of the Wandering Jew, is closely akin to the tarrying St.
John, whereas Ahasuerus is the creation of the modern purveyors of the
legend in the Renaissance German Ahasuerus Book.

53. Except in the art-form of the legend, the parentage of Ahasuerus
is not stressed, though it is often mentioned in popular literature after
1600. The French *Historie Admirable* (*ca.* 1650 ff.) associates him with the
tribe of Naphthali; his father in the many editions is either a cordwainer
or a carpenter, rarely himself a shoemaker.

54. See especially Erno Railo, *The Haunted Castle* (London, 1927), 194–
243. In the heart of the English romantic age, the most distinguished
English contributions were those by M. G. Lewis, *The Monk* (1795);
Shelley's *Queen Mab* (1813), *The Wandering Jew's Soliloquy* (posthumous,
1887), and particularly *Hellas* (1822); George Croly, *Salathiel: a story of
the past, present, and future* (1827); and Caroline Norton, *The Undying One*
(1830). Of course Coleridge owes something to the Wandering Jew for
his picture of the Ancient Mariner; and he appears in a minor part in
Byron's *Cain* (1821) and in Wordworth's *Song of the Wandering Jew*
(1800).

55. A. R. Wright, *English Folklore* (New York, 1932), 117–118.

56. The best account of English works in this category will be found
in Railo (note 54).

THE WANDERING JEW
IN AMERICA

Rudolf Glanz

When Europeans came to the New World, they brought their legends with them. The Wandering Jew was no exception, and, in a country where an ever expanding frontier was marked by all sorts of wanderers, the legend remained popular. The American experience created a new context for the Wandering Jew which in turn generated additional folklore texts in a variety of genres. Drawing from folk speech and similes as well as from newspaper accounts, Rudolf Glanz, a specialist in Jewish folklore, skillfully demonstrates how an Old World legend is adapted to a new environment.

Although only an episode in the crucifixion story, Ahasuerus becomes a symbol of the itinerant fate of the Jewish people, by way of the thought association of the crucifixion with the Jews. Among the many wanderers in the folklore of the most diverse peoples, there is hardly one who can compare to Ahasuerus, either in the folk phantasy or even in the literary treatment of the folk motif of Ahasuerus.[1] Furthermore, if we follow the folk motif itself in its migration through countries and continents, through its adaptations, revisions and recreations,[2] we find that there is

Reprinted from Rudolf Glanz, *The Jew in the Old American Folklore* (New York, 1961), pp. 30–41, 193–5.

hardly any other wandering folk motif which in its ubiquitousness still so clearly reveals its origin and its true significance despite such rich modulations. Thus the story of the eternal, wandering Jew migrates to America, from the very outset firmly aiming to make its fate in Europe also its fate in the New World. Here it gains a popularity that seems altogether unmatched in its European counterpart. The image of the wandering Jew establishes itself in language and idiom of the nascent American nation with an altogether surprising plasticity and creates one of the most popular comparisons of the new continent, simultaneously fertilizing folklore and individual wit and humor.

Since we are dealing here with a literate nation, we ought to investigate at first to what an extent the American literature itself, through the medium of periodicals which were available to the population, may have brought the wandering Jew before its readers. Such presentations, especially as newspaper material, can hardly have failed to affect the folk phantasy, although it is difficult to prove here a direct connection. It is easier, however, to recognize the effect of such printed material in the subsequent creations of the folk phantasy which, in the form of contributions by anonymous reader-authors, were submitted to the very same newspapers—as fictitious or true letters from readers. Thus the circle closes, folklore remains also here the magic carpet on which the material is brought into the newspaper and from the newspaper to the creative mind.

Already in Europe, the appearance of the wandering Jew whom credulous souls, especially in remote areas, thought to have spotted time and again, was considered newsworthy. In addition to unaccustomed types of wanderers, there were, in Europe's historic beggar circuit, many fraudulent beggars. Among them an enterprising crook would occasionally peddle the wandering Jew in order to obtain alms from the rural population. A case of such an undertaking, elaborated with additional Biblical trimmings, was reported from England in the American press:

> A few years ago there was a fellow with a long beard in London, who professed himself to be the Wandering Jew. He did not adhere to the legend, which was of little consequence, as his visitors were not likely to be better informed than himself, but laid

claim to higher antiquity than the Jerusalem shoemaker, and declared that he had been with Noah in the ark. Noah, he said, had refused to take him; but he got in secretly, and hid himself among the beasts, which is the reason his name is not mentioned in the Bible; and while he was there, the he-goat had given him a blow on the forehead, the mark of which was visible to this day. Some persons asked him which country he liked best of all that he had visited in his long peregrinations; he answered "Spain," as perhaps a man would have done who had really seen all the world. But it was remarked as rather extraordinary that a Jew should prefer the country of the Inquisition. "God bless you, Sir!" replied the ready rogue, shaking his head, and smiling at the same time as if at the error of the observation, "it was long before Christianity that I was last in Spain, and I shall not go there again till long after it is all over."[3]

Also later on, after the appearance of the above story, newspapers still carried reports on the wandering Jew in England.[4]

Meanwhile folk imagination had been sufficiently awakened in America to encounter the wandering Jew in the tremendous expanses of the new continent, and from now on he is being also sighted here, as in Europe first in a rural setting:

> . . . a good-natured naive German farmer who lives in Cambria County in Pennsylvania, told me a few years ago in all seriousness he had seen him hurry past his farm. And since that long-nosed, greybearded wanderer did not carry a long bag on his back, and since he did not peddle ribbons and shoe laces, he must have been the real old Ahasuerus.[5]

Of considerably greater significance are newspaper reports about his appearance in New York. In the mind of the Westerners who were spreading across the continent, the city had an aura of fabulousness, and news emanating from it that stressed the miraculous were widely covered in the Western press. Besides the New York reports, Ahasuerus' appearance received even greater emphasis where the press served a religious denomination that was just searching for confirmation of its teaching from the outside world, and that wove interpretative material around the news that served this purpose. The following report from the *Deseret News*, the unique main organ of the Mormons in Utah, bears all these features:

The Wandering Jew in New York

A sensation was created in William Street on Thursday Morning, by the appearance of a man on the pave with a long floating beard, and dressed in loose pantaloons, with a turban on his head. He carried in his hand a little manuscript Hebrew book, out of which he read to the crowd which gathered around him. He represented himself as the veritable Wandering Jew. Nobody knows who he is and where he came from. A learned Jewish Rabbi was sent to converse with him, which they did in the Hebrew language, and the stranger was found to be perfect in his knowledge of that most difficult tongue.

The Rabbi tested him in the Arabic, in Phenician and in the Sanscrit, but soon found that the aged stranger by far surpassed him in intimacy with them all. The Rabbi invited him to his house but, said the stranger, "nay, I cannot stop. The Crucified One of Calvary has pronounced the edict, and I must not rest. I must move on—ever on!" He was last seen on Thursday, but to where he departed no one can tell.[6]

It can be seen here how this denomination established a testimonial for the basic facts of its new doctrine, the revelation on American soil of the "Book of Mormon." Similarly, testimony about Ahasuerus is not omitted either in the following second report about the appearance of the Wandering Jew in New York. Information about his birth, descent, and even the fate that Jesus pronounced about him, is this time recorded in writing. Moreover, the religious instructions that are connected with the Wandering Jew are much more extensive this time:

Quite an excitement, it is reported, was recently caused in the village of Harts Corners, a few miles from New York, by the appearance of the veritable "Wandering Jew." Now an ordinary wandering Jew would not be at all likely to create any surprise, seeing that they are to be met with in every quarter; but the case would be quite contrary—even in a community of beer- and tobacco-loving Dutchmen, the very embodiment of all that is imperturbable, if the genuine Ahasuerus—condemned by the Great Teacher to walk the earth until the day of judgment—were to make his appearance in their midst. So nobody can wonder at the excitement displayed by the people of Harts Corners on the appearance of this very notorious and venerable character in their midst!

The discovery was made under the following instances: On the

2nd instant, as two little boys were going a-fishing, their attention was arrested by deep groans which seemed to emanate from an old shanty they passed on their way. The boys entered the shanty and there beheld a venerable-looking individual with a long white beard, dressed in black flowing garments, seated in one corner, apparently in pain. They manifested a desire to assist him, but were frightened off by the old fellow lifting his staff in a frightening manner. The youngsters retreated and soon returned with a number of the villagers, who, on entering the shanty, saw an individual with a large hooked nose, larger ears and finger nails about an inch long—there was no tail visible at least. They asked what ailed him, and he replied that he had fallen on a stone and severely hurt his leg. In the course of conversation he also informed them he had no home, and that his last friend had departed this life long before the light of heaven illumined the soul of any among them, and that the voice of the only one he loved was silent in the tomb before printing was invented, or America had ever echoed the cry of liberty.

Exclamations of "cracked" escaped several of the crowd, which aroused the indignation of the Jew who asked them why they had come there if they did not believe him. They replied they came because they had heard there was a man in trouble and they wished to assist him. To this he replied, "man *can not* and Heaven *will* not." He then gave them a short account of his recent travels from Siberia to America via Behrings Straits, through the wilds of Alaska, etc., saying that the first kind word he had heard during the whole journey was from the party he was then addressing. He then bade them adieu and departed.

In his hasty departure on this occasion as he is said to have done on many others, he left a memento by which his identity was fully proven. This time it was an old volume of extracts from the Babylonian Talmud in the Hebrew character. On a fly leaf was a short account of his birth, parentage, the sentence of the Saviour and his subsequent wanderings, all clearly proving that he was the identical *bona fide* Wandering Jew. This remarkable book, proving the identity of poor Ahasuerus, is now in the possession of one Michael O'Grady (sic), a switch tender and farmer, living a short distance from the place where the Jew was discovered. By applying to him, any one sufficiently interested may doubtless obtain further details in relation to this—the very "last sensation"; of course they may.[7]

Such newspaper reports "document" the appearance of the wandering Jew in the same manner as they do other facts of life, but simultaneously give what is due to the imaginary vision of folklore. Characteristically this happens in remote regions of the continent which hardly ever have seen a real Jew, and where they express a concept of the "wandering Jew" without having been influenced by any real type of Jewish figures, and where at the utmost they have heard of the German-Jewish peddler. This is how he is seen in Mormon folklore:

> So he talked German to them: "Mann heisst mich den ewigen Juden."—Man calls me the everlasting Jew. Well, they paid no attention to it, but when he got away it came to them, "Well, that must be the rovin' Jew."[8]

In a further step toward popular fiction, a deserted landscape is imagined in which the wandering Jew creates a sensation through his appearance, such as in the following Pennsylvania Dutch poem:

> Backmult–Wälli,
> . . . Es kummt ken Kremer in das Dahl
> As juscht der eewig Jud;
> Den findt mer, dann bal üwerall—
> Geht eewig net Caput.
>
> . . . Die Jude hen sich Götter g'mcht
> Fon Gold, trotz Moses *Law;*
> Mie liewer Leeser, nem's inacht—
> So dhun fiel Chrischte a'h.
>
> Backmult Valley
> . . . No merchant comes into the valley,
> As just the wandering Jew;
> You find him almost anywhere—
> He just never goes to pieces.
>
> . . . The Jews fashioned idols for themselves
> of gold, despite Moses' law;
> My dear reader watch out—
> Many Christians do it, too.[9]

Here we find the wandering Jew already in transition to a new motif. He has already acquired a secular purpose, while it had been the very essence of his previous distinction that he did not trade, and that his long bag served only to illustrate his long travels. But on the long way across the American continent the resemblance of his bag to the peddler's bag of the German-Jewish immigrant continuously increases, and we have already found this hinted in our poem. If we take this as our point of departure, we come to understand why the legendary features of the wandering Jew blend so fully with those of the traveler for temporal gain in the figure of the Jewish peddler that has been treated so often in the literature, that in the end the long bag full of the sufferings of the eternal wanderer is forgotten over the peddler's bag.

The direct reminders of the golden calf in connection with the wanderer increase in strength as we move to the West where we can read the following as early as 1833:

The Wandering Jew
. . . Beneath the dreadful ban of God,
Judea's sons are scattered now—
The blasted wreck of former days—
And to the god of mammon bow.[10]

Such voices swell into a chorus once gold has been found in the Far West and the Jews are streaming to California. Poetical outbursts about the Golden Calf become more frequent, and the connection between the gold curse and the crucifixion curse becomes so tangible that it lays the foundations for the concepts that later on will make all of America quiver about the "cross of gold."

Literary concern with the wandering Jew starts early in America, and his motif is already worked into the offerings of the primitive theater in the 18th century.[11] Later on Europe's ballad-type material about him is reproduced with emphasis on its old age:

An lately in Bohemia,
With many a German towne;
And now in Flanders, as 'this thought,
He wandreth up and down:
. . . ballad . . . not less than three centuries old. . . .[12]

In the direct literary elaboration that follows later on, the side show of the Mammon motif in the travels through a materialistic-

minded world is by no means forgotten, and can be broadly illuminated as in the following:

> Letters of Salathiel, the wandering Jew, to Solomon ben Israel of
> Jerusalem.
>
> New York, June 1, 1836
>
> My Brother,—I call you my brother, for you are the only living
> man to whom I have communicated the terrible secret of my
> protracted existence. You only know the extent of my wander-
> ings; you alone have the means of conjecturing what may be the
> nature of my joy and sorrows, my feelings and habits; you are the
> only one who can in any degree sympathise with me; and to you
> alone will I communicate my views of what claims my notice in
> this new world, to which I have at length found my way.
>   . . . Of course I brought no letters with me, except a single
> letter of credit from Verrazani to a banker here, who, from my
> familiarity with the language, probably takes me for an English
> Jew; and from his conversation I suppose he has settled it in his
> mind that the object of my visit is trade, whenever I shall become
> sufficiently acquainted with the country to take an active part in
> its commerce. I believe I shall humor this notion of his, especially
> as it appears to be hardly possible for the people here to under-
> stand how a man can have any other object in this world than to
> make money, as they phrase it.[13]

The motif of the Wandering Jew evinces its popularity not only
by its repeated utilization in magazines,[14] but also through direct
testimony as to its frequent occurrence as a topic of conversation.
If this can be accepted as a fact, it would mean that a statement on
his frequent appearance as a topic of conversation often precedes
the further elaboration and application of comparisons with the
Wandering Jew:

> . . . the "Report of our Spring Races in '38"—that solemn docu-
> ment, which seems to have been as much talked of, and sought
> for, as the lost Pleiad, or the "wandering Jew."[15]

The reading of a literary standard work, Sue's master novel *The
Wandering Jew* lends itself to a standard pastime:

So we went, talking on morals and politics, reading the *Wandering Jew*, and playing poker until dinner came. . . . *The Wandering Jew* did very well as long as it lasted.[16]

In the process of developing into a general simile, the comparison at first refers to the element of mobility in space and in time which may be used as a basis for comparison with the eternal wanderer. In the following example it is the boundlessness of the high seas that the sailor has traversed:

. . . I began to be fascinated, and found myself comparing him to the "old man of the sea," and the "wandering Jew."[17]

But the imagined expanse may also be traversed in a comparison of one's self:

. . . I'm a kind of a wanderin' Jew of a blue devil—come, let's go and take a drink.[18]

The element of time may be added to that of space, or it may appear as an independent basis for comparison:

I shall be as old as the Wandering Jew soon.[19]

Once the simile has been developed with its spatial and temporal infinity, its application to cosmopolitanism follows logically:

I heard somebody say,
if I recollect right,
That he wasn't a Jew
but a Cosmopolite;
A 'Wandering' Jew, . . . [20]

But in most cases the application of the comparison draws its particular vigor from the specificity of the compared wandering element in a person or a given situation.

Oftentimes the task may be combined with a particular situation out of which it has grown, and nicknames may originate for certain persons:

For instance, a St. Louis reporter dispatched to cover the debates between Orr and Jackson was nicknamed "The Wandering Jew."[21]

But also a task as basically different from journalism as that of a railroad builder may earn the nickname:

Belongs to Hon. Otto Mears, known in this country under the enviable title of 'Pathfinder' and the 'Wandering Jew'! Mr. Mears is the president of the 'Denver and Rio Grande Southern' and of the Silverton and Ironton Railroads. . . .[22]

There are numerous cases in which the comparison is based on the person's occupation only:

The stationery-Man. . . . He is, I believe the Wandering Jew of the paper trade.[23]

Or that itinerant tradesman, the glazier, with his cry of:

Glass put in![24]

"Old clo' " without fail evokes the thought association to the "Wandering Jew," with "old clothes undesirables to wandering Jews,"[25] forming the apex of the memory of situations in which clothing "makes" people.

General compassion with the appearance of a professional who is poorly off may subject also him to comparison:

. . . the schoolmaster has long been deemed as little deserving of pity as the Wandering Jew.[26]

But even if such compassion is denied him on the basis of his poorly remunerated profession, he may still be granted such compassion on general human grounds:

Others seemed to agree that he was a son of the Wandering Jew, but with no inborn purpose of evil. . . .[27]

In contrast, cases where human qualities make the comparison possible must be severely called to account:

> And when we see a man, regardless of results, seeking like the
> fabulous Wandering Jew, a peripatetic immortality, and a despic-
> able prominency, at the sacrifice of all we hold dear and sacred
> . . . it becomes our duty to call him to a strict account . . . .[28]

Still the view prevails that he who lives long, experiences much
evil, and that evil must remind one of him because he who lives
eternally and keeps wandering, is exposed to more evil than any-
body else. Hence he who has suffered very much has the feeling
as if he had lived since ancient times, like the wandering Jew:

> Mr. Editor: I am that unfortunate personage, to whom all the
> mischief is attributed, that is perpetuated in this mischievous
> world: alas! that I should live to this day, to see the dreadful
> aggregate continually accumulating, and the burthen never
> lighted! I am not the wandering Jew, yet I have lived from the
> earliest ages.[29]

At the height of misfortune when all social ties dissolve and
man is left all by himself, then only the wandering Jew is chosen
as his only companion in suffering:

> Karl Konstant Kain, the last of Kains, . . . he has reached, at this
> period of his existence, a climax of loneliness and gaunt despair
> that would have rendered him a fit companion for the "Wander-
> ing Jew," and a most unfit one for anything less ludicrously
> ideal."[30]

In being used as the prototype of the ridiculous, the Wandering
Jew again runs through the entire gamut of human emotions. A
person may be accused of physical resemblance to him,[31] or may
simply be considered to be identical with him.[32]

A special kind of humor is produced by crossing the wandering
Jew with the Lost Tribes:

> . . . this wandering Israelite might be lost.[33]

The humorous comparison seems to reach its peak with the wandering preacher who changes his pulpit from one denomination
to another, as was the practice at the beginning of the Inter-Faith
movement, and who delivers a sermon, of all subjects, on

"The Wandering Jew!" Strange as it may seem the Wandering Jew lately made his appearance in a Christian pulpit in Chicago. . . . In short he was the Rabbi Felsenthal, Ph.D.; his audience was the Young Men's Christian Union of Chicago; and his sermon was entitled "The Wandering Jew—" in which he eloquently discoursed on the wanderings of his race.[34]

The impossible, an attempt to heighten the peak of humor, is still made through a transvestism. The element of wandering appears then a little inconsistent, like the character of a woman:

They have no notion, not they, of rambling hither and tither like the Wandering Jewess.[35]

The comparison is applied to lower forms of life only in exceptional cases.[36] But occasionally it is applied to inanimate nature where an element of instability has intruded. Even a building temporarily assigned to a roving court may be *The Wandering Jew* in comparison with other public buildings.[37]

Meditative souls, keeping the "Wandering Jew" before their eyes, could also arrive at a kind of criticism or self-criticism of the Yankee, thus adding a new dimension to the Jew-Yankee comparison. Thomas Lake Harris, for example, calls the Yankee in his push across the continent rootless like the Jews.[38]

In summing all this up it may be stated that the Wandering Jew mirrored the thoughts of the American nation about one's fellow men and about situations, and finally about the nation itself. Thus the wandering Jew himself filled the full function of the Jew in American folklore, viz., being a known phenomenon to provide a standard to be applied to the unknown that so often seemed to pose a threat.

NOTES

1. L. Neubaur, *Die Sage vom ewigen Juden* (Leipzig, 1893); Eduard König, *Ahasver, "der ewige Jude"* (Gütersloh, 1907); Werner Zirus, *Der ewige Jude in der Dichtung*, vornehmlich in der englischen und deutschen (Leipzig, 1928).

2. *Folk Travelers: Ballads, Tales, and Talk*, Mody C. Boatright, Wilson M. Hudson, and Allen Maxwell, eds. (Dallas, 1953).

3. "The Wandering Jew," *New Yorker* 2 (1836–37): 312.

4. "The Wandering Jew in England," *Criterion* 1 (1855–56): 204.

5. Karl Knortz, *Nachklänge germanischen Glaubens und Brauchs in Amerika* (Halle a. S., 1903), p. 41.

6. *Deseret News*, vol. 7 (1856), p. 107.

7. *Deseret News*, vol. 17, p. 257.

8. "The Legend of the Three Nephites Among the Mormons," *Journal of American Folklore* 53 (1940): 31. See also Austin E. Fife, "The Legends of the Mormons," *California Folklore Quarterly* 1 (1942): 125, for a second version: "How the Wandering Jew appeared to an early settler in Nevada."

9. H. L. Fischer, *Kurzweil un Zeitvertreib* (York, Pennsylvania, 1882), p. 107.

10. *Western Monthly Magazine* 1 (1833): 273.

11. *Diary of William Dunlap (1766–1839)*, Dorothy L. Bark, ed. (New York, 1930), p. 252.

12. *Pictorial National Library*, vol. II, "Ancient Ballad of the Wandering Jew," (Boston, 1849), pp. 300–302.

13. *Gentleman's Magazine* 1 (Philadelphia, 1837): 202–205.

14. "The Wandering Jew," *Brother Jonathan* 1 (1842): 441; "Ahasverus," *Northern Monthly*, 2 (1867–68): 315–21; "Editor's Easy Chair," *Harper's* 55 (1877): 300.

15. "Sporting Epistle from Alabama," *Spirit of the Times* 10 (1840): 379.

16. Dr. Thomas L. Nichols, *Forty Years of American Life*, vol. 1 (London, 1864), p. 164.
The first appearance of Sue's novel is announced as a sensation: "Numbers 8, 9, and 10 of *The Wandering Jew* have just been issued by the *Harper's* . . . No. 13 of *The Wandering Jew*—Sue's last and most exciting publication." *Spirit of the Times* 15 (1845–46): 45, 201.

17. George J. Miller, "Trout Fishing in Nova Scotia," *Sportsman's Magazine* 2 (1897): 138.

18. "Tom Johnson and Bill Jones . . . ," *Spirit of the Times* 17 (1847–48): 157.

19. Henry L. Boone, *Yankee-Jim, the Horse-Runner* (New York, 1870), p. 43.

20. "The Tall Son of York and His Correspondents," *Spirit of the Times* 21 (1851–52): 338.

21. M. J. Hubble, *Personal Reminiscences and Fragments of the Early History of Springfield and Greene County, Missouri* (Springfield, Missouri, 1914), p. 84.

22. "State of Colorado," *Jewish Voice* 14, no. 8 (1893): 8.

23. "The Street Employments of New York," *Knickerbocker* 54 (1859): 402.

24. Parker "Paddy" McGoff, "Scenes of My Childhood," *New York Folklore 2* (1946): 250.

25. "American Student Life: Or Some Memories of Yale," *Knickerbocker* 48 (1856): 555.

On the other hand, the eternal wanderer himself is in need of apparel: "He said he wanted to buy a new suit of clothes. That what he had on he had bought in 1807 in Germany, and it was beginning to get threadbare." C. Heber Clark, *Elbow-Room . . .* (Philadelphia, 1876), p. 320.

26. "Recollections of a Schoolmaster," *Maine Monthly Magazine* 1 (1837): 241.

27. Sam Slick, Jr. (S. A. Hammett), *Courtship and Adventures of Jonathan Homebred . . .* (New York, 1860), p. 18.

28. C. Aubrey Angelo, *Idaho . . .* (1865), p. 17.

29. James Hall, *Illinois Monthly Magazine* 1 (1831): p. 537.

30. James Melville Beard, *K. K. K.: Sketches, humorous and didactic, treating the more important events of the Ku Klux Klan movement in the South.* (Philadelphia, 1877), p. 181.

German Socialists in America were prepared to provide a collective trailblazer for a collective Ahasuerus to bring about "the salvation of the Jews by Germandom. . . . Ahasuerus [saved] by the awakening revolutionary Michel." *Der arme Teufel* 11 (1894–95): 205.

31. "He is a rather striking figure, . . . bears considerable remembrance to Cagliostro or the Wandering Jew." *Squints Through an Opera Glass* (New York, 1850), p. 18.

32. "Some took him for the Wandering Jew." *Streaks of Squatter Life* (Philadelphia, 1858), p. 139.

33. *Ubiquitous* vol. 1, no. 5, p. 3.

34. "The Wandering Jew," *Golden Age* 2 (Sacramento, April 30, 1872), p. 4.

35. "Behind the Scenes," *Spirit of the Times* 14 (1844–45): 21.

36. David E. Lick and Thomas R. Brendle, "Plant Names and Plant Lore Among the Pennsylvania Germans," *Pennsylvania German Society Proceedings* 33 (1926): 108, "Der Eee Wich Judd . . . Ee Wich Jud De Graut . . . Everlasting Jew Herb."

37. Charles C. Lowther, *Dodge City, Kansas* (Philadelphia, 1940), p. 175.

And only "a modern Wandering Jew" could seek a sinecure like the office of the United States Attorney for New Mexico. W. H. H. Davis, *El Gringo: Or, New Mexico and Her People* (New York, 1857), p. 388.

38. Herbert W. Schneider and George Lawton, *A Prophet and a Pilgrim* (New York, 1942), p. 360.

THE COBBLER OF
JERUSALEM
IN FINNISH FOLKLORE

Galit Hasan-Rokem

Most discussions of the Wandering Jew cite mainly printed texts without recourse to archival collections of oral tradition. In this essay, the rich holdings of the folklore archives of the Finnish Literary Society (founded in 1831) make it possible to define and analyze the image of the Wandering Jew figure in Finland. The occurrence of the image in a wide variety of genres is documented, and the legend is examined from structural and functional perspectives.

Introduction

The Wandering, Eternal Jew, who in Finnish folklore goes by the name of the Cobbler of Jerusalem, wanders between a number of different folklore genres. The way his figure is described, as well as the importance he assumes in the item of folklore, is clearly related to the specific genre. It would not be difficult to show that the subject is not of Finnish origin, but the popular nature of this figure in Finnish folklore is powerful enough to contradict the

Reprinted from *Jerusalem Studies in Jewish Folklore*, 2 (1982):124–48. The translation from Hebrew into English was made by the author.

contention of the German *Encyclopedia Judaica* that "Die slavischen und die finnischen-ugrischen Völkern scheinen also die Sage vom ewigen Juden nicht zu kennen."

My work is based on Finnish sources from several collections[1] and on comparative Scandinavian and European material, mostly from printed sources.[2]

History of the Tale

The birth date of the Cobbler of Jerusalem is quite well known; he entered European consciousness on the pages of a chapbook that was printed in northern Germany in the year 1602 and signed with a pseudonym.[3] The chapbook was very soon well distributed in central and northern Europe. The first Danish translation was published in 1621;[4] in Sweden it was first printed in 1643;[5] and even in Iceland the book was already translated in the first half of the seventeenth century.[6] Its dissemination in the Scandinavian countries was quite remarkable: Sweden saw at least nineteen editions (printings), and in Denmark there were at least four of them.[7] What was it that so stirred the imagination of northern Europeans?

The chapbook[8] describes in detail how Paulus von Eitzen (one of the prime students of Melanchton of Wittenberg, who was Martin Luther's teacher) in the year 1547 met a strangely dressed man in a church in Hamburg. He was in his fifties presumably, and his behavior was exceedingly pious and modest. The man revealed that he had been a cobbler in Jerusalem and that he had refused to allow Jesus to rest on the wall of his house when he went by bearing his cross. That is the reason why the man has been punished with eternal wandering until doomsday. This Jew, whose name was Ahasverus, saw himself as a living witness for the guilt of the Jews for Jesus' sufferings. The learned men of Hamburg talked to him at length, and his knowledge of history and languages made a great impression on them. They were also impressed by his deep piousness and Christian religiosity. Any alms over two pfennig he would instantly turn over to the poor.

The tale goes on providing witnesses of the appearance of the same Jew in Lübeck, Danzig, Königsberg, and other places, among them Madrid, where he was reported in the year 1575. The printer himself testifies that he had heard with his own ears from hundreds of people that they had met him, in Poland and in Moscow among other places, and he, the printer, promises to announce to his readers instantly if he himself happens to run into the man.

The intent of the chapbook seems pretty clear. It tries to convince the local Jews to convert to Christianity,[9] and also legitimizes the harassing of Jews as well as the looting of their houses and the seizure of their possessions.[10]

The use of popular legends as anti-Jewish propaganda is not a new phenomenon in the Reformation era. There are a number of earlier popular legends partly of a religious character in this vein.[11] Supernatural motifs such as the liaisons of the Jews with Satan and their familiarity with black magic belong to the same types of materials spreading prejudice and hatred.

The earliest printings of the so-called Volksbuch of Ahasver belong to the wake of the Lutheran Reformation, during which quite militant religious polemics were not unusual. The "youthful" years of Ahasver's wanderings are accompanied by the cannon blasts of the Thirty Years' War, a war with heavy religious overtones. The author of the present Volksbuch was presumably a Protestant.[12] Similar chapbooks were in circulation for communication and propaganda purposes, but few reached the wide distribution of the "Wandering Jew" chapbook.[13] A Danish scholar seems to think that the Volksbuch was not particularly efficient in achieving its propagandistic purposes.[14] He assumes that its principal function was indeed missionary, and he almost completely overlooks its racist and Jew-baiting message.[15]

The Volksbuch arrived in some countries even before the Jews themselves had settled in them. Thus in Denmark the chapbook was translated in the year 1621 although the first Jew settled there only in 1622, as far as we know.[16] Some Jews arrived in Sweden between 1680 and 1685 (although they attained a formal certificate for residence only in 1721),[17] but the tale of the Wandering Jew had arrived there by the year 1643. In Iceland, where the Jewish population remains scanty and minimal to this day, the Volksbuch was translated by the first half of the seventeenth century.

The tale as we know it from these literary versions has its roots in European folklore. Anderson has pointed out that the seventeenth-century tale about Ahasver includes many elements from earlier legends and myths, and his findings draw heavily from earlier research stating the same facts. Anderson shows the great influence of Italian folklore on the prototypes of the Ahasver legend[18] by discussing several forms of the protolegend, such as the Buttadeo legend and others. Anderson assumes that the plot nucleus of the legend came into being during the Crusades somewhere in the vicinity of Jerusalem, where the legend would have had a special local flavor.[19]

Two elements are innovations of the 1602 version: the name Ahasverus and the occupation of cobbler. These two elements seem to be among the most stable elements of the central and north European traditions. The name has been explained by the Purim-Shpiel, the traditional Jewish folk-drama based on the biblical Book of Esther, in which the Persian king Ahasverus figures,[20] but the occupation still puzzles scholars. Anderson points out the ironical aspect of a shoemaker having to wear out his shoes in this endless manner without ever apparently having time to practice his trade.[21] Finnish folklorist Lauri Honko assumes a relationship between Ahasver's trade and the fact that in medieval society the guild of the shoemakers was a wandering group of tradesmen.[22] In Finland, wandering or itinerant cobblers were still active at the beginning of this century.

The Volksbuch—the Chapbook of the Wandering Jew—in Finland

In Finnish collections, I have found three small chapbooks in which the story of Ahasver is related in prose, printed in the years 1892, 1903, and 1907. It is not difficult to prove that these are translations of Swedish translations of the original German chapbook.[23] In one of the Finnish translations there is an exact repetition of a local Swedish addition which was printed earlier in a Swedish version from the town of Jönköping. In this detail, the colorful and exotic appearance of the Cobbler in the market of the town of Värnamo is described. The Nordic folklore has garbed Ahasverus in the following outfit, very different from the austerity of the German version: he wears among other things a coat made of horsehair, trousers made of camel skin, and a tiger skin hat.

The 1903 Finnish edition seems to have been popular enough to have been reprinted in 1907. That edition contains a remarkable piece of news: The Cobbler of Jerusalem was seen among the soldiers of the Italian army in Tripoli (Libya). The printer warns the readers that there might be some inaccuracies in the account, since the story has traveled such a long way. In the same paragraph, he also mentions that the Cobbler was seen in England in the eighth century. This seems like a distant echo of a well-known mention of a cursed wanderer in the chronicle of Roger de Wendover.[24]

Whereas the Finnish chapbooks mention the name Ahasverus, this name is not found in the oral versions. So although we can state quite confidently that the core and main part of the elements of the story were transmitted to Finland from Germany via the Swedish translations of the Volksbuch, the name apparently did not enter oral tradition. Perhaps it was too difficult and strange for the narrators to remember it. The emphasis was therefore transferred to the occupational aspect instead. The fact that the Wandering Jew is a shoemaker is in any case a constant element in Finnish tradition, and indeed this is the name by which he is commonly identified: the Cobbler of Jerusalem.

The elimination of the term "Jew" from the standard recognized epithet for our hero correlates with the near total disappearance of anti-Semitic elements from the Finnish folklore surrounding this figure. This, more than the fact that there are not many Jews in Finland, explains the disappearance of the anti-Semitic elements, since we saw that the Volksbuch reached most Scandinavian countries before the Jews settled there. The Finnish folklore related to the Wandering Jew includes a variety of elements not to be found in the German editions of the Volksbuch and its translations, but elements which do exist in the Continental folklore on the subject. These elements have probably been transmitted through oral tradition or by independent invention to which we shall return later.

The Cobbler of Jerusalem in Finnish Oral Tradition.

The Legend

The legend, or the sacred tale, is a folk narrative genre in which the violation of the rules of normative religion is punished by a representative of the supreme force, or the following of these rules is rewarded by the same. The term *legend* has in the context of this essay been reserved for that part of the complex of tradition related to the Wandering Jew in which the encounter between Ahasverus and Christ is described as well as the curse meted out by Christ.

The Cobbler of Jerusalem occurs in Finnish folklore in a variety of genres. Sometimes the relationship between these genres is genetic, that is, one genre generates another. For example, the narrative generates a proverb or the legend generates a folk belief. Sometimes the relationship between the genres is symbiotic; that is, they are linked together in one sequence. However, the most persistent of all the genres is the legend about Jesus and the Wandering Jew. But only in seventeen texts (out of fifty-nine which constitute the whole corpus discussed here) does the legend appear without the accompaniment of another genre, and even in these seventeen texts there is a reference to the existence of a proverb, i.e., another genre. The legend about Christ's sufferings serves a clear religious function by itself. In other cases, we may discern conglomerations of various genres such as a proverb, a legend, and a folk belief (e.g., see text no. 40—for details of the texts cited, see Appendix 1). The different genres become structural elements of the complete tradition complex which tends to cluster around this theme.

The legend is not only the most constant of the genres involved, but it is also the most widely distributed, and it is included in one form or another in forty-four of the fifty-nine texts, albeit in some instances just by means of a reference (14, 41, 43), summary (40, 33), or fragment (39, 40). Other genres that figure in the generic combinations of the theme in Finnish folklore are the warning tale, which is related to the didactic function of the tradition, the proverb, the folk belief, the belief tale, and the memorate.

The legend itself may be analyzed as being composed of two main episodes:[25] the sin and the punishment. In the present discussion of the legend, a basic structural unit will be considered which in order to avoid previous associations in structuralist research will be labeled as neutrally as possible. Let us call it an element. The element may not be divided into smaller parts than itself in the framework of this legend; that is, parts of it will not appear independently, and the element itself can be linked to other different elements in the narrative. The element is not necessarily in any order of sequence despite being linked to some of the other elements. This definition of the element defines so to speak the minimal and maximal limits of the unit. The element in this narrative may be a description, an act, a quality, or an utterance. The elements are listed systematically in Appendix 2. Here we shall discuss the results of the analysis.

The protagonist of the legend is Jesus Christ. The elements concerning his activities in the narrative are the most constant, and they take up the longest time in the story. His behavior in the legend is stereotypical[26] although the legend is generally varied in its plot elements. The elements involving the behavior of the Cobbler, on the other hand, are varied. Only in five cases is the behavior of the Cobbler motivated: by his richness, by his being "a rich Jew" (one of the rare occurrences of his ethnic background in the texts), the general viciousness of shoemakers, his fear of the storming masses. The Cobbler himself is occasionally described as being in the midst of mending Pilate's shoes (29 and another six texts) or holding his own child in his arms. These elements are usually connected to related elements in other genres symbiotically connected with the legend. In those cases where the legend is accompanied by folk beliefs and belief tales, the importance of the Cobbler grows and the elements concerning him are emphasized more since in those genres, unlike in the legend, it is he and not Jesus who is the central figure. The sin is followed by the punishment which is focused and textually embodied in the verdict uttered by Christ, a verdict which proves to bear a magic quality insofar as it has predictive power. Here we are already past the dramatic climax of the narrative. The severity of the deed leaves us in suspended expectation for the appropriate reaction, and when the verdict is given, the suspension is relieved. This suspension is crucial for the dramatic quality of the narrative, and consequently in none of the texts does any element occur between the elements of sin and verdict.[27]

Christ's words constitute the conservative element of the legend tradition, and this element is a highly formalized and repetitive feature of the texts. It is possible that the holiness with which this utterance must be imbued in the legendary tradition serves as a conservative force in the process of transmission. The utterance must conform. In some ways, it could be argued, it is the stylistic character of the passage in question which has such a conservative effect on the tradition bearers as it includes, in addition to rhyme, contrastive parallelism and other formulaic elements.

The span of the punishment as defined by Jesus is "until doomsday" (in ten of the texts), "to the end of the world" (seven texts), or "until I return to this world" (three texts). Some additions to Jesus' utterance refer to folk beliefs, such as the fact that the Wandering Jew is carrying his cobbler's tools on his back or that he lives to be a hundred years old or alternatively that he lives forever, in such wordings of the verdict as: "Take your cobbler's tools," "You shall not die," "You shall live forever." The folk beliefs expressed in the texts will be discussed more extensively later in this essay.

It is interesting to note that the different forms of Jesus' verdict do not have any discernible geographic distribution so as to create local redactions in the manner described by the historic-geographic analysis of folklore. The fact that eternal life is meted out as a punishment in this legend points to a worldview in which eternal life is assumed to be a negative state rather than a desideratum. In folktales, eternal life is usually presented positively as a wish fulfillment and even more so in myths, where eternal life is very often the positive result of a tremendous effort or an unusually heroic deed accomplished by the protagonist. This would suggest that in this legend we have a moralistic and superego-colored way of thinking in contrast to the fulfillment of secret wishes and the liberating of usually repressed fantasies that we more often associate with folk narratives. The characterization that Jesus is given in the legend is not of the ideal all-merciful overseer of human sins who calls in the Gospel for the other cheek to be turned to the assaulter. The curse expressed in the verdict points to a rather strict "eye for an eye" code of vengeance, more like the not-so-exact image that Jewish law is given in Christian imagination. The Danish scholar Nyrop credits this disposition in the characterization of Jesus to the fact that the sources of the legend are not really evangelical but later medieval in origin.[28]

The element of punishment includes a motivation for the specific character of the punishment in seven texts. In all the other cases it follows the sin with no connective and no motivation. The motivations in those cases where they are supplied are of a psychological nature: "he was overcome by a forceful lust of wandering," "his conscience pushed him to go," "the earth was burning under his feet," "the man lost his wits." There is, however, no correlation between the mention of a psychological motivation in the punishment and psychological motivations for the sin in the first episode, so that it is not possible to single out versions of a general, more 'psychological' type.

The elements concerning the very wandering of the Jew are problematic to isolate since it is not always clear when they are an organic part of the legend and when they are rather part of the following folk belief or belief tale. In the cases where the element of the wandering is unambiguously a part of the legend, it is always its concluding element.

By tabulating the elements (Appendix 3), it is possible to determine which is the favorite sequence of elements in the Finnish versions of the legend. The statistically most widely distributed combination is as follows: Jesus bears the cross and leans on the wall of the Cobbler's house. The Cobbler drives him away. Jesus says to the Cobbler: "I shall rest, but you will wander in the world (till doomsday)."

Folk Beliefs

We have shown that the legend is a constant genre in Finnish folklore about the Wandering Jew, both thematically and rhetorically. The folk beliefs about the same theme are, however, very varied, and the materials are often quite fragmentary and incomplete. Eschatological beliefs are of special importance and interest among the Finnish folk beliefs about the Cobbler of Jerusalem. Finnish folklorist Lauri Honko contends that these beliefs also give a special insight into the function of the legend and serve as the functional basis for the dissemination of the legend and the other folk literary genres related to the theme. In the above historical survey, the anti-Semitic function of the legend in its central European, especially the German, setting was mentioned. The Scandinavian materials, especially the Finnish texts, do not lend themselves to a similar kind of function. Therefore, the question of the function has to be put to this material separately within its social and spiritual setting, although the narrative elements of the legend itself may not be different from the central European material. This is an interesting illustration of the need to look beyond the boundaries of the text in order to analyze the function of folklore. Honko's suggestion is that the Wandering Jew was left by Jesus in this world as a living witness that He was in this world and that He will return at the end of days. That the appearances of the Cobbler are closely associated with wars and other catastrophes supports the notion that the theme raises questions of extreme existential character.

That the legend deals with the basic order of the world is attested in the text by the sacred quotation of Christ's words, which assumes the status of a 'holy script', and as we have seen also is the raison d'être of the legend in the popular tradition as well as the most stable textural element, perhaps even the generative nucleus of every separate narrating of the plot. Although the highly normative, Christian function of the legend seems obvious, it is always advisable in folkloristic materials to consider also the less obvious functions. Indeed, it is sometimes thought that the most important sociopsychological function of folklore is precisely to carry those less obvious, hidden meanings. If we apply a somewhat psychoanalytically oriented model to the legend, we might well interpret its contents as follows: Jesus, who is in this case a severe and punishing father figure, is confronted with the rebellious son, the Cobbler, whose rebellion is punished by the father in a manner that actually turns out to be a wish fulfillment: eternal life. That is, the Oedipal rebellion is necessary to ensure growth and life. This interpretation assumes an identification with the Cobbler rather than with the sufferings of Christ, which is actually reflected also in the descriptive and emotive passages of many of the texts, thus turning it into almost an antilegend, or a subversive legend. The paralegendary tradition of the Wandering Jew stresses this interpretative potential of the legend even more, and it becomes the main theme in many of the literary renditions of the work, especially those of the Romantic school.[29] In the legend itself, Jesus assumes the traditional archetypal role of the returning hero, such as Elijah the prophet in the Jewish and Moslem traditions and Väinämöinen in the Finnish pre-Christian tradition. The legend, the static part of the tradition, describes the mythological era of Christianity, the era in which Jesus formed the order of the world by his word. The Cobbler of the legend wanders in the world as a concrete remnant from that mythological era, comparable to such etiological-mythological motifs as the rainbow being a remnant of the mythological era of the creation of the world, which is the mythological era of Judaism. (Strictly speaking, the whole world should be considered as such a remnant, a sign of God's activity in the world, but that is another matter.) That is why in many tales there is a prediction which relates the end of Ahasver's wanderings to the end of the world, yet another era to come.

In the German and the Swedish versions of the Volksbuch, the eschatological motifs are only vaguely referred to, the end of the world being more of a theological term and not a pictorial imaginative literary element. In Finnish folklore the subject was developed and elaborated. In proverb form, it may reveal the existence of a folk belief, such as: "When the Jerusalemite Cobbler has gone

around the whole world, the end of the world comes" (in texts
47, 52, 55). In a more detailed form it sometimes includes other
eschatological motifs from Finnish folklore, such as the following,
very popular one: "When the church will be full of people, the
roof will fall down; then comes the Cobbler of Jerusalem and the
end of the world is there" (46). The belief may also assume a more
local coloring: "The end of the world comes when the Cobbler of
Jerusalem will be able to go through the church of Mynämäki; a
churchful of people will die and the blood will be so deep that a
nine 'tuuma' [a unit of length of approximately one inch] log will
float in it" (53).[30]

In a Danish folk belief it is said: "The world will be destroyed
when the Cobbler of Jerusalem comes to Denmark."[31] In Finland
too the appearance of the Cobbler in the place where the tradition
is transmitted may serve as sign for the end of the world: "When
the Cobbler of Jerusalem comes to Nousiainen's Nummi, that is
the end of the world" (38). In this case, the narrator mentions this
as one of many events signaling the end of the world. He adds
several others, some of which he himself doubts: "When I was a
child, it was said that he is already near, but it seems to have been
a false belief. . . as he has not yet reached Nousiainen's Nummi
although it was said fifty years ago that he was somewhere
nearby" (38). In a neighboring village, the ethnocentric belief is
even more stressed as it is assumed that the Cobbler also started
his wanderings from there (56), in clear contradiction to the information supplied in the legend, where the wanderings naturally
started at the locus of Christ's suffering, at the hometown of the
wanderer, that is, Jerusalem.

In some texts, it is stated that the appearance of the Cobbler in
a country may serve as a prophecy for hard times or a war (26,
31, 32, 42); in the Danish tradition we find similar notions.[32] The
Finnish texts include the belief that before the end of the world
the Cobbler will have visited every single corner of the earth (37,
47, 52, 55). A legend (the term being used here as it usually is in
folkloristic terminology and not as the specific term that has been
employed throughout this paper, which would more properly be
referred to as saint's legend) in which the Cobbler's appearance on

the German front during the war is reported combines this appearance with the belief that he is immortal: "They put him in front of a cannon and fired at him but the bullets did not hit him."[33]

Sometimes the connection between the tale of the Cobbler and other eschatological beliefs is rather mechanical, such as, "The elders say they have seen him and he asked them: 'Do the ears of rabbits still have magic, because when the ears of a rabbit become white, the end of the world has come and the Cobbler of Jerusalem will come to his rest.' " Sometimes such beliefs are encapsulated in memorates: "Once the Cobbler of Jerusalem came to a house and carried his tools. The neighbor came in and brought with her fresh bread as a present to the lady of the house. When the Cobbler of Jerusalem noticed this, he said sadly, 'Oh, oh, there is a long time yet to the end of the world if neighbors still bring bread to one another,' and he went from the house" (45).[34]

This memorate assumes a belief according to which the deterioration of relations between neighbors or human relations in general are signs of the end of the world.[35] The Cobbler is therefore characterized negatively as deploring the still good relations between neighbors as they prolong the safe continued existence of the world and consequently his own wanderings. The legend in this instance assumes a definite didactic function insofar as it promotes good relations between neighbors and people in general as such relations are presumed to postpone the end of the world.

The Memorates[36]

Memorates in general present a supranormal experience as a fact, and therefore create a considerable amount of social pressure which is concentrated on the narrator, whose only proof is usually his own belief and its correlation to beliefs current in his sociocultural milieu.[37] The memorate mentioned in the last paragraph is chronologically interesting as it is earlier than all the above-mentioned chapbooks in Finnish (annotated in the archives in 1886). The tradition may therefore have existed orally in Finnish before it was circulated in written form. Since there is a parallel memorate tradition from Finland in the Swedish language which is from an earlier date, 1883, it is logical to infer an oral transmission inspired by one of the Swedish versions of the chapbook.

Another memorate, from the year 1936, recites an experience that took place thirty years before the recording of the narrative. The encounter with the Cobbler took place on the night of Saint Sylvester, New Year's Eve (44). This day is also mentioned as the day of encountering the Wandering Jew in a Swiss tradition.[38] The Danish tradition tells about meetings with him on Sundays,[39] on Christmas Eve,[40] and on the night of Saint John's Day, i.e., Midsummer.[41] In Finland, the saying goes, "This man is so accursed that he has no rest but on Christmas" (48). In this memorate, the narrative serves as a motivation for a folk belief and it seems that the narrator is not sure that his audience is familiar with the background and he is eager to provide it. In another case, the narrator is from northern Ingria (situated between Finland and Estonia, the original population spoke a Finnish dialect or a closely related Finno-Ugric language), and he told a memorate in the year 1939, quoting his father. In this case, too, the legend is the central genre of the narrative complex, and the memorate is told in order to enhance the folk belief. In another narrative from northern Ingria (3), also quoting the father of the narrator, the Wandering Cobbler is endowed with a special name: Nicodemus of Cyros or Nikko of Jerusalem.[42]

Usually the memorates include rich materials concerning the appearance of the Cobbler and his clothing, thus expressing the visual fantasies that have been evoked by this figure or that have been connected to him: "His clothes are torn and his hair and beard are overgrown" (49). His person is wrapped in mystery and sometimes the identification of him as the actual Cobbler of Jerusalem is only hypothesized (49). This phenomenon is current in other Scandinavian traditions as well, in Denmark, in Norway, and in Sweden.[43] The memorates may well be based on real experiences, as it is quite probable that old long-bearded men wandered through the countryside once in a while and needed the charity of the local population in order to survive. Their interest in promoting a tradition which relates the hospitality for such figures to a folk religious norm would be perfectly understandable in terms of self-interest. It is somewhat more difficult to accept the supposedly scientific theory of the "nevropathes voyageurs" presented by the Dane Nyrop, which is based on the research on cases of hysteria reported by Charcot and Meige. Meige thought that he had found a specific Jewish mental disease involving an abnormal urge to wander, which according to him provided a realistic basis for the legend of the Wandering Jew![44] Lauri Honko's hypothesis that the Cobbler of Jerusalem might be perceptually related to the itinerant village cobbler seems more plausible and convincing. The supranormal experiences mentioned in the tales and memorates where the Cobbler of Jerusalem is encountered are explicable on the basis of the eschatological beliefs found in the chapbook traditions about this figure.

Belief Tales

In the belief tales, as in the memorates, the appearance of the Cobbler in various places is the central theme. The details that most narrators seem to be interested in are details concerning the Cobbler's outfit and his general looks. From the Volksbuch stems the behavioral detail of the refusal of the Wandering Jew to accept alms; when he receives them, he turns them over to someone in need, since the Lord himself cares for his livelihood. The theme was altered and exaggerated in Finnish folk tradition: "He needs no food, no drink" (41); "He is not allowed to receive food, clothing, money, nothing" (30). The same occurs in Denmark.[45] In Denmark and Sweden, there are parallel legends in which the Cobbler asks to be given bread.[46] Anderson thinks that the motif in which the Cobbler is portrayed as thirsty and asks to drink is characteristic of the English folklore on the subject.[47]

In Finland too at least one thirsty Cobbler of Jerusalem is mentioned: "Kalle Honkala, an old bachelor, lived alone in his hut. A small old man, all covered with moss came there, sat down beside the fireplace to warm himself, complained about his tiredness, and asked to drink something" (51). The mossy covering of the man which is found in Finnish tradition is also reported in Danish,[48] Norwegian,[49] and Swedish tradition.[50] Another descriptive detail associated with the Cobbler in Scandinavian traditions is his tools

in a sack, especially the lasts.[51] This detail strengthens the theory
which connects the distribution of the theme to the wanderings of
actual village cobblers (see L. Honko's suggestion above). In one
of the Finnish versions, the belief legend mentions the tools of the
Cobbler and connects them to the saint's legend by telling that
when Jesus reached the house of the Cobbler, he was busy mending Pontius Pilate's shoes. This connection achieves two things: a
motivation for the descriptive detail of the tools that the man is
carrying around and a connection between two great sinners in
the same narrative plot.

In some of the legends there are specifically religious motifs,
such as "You can identify the Cobbler of Jerusalem since his footsteps have the sign of the cross" (32). This is also mentioned in
Danish tradition,[52] where the Cobbler is held as one who has the
power of prophecy and soothsaying.[53] In Finland the point is
made that he prophesies the downfall of rulers and mighty men
(30).

The age of the Cobbler ranges somewhere between 30 (34) and
200 (36). It is also mentioned that every hundred years he returns
to the age he was when his wanderings started.[54]

Folk Songs

In addition to the prose chapbooks about the Wandering Jew or
the Cobbler of Jerusalem, there is also a chapbook which includes
a folk song entitled "The Cobbler from Jerusalem."[55] This song
is composed of sixteen verses of four lines each and describes an
apocalyptic scene saturated with traditional motifs and descriptions from apocalyptic scenes in Finnish folklore. This particular
description of the end of the world brings in the angel Hamael and
the epic heroes Väinämöinen and Joukahainen, who are known to
Finnish audiences. There are also references to others from the
Kalevalaic epic poetry and to such folktale figures as the Old Man
of the Mountain or the Lady of the Forest. Naturally there are also
some religious stereotypes in such descriptions, e.g., the Holy
Spirit in chains, and the inmates of hell keeping a feast. This poem
or song exemplifies what was said above about the relationship
between traditions concerning the end of the world and the tradi-

tions about the Cobbler in Finnish folklore. The Cobbler is for understandably natural reasons anticipating this event since it will finally put an end to his suffering, and he will, as has been predicted, also see it. The subject of the song-poem is still essentially the end of the world, and the Cobbler of Jerusalem, whose name it bears, is the poetic first person "I" of the poem and is not mentioned in the text itself. The popularity of the text is proven by the fact that it was reprinted in a second edition.[56] A poem like this becomes a factor in the formation of oral tradition—in this case in establishing the association between the Cobbler of Jerusalem and the apocalyptic theme in folklore. The Finnish folksong archives have a number of fragments which include verses similar to the ones in the printed chapbooks which supports the view that printed versions can become 'folklorized' also in an oral tradition.

The Epic Song

An interesting epic song from northern Karelia[57] describes Passover in the home of the cobbler Issaschar in Jerusalem. The family's poverty is described, and there is a definite tone of pity throughout the poem, especially with reference to the oppression of the Jews in general and this family in particular by the Romans. The role played by the Jews in the crucifixion of Jesus is rather unusual for a folk tradition. They follow the scene in weeping and sorrow. The sin of the Cobbler is not mentioned in the poem but since the text ends with the departure of the man for his wanderings, there is another motivation given. Issaschar admits having spoken some evil things, and it seems that blasphemy concerning Jesus is meant here or something equivalent which is not mentioned in the text itself. The epic poem is actually a parallel of the prose legend, a parallel different from most of the prose narratives we have reviewed since it lacks the element of the sin. The merciful approach to the cobbler culminates in the didactic decree: "When a poor beggar begs for a piece of bread, remember that he needs your grace and have mercy."[58] The style, the form, and the biblical names—such detailed information—all point to a written source for this text.[59]

The legend has been rendered in poetic form in other countries

in Europe. The French scholar Gaston Paris contends that the
French poem is the most widespread of the poetic versions.[60] The
adaptability of the theme of the Wandering Jew to different genres
is influenced by generic preferences in different cultures. Thus in
England there is a Wandering Jew in ballads,[61] and in Finland there
are a number of allusions in one of the favorite genres of Finnish
folklore: the proverbial comparison.

The Folktale

The folktale which has the Cobbler of Jerusalem as its hero is
rather peculiar (57). The cunning hero buys himself a fur coat that
makes him seeing and unseen, and slippers that carry him to every
place that he can think of.[62] The coat and the hat become torn
after a while, "but the shoes are never worn out, and in them the
Cobbler of Jerusalem will pace to the end of the world." In a
Swiss belief tale, it is also mentioned that the Wandering Jew has
shoes that never wear out.[63] It is possible that in this folktale there
is an amalgamation of the eternal wanderer motif with some other
folktale figure who owns shoes which never wear out.[64] The quality of seeing and not being seen is also a specific trait well known
from the international folktale repertoire and is also reported
among the folk beliefs concerning the Cobbler of Jerusalem in
Finland (31).

In the central European tradition, it is possible to discern even
more clearly the connection between folktale motifs and the popular descriptions of the Wandering Jew.[65] Scholars who have been
especially interested in comparing common motifs of all folk narratives in the world have tried to show a connection between the
mythological motifs concerning the German Wotan as well as the
Indian Buddha, which have supposedly been transmitted through
the folktale figure of the Wandering Huntsman to the Wandering
Jew of the legend.[66]

Proverbial Comparisons

Among the Finnish proverbial genres in which the Cobbler of
Jerusalem appears the most widely distributed is the proverbial
comparison. The genre of proverbial comparison is generally in-

terspersed with motifs involving exotic figures and faraway places, not to mention saints and biblical figures.[67]

The Finnish proverbial comparisons that I have seen included twenty-seven in which the Cobbler of Jerusalem is mentioned. Most of these comparisons are based on the above-mentioned characteristics that are usually associated with him in the folk imagination: "Wanders like the Cobbler of Jerusalem" (six versions), "Goes around like the Cobbler of Jerusalem" (four versions), or "Walks-runs-walks around-goes in circles" (six versions). From his unceasing movement are derived the following: "Fussing like the Cobbler of Jerusalem," "Flying around like the Cobbler of Jerusalem." The idiom "Jumps around the world like the Cobbler of Jerusalem" includes reminiscences of the final motif of the legend, and also resembles the formulaic sentence which ends the legend itself.[68]

We have already mentioned how central to folk tradition the motifs describing the appearance and dress of the Cobbler are. The proverbial comparison "A beard like the one of the Cobbler of Jerusalem"[69] is based on the beliefs regarding the appearance of the Wandering Jew figure. This proverbial comparison has a close parallel in "A long beard like the one of the Cobbler of Jerusalem who wanted to swallow a horse and only the tail was left on earth."[70] In this idiom we may trace a humorous attitude towards the Cobbler, not very common in the rest of the material that has been analyzed.

Three proverbial comparisons deal with the working space of the Cobbler of Jerusalem. Features include the doors of the space being wide open[71] and the temperature in it being extremely cold.[72] The workshop is imagined to be very big, as is expressed by the comparison "A nose like the workshop of the Cobbler of Jerusalem."[73] Maybe the fantasy about the immense size of the workshop implies that there is really no workshop at all, and that his being a wanderer means his workshop is actually the whole world and thus his shop is therefore as wide as the entire world.[74] And in a less hyperbolic manner, the comparison may be taken to refer to the fact that the Cobbler spends his nights under the bare skies, since according to some folk beliefs he can never rest inside a house (21).[75]

In a proverbial comparison from Finland but in Swedish, it is said, "Goes around like the Cobbler of Jerusalem."[76] In the records of folklore traditions of other peoples regarding the theme of the Wandering Jew or the Cobbler of Jerusalem, this specific genre, which as we have seen is a favorite genre with the Finns, has not often been reported.

Proverbs

Some of the folk beliefs already mentioned are sometimes found in proverb form, e.g., "When the Cobbler of Jerusalem will have gone around the whole world, comes the end of the world" (47, 52), and "Hard are the wanderings of the Cobbler of Jerusalem" (58).

What is the relationship between the proverb and the legend? It is quite safe to state that the proverbs and proverbial expressions concerning the Cobbler of Jerusalem do not have an independent existence in the cognitive systems of the bearers of that tradition, but always refer directly or indirectly to the legend and belief materials about the same figure, and are in fact some sort of summarized versions of the narrative material about the same figure in Finnish tradition. In the proverbs as in all the other genres of folklore excluding the legend (saint's legend), the Cobbler is the central, main figure. In the saint's legend, in contrast, it is Jesus who is the central figure. The narrators of the legends and the belief tales are very often conscious of the existence of the proverb, and very often they end their narration by referring to it and by explaining its genesis from the narrative material. In ten versions of the narratives, the source of the proverb is explicitly said to be the narrative. In three of these cases, the wish to explain the source of the proverb constitutes the principal motivation for the narration itself, and this rationale occurs at the very beginning of the narrative (5, 14, 40). It is therefore reasonable to suppose that the proverb and the proverbial expressions are actually more widely distributed in the folk tradition than the narrative material, and it consequently makes a good point of departure for the narrators. Here we have a clear case where there might be a conflict between the findings in the archival material and the actual state of the distribution as it is reflected in oral tradition. Such contradictions may be explained by the fact that the collected material, especially that from the beginning of the twentieth century and the end of the nineteenth, which is very well represented in the material being discussed here, often reflects the prejudices and esthetic preferences of the collectors of that time. They had an approach that was different from the one current in the second half of the twentieth century, with its interest in the problematics of source criticism.

The ending with the saying is even more popular than its occurrence in the opening of the story, as we can see from seven versions (1, 3, 4, 11, 12, 35, 42). In one of these, the narrator gives the following explanation for the use of the saying: "And therefore always, when there is a vagabond or a wanderer it is said . . . he goes around like the Cobbler of Jerusalem." All the sayings which appear in the narratives belong to the genre of the proverbial comparison and are parallels of those found in the printed collections of this genre, where they are reproduced independently, lacking the context of the narrative.

The Riddle

In the texts I have examined, I found only one riddle which mentions the Cobbler of Jerusalem. The question is: "Who has been going in the world all the time since the crucifixion of Jesus?"[77] and the right answer is: "The Cobbler of Jerusalem." This riddle is of the kind which requires a special type of background knowledge in order for the audience to be able to answer it. In this case, the special knowledge consists of the legend of the Wandering Jew. This genre of riddles was typically employed by clerical educators to check on the parish's knowledge of sacred traditions. The lack of many texts concerning the Cobbler of Jerusalem suggests that this theme may not really have been well absorbed into the riddle genre in Finnish folklore.

The wording of the proverbial materials referring to the Cobbler of Jerusalem discussed above suggests an interesting comparison. There is a quite popular riddle for a clock: "What goes and goes and never reaches a destination?" If this were a riddle based upon special knowledge, the Wandering Jew or the Cobbler of Jerusalem would be a perfectly acceptable answer, but since this riddle is constructed around a metaphor, as most riddles are, the only correct answer remains: the clock.

Games

In the collections of the Finnish Dictionary Foundation, there are three items which include games bearing the name The Cobbler of Jerusalem. In one of the game notations, only the name has been preserved, accompanied by the remark that it is an indoor game for grownups.[78] Something similar to the well-known game of Musical Chairs might be conjectured. I have in fact one oral report confirming that this game, which is current in birthday celebrations in urban middle-class culture in Finland, does have the name of The Cobbler of Jerusalem.[79] The game consists of a group of players who circle around a group of chairs, one less in number than the number of participants. Music is played, and when the music stops, every player tries to find a chair to sit on. The person who is left without a chair at the very end of the game is the Cobbler.

In the collections of the Finnish Dictionary Foundation, there are two more games by this name. One is an outdoor game played by children, based on jumping between different, round, drawn areas.[80] The last one is a game for grownups for holiday eves. One of the participants goes among the others, holding a stick in his hand, and repeats the following: "I am that old Cobbler from Jerusalem. I have no work, no food, my shoes are torn, will you give me one of your daughters?" Although the other games mentioned before include some associative reference to the traditional motifs concerning the Wandering Jew, this last one seems to have the most direct reference to the standard narrative tradition. The role played by the Cobbler of the game is consonant with what the audience may have known about the figure from other sources. The game may also reflect fear of intermarriage with Jews.[81] In Denmark, on Shrovetide Eve, rural folklore figures were enacted, among them the Wandering Jew. The man who acted that role was dressed up in a long white wig and carried a bunch of lasts. He went among the audience and begged for alms[82] (in complete contradiction to the above-mentioned belief that the Wandering Jew would never accept alms!).

Summary

The theme of the "Wandering Jew" came to Finland through the Swedish translations of the German Volksbuch. During the wanderings of the "Jew" from central Europe to the northern part of the continent, the anti-Semitic function of the legend diminished until it has almost disappeared in Finnish folklore. In all the Finnish materials which have been considered here, we found only two references to the ethnic background of the Cobbler.

The folkloristic complex of genres clustering around the theme of the Wandering Jew is a good example of the interrelationship between folklore and booklore. This is not unusual, as the Finnish folklorist Martti Haavio has shown, when there is a reference to sacred traditions, and when the local folklore creates new combinations which may not have been encountered in folklore about the same theme elsewhere.[83]

The structural analysis of the saint's legend exhibited a stable structural and thematic tradition in that genre. The variations that were found did not reveal any defined geographical distribution so that we cannot really talk about any local redactions of the legend along the lines of the basic assumptions of the historic-geographic school (also called, in fact, the Finnish school since the founders were Finnish). The most popular combination of the elements of the legend again emphasizes the direct contact with the literary sources, i.e., the Volksbuch. Of all the genres discussed, the legend bears the strongest connection with booklore.

The folk belief material examined here concentrates mainly on the relationship between the Cobbler of Jerusalem and the end of the world. The encounter with the figure or his visit to a specific settlement supplies the greater part of the experiential data for this tradition. Here too there is a clear enough connection to the Volksbuch but also more ethnocentric material and local color. This is true about Finnish as well as other European belief traditions concerning the Wandering Jew. It appears likely that the description of this figure in folk beliefs bears resemblance to other characters in the belief traditions of each of the cultures. In the songs, the eschatological theme prevails. Proverbs, riddles, and games are not very numerous, but all are related to the theme of endless movement and the curious appearance of the Cobbler of Jerusalem.

We have found that the primary function of the tale in Finland is to conserve and confirm certain Christian norms concerning the order of the world and history. This includes the formative role of Jesus in history and the firm belief in the Second Coming. A secondary function we observed relates to the strengthening of certain social norms, such as promoting kindness among neighbors.

The material itself is open to other kinds of approaches. A relevant question would be: from which other figures from folk tradition has the Wandering Jew borrowed either outward or inward characteristics? The comparison between this specific legend and other Finnish legends might well yield more insight into this story. In the other genres, the relative scarcity of archival materials does not really allow for much in the way of comparison. As for the paucity of reported traditions, we cannot know whether this reflects an actual lack of existing folklore or simply the possibility that the Cobbler of Jerusalem was never very high on any Finnish collector's agenda.

Although the Wandering Jew seems not to be one of the major themes of Finnish folklore, it is interesting nonetheless to see the variation in genres that has been created around it. The Wandering Jew has also been a popular figure in Scandinavian literatures, but that is quite a different story.[84]

NOTES

1. The several collections are:
Fifty-nine texts from the Finnish Folklore Archives at the Finnish Literary Society. These consist mainly of legends, but also some memorates, folktales, proverbs, and riddles are included.

Three prose narratives and twenty-one songs from the chapbook archives of the library of Helsinki University.

An epic poem from a private collection.

Twenty proverbs from Matti Kuusi's book *Suomen Kansan Vertauksia* (The Proverbial Comparisons of the Finnish People).

Three games from the collections of the Finnish Dictionary Foundation.

The Finnish material concerning the Wandering Jew which is mentioned in the most comprehensive monographical study of the subject, G. K. Anderson's *The Legend of the Wandering Jew* (Providence, 1970), is only marginally related to the subject. See his note 2 on page 103. It refers to wandering heroes such as Väinämöinen from the Kalevala epic poetry, but there is no reference to the folkloristic material discussed in the present article.

The first version of this paper was written as a seminar paper for Prof. Matti Kuusi in 1969 in Helsinki.

2. A. Aarne and S. Thompson, *The Types of the Folktale*, 2d rev. (Helsinki, 1977), no. 777; G. K. Anderson 1970; E. Dal, "Ahasverus in Dänemark," *Jahrbuch für Volksliedsforschung* 1964, pp. 144–70; R. Edelman, "Ahasverus, the Wandering Jew, Origin and Background." *Reports of the IV World Congress of Jewish Studies* (Jerusalem, 1968), pp. 115–19. I have also seen around 150 texts from Sweden, courtesy of my friend and colleague Bengt af Klintberg. A number of Estonian texts were sent to me from the Soviet Republic of Estonia, with the kind help of the late Marie Luht of the Folklore Archives of the Finnish Literary Society. Other works will be quoted where relevant.

3. Anderson 1970, pp. 42–48; L. Neubaur, *Die Sage vom Ewigen Juden* (Leipzig, 1893), pp. 53–55. Anderson mentions in his book, p. 41, some texts from the second half of the sixteenth century; the cobbler motif is not included in them, and they may not have influenced the Finnish tradition.

4. K. Nyrop, *Fortids Sagen och Sange* II, *Den Evige Jøde* (København, 1907), p. 22; Anderson 1970, p. 66.

5. H. Schück, *Ur Gamla Papper* (Stockholm, 1892), I, p. 14.

6. L. Neubaur, "Zur Geschichte der Sage vom Ewigen Juden," *Zeitschrift für Volkskunde* 22 (1912):48.

7. Schück 1892; Nyrop 1907.

8. The summary following P. O. Bäckström, *Svenska Folkböcker, Sagor, Legender och Äfventyr* (Stockholm, 1848), pp. 212–16; Anderson 1970, pp. 45–47.

9. Nyrop 1907, p. 119; Neubaur 1912, p. 40, note 4.

10. G. Paris, *Legendes du Moyen Age* (Paris, 1908), pp. 167–68. This tendency is strengthened in the second half of the seventeenth century. Anderson 1970, p. 53.

11. T. Percy, *Reliques of Ancient English Poetry* (London, 1846), I, p. 29.

12. Anderson 1970, p. 44.

13. Paris 1908, p. 166; Anderson 1970, p. 45; H. Dübi, "Drei spätmittelalterliche Legenden," *Zeitschrift des Vereins für Volkskunde* 17 (1907):144.

14. Nyrop 1907, p. 35.

15. Nyrop 1907, p. 119.

16. Neubaur 1912, p. 40.

17. S. Jacobsson, *Taistelu ihmisoikeuksista* (Jyväskylä, 1951), pp. 20–22.

18. Anderson 1970, pp. 11–37.

19. Ibid., p. 17.

20. Ibid., p. 50.

21. G. K. Anderson, "Popular Survivals of the Wandering Jew in England," *Journal of English and Germanic Philology* 46 (1947). Reprinted in the present volume.

22. Lauri Honko's ideas here and in the following were orally communicated in Helsinki in March 1969.

23. For more details concerning the Swedish tradition on the subject, see af Klintberg 1968. Reprinted in this volume.

24. Roger de Wendover, *Flores Historiarum*, ed. H. R. Luard (London, 1890); Anderson 1970, pp. 18–20.

25. There is resemblance between this plot-scheme and the minimal four-motifeme sequence suggested by A. Dundes in his *The Morphology of North American Indian Folktales*, Folklore Fellows Communications 195 (Helsinki, 1964), pp. 64–66.

26. See Appendix 2, elements a1, b1, f1.

27. Exceptions: Text 14 seems to be a mere summary and includes no reaction of Jesus whatsoever; text 17 is a belief account which only refers to the legend; text 18 is a memorate which refers to the legend; and in text 42, the Cobbler's sin is not mentioned either.

28. Nyrop 1907, p. 144.

29. Anderson 1970, pp. 174–227.

30. Also in other eschatological beliefs in Finland there is a church or a valley filled with blood as a sign for the end of the world: L. Simonsuuri, *Myytillisiä tarinoita* (Helsinki, 1947), p. 229. The Danish tradition has a horse wading in blood in Armageddon: S. Thompson, *Motif Index of Folk Literature* (Copenhagen, 1961), motif A 1080.1; H. F. Feilberg, *Bidrag til en ordbog over jyske almuesmål* I, 600 a.

31. E. T. Kristensén, *Danske Sagn* (Aarhus, 1892), II, p. 269, no. 91.

32. Ibid., p. 268, note no. 84.

33. On the other hand in one of the legends somebody thinks that the Cobbler is a "fire-fox" (a known figure in Finnish belief legends) and the

fox itself begs "Do not shoot me, I am the Cobbler of Jerusalem." On the inclusion of the Wandering Jew in local belief tradition and legend see also af Klintberg 1968.

34. A parallel from Finland in the Swedish language in V. E. V. Wessmann, *Finlands Svenska Folkdiktning* II. *Förteckning över sägentyperna* (Helsingfors, 1931), p. 631, no. 933.

35. Cf. in the Jewish tradition in Mishna Sota, Ch. IX, 15.

36. I included in the memorates narratives that were told about the experiences of the father or the mother of the narrator himself. Although the experiences of the older generation may at times be dismissed as old people's talk, it is still contended that a memorate learned from such a near person carries a considerable weight of authority. The Danish tradition has a similar narrative: Kristensén 1892, p. 269, no. 97.

37. Sometimes also in tracks and other signs, which are naturally open to conflicting interpretations.

38. E. L. Rochholz, *Schweizersagen aus dem Aargau* (Aarau, 1856), II, p. 306, no. 489; in another tradition on Good Friday, L. Jaccod, "Les Trois Pommes de Paques," *Augusta Praetoria (Aosta) Revue Valdotaine*, 1 (1919):167, reprinted in this volume.

39. Kristensén 1892, p. 268, no. 87.

40. Kristensén 1892, p. 268, nos. 84, 88. Also, E. Kristensén, *Jyske Folkminder* 6te samling, *Sagn og Overtro fra Jylland* (Kjøbenhavn, 1883), VIII, p. 233, no. 319.

41. Feilberg, II, p. 40.

42. There is a possible association to Nicodemus from the New Testament, the Pharisee who defended Jesus in the Synhedrion. In the narrative the relationship to Nikko is merciful, almost positive. It is also possible that there is an association to Simeon from Cyrenaica who as a complete reversal of the Cobbler of Jerusalem helped Jesus with the cross on the Via Dolorosa. Neubaur also mentions a text which refers to Nicodemus the Pharisee: L. Neubaur, "Einige Bemerkungen zur Sage von Ewigen Juden," *Zeitschrift für Bücherfreunde*, 9 (1917):311.

43. Kristensén 1892, p. 270, nos. 95, 99; J. M. Thiele, *Danmarks Folkesagn* (Kjøbenhavn, 1843), II, p. 311, no. II; Th. S. Hauknaes, *Natur, Folkeliv og Folketro i Hardanger* (Voss, 1887), IV, p. 573; A. A. Afzelius, *Svenska Folkets Sago-Häfder* (Stockholm, 1844), I–III, p. 134.

44. H. Meige, *Le Juif-Errant à la Salpêtrière, Étude sur certains névropathes voyageurs* (Paris, 1893).

45. Kristensén 1892, no. 95.

46. E. Wigström, "Allmogeseder i Rönnebärgs Härad i Skåne på 1840–talet," *Svensk Landsmålstidskrift* VIII No. 3 (1891), p. 154, no. 493; A. Hazelius, *Samfundet för Nordiska Museets främjande* (Stockholm, 1890), p. 24; Kristensén 1883, p. 233, no. 319.

47. Anderson 1947, pp. 370–71: "The thirst of Ahasverus in these tales is appropriate in a land fond of its ale and tea."

48. Kristensén 1892, pp. 268–70, nos. 84, 89, 95, 97; *Skattegreveren* I (1884), p. 8, no. 5.

49. Th. S. Hauknaes, *Natur, Folkeliv og Folketro i Hardanger* (Eidfjord, 1884), I, p. 179.

50. af Klintberg 1968.

51. In Norway: Hauknaes 1887, p. 573; Th. S. Hauknaes, *Natur, Folkeliv og Folketro i Hardanger* (Kvindherred, 1888), VI, p. 190. In Sweden: af Klintberg 1968. In Finland (in the Swedish language): Wessmann 1931 p. 631, no. 933. In Iceland: J. Árnasson, *Islenzkar Pjodsogur og Aefintyri* (Leipzig, 1864), II, p. 47.

52. *Skattegreveren* II (1884), p. 27.

53. Thiele 1843, p. 331, no. I.

54. And in Denmark: Kristensén 1892, p. 268, no. 86.

55. In the collection of printed folksongs of the library of the University of Helsinki: Arkkiveisuja 1818–1826, no. 24.

56. Arkkiveisuja 1818–1826, no. 21 (bound together with the first edition although printed in 1828).

57. In the collection of orally transmitted folksongs: SKS, Kansanlauluarkisto; Kiihtelysvaara. Antti Rykönen 307. This hymn has a strong connection with the chapbook versions of the folksong. Another song is clearly related to the legend: SKS, Kansanlauluarkisto; Muurla. V Saariluoma 1908, 1914. In this song the events are described from the point of view of the Cobbler himself.

58. Tohinajärvi. Aino Juvonen. 18.5.1954. The song was kindly made available to me by Olli Juvonen to whose private collection it belongs.

59. Olli Juvonen (see the former note) shares this view.

60. Paris 1908, p. 176. Contrary to the view that there was no English prose version of the legend, see Anderson 1970, pp. 63–65, for a prose translation of the German Volksbuch dated 1620. But Anderson also says that the prose versions are scarce both in chapbook and oral folk tradition. Ibid., pp. 94–95.

61. A Danish ballad on the subject: E. T. Kristensén, *Jydske Folkeminder 11te samling. Gamle Viser* IV samling (Viborg and Kjøbenhavn, 1891), p. 204.

62. This tale type is very well distributed in Finland. Aarne & Thompson 1977, no. 518.

63. Rochholz 1856, p. 306, no. 489.

64. In some European legends the Wandering Jew strolls barefoot. A. Birlinger, *Volkstümliches aus Schwaben* (Freiburg, 1861), I, p. 211, no. 322.

65. Anderson 1947, p. 370; Schück 1892, p. 21.

66. Rochholz 1856, p. 308; E. Meier, *Deutsche Sagen, Sitten und Ge-bräuche aus Schwaben* (Stuttgart, 1852), p. 115.

67. Kuusi 1967, p. xi in the Introduction.

68. Ibid., pp. 257, 258, 210, 845, 315, 280, 276, 154, 917, 120, 224, 360, 917. In the collections of the Foundation of the Finnish Dictionary: SS. PL: Urjala, Hannes Mäkelä, 1932, SS. PL: I Onttonen, H. Rautu, 1955. SS Hakusanoitettuja Sananparsia Mikkeli. J. Valkonen. SS Sav. Osak. keräyttämä, 1932. SS.PL: I Kalajoki. J. Sauvala, 1952 SS. Sana-nuotta 1960 Sääminki. OF. Kuvaja ("Jerusalemi"). SS.PL.: II Hyrynen. H. Vieremä, 1959. SS Hakusanoitettuja sananparsia. Marttila. Toivo Alho, 1931 ("Jerusalemin Suutari").

69. Kuusi 1967, p. 553.

70. Ibid., p. 593.

71. Ibid., p. 855.

72. Ibid., p. 705.

73. Ibid., p. 269.

74. Kuusi's notes for the relevant proverbial comparisons.

75. Also in Denmark: Kristensén 1892, p. 268, no. 84.

76. V. Solstrand, *Finlands Svenska Folkdiktning* (Ordstäv and Helsing-fors, 1923), III, p. 351.

77. Ahlainen. Lempi Törne AK 19:75. 1967.

78. SS.PL: II Kuhmoinen. Leena Lättilä 1965.

79. Oral communication from Finnish folklorist Tellervo Venho.

80. SS.PL: I Valkeala, Sirkka Kärkönen 1960.

81. The sexual behavior of Jews is sometimes admired, sometimes feared. This appears in several genres in Finnish folklore, notably the proverbial comparison and the anecdote.

82. *Skattegreveren* 1886, p. 228.

83. M. Haavio, *Kansanrunojen maailmanselitys* (Porvoo and Helsinki, 1955), p. 118.

84. E.g., Pär Lagerkvist's *Ahasverus' Death* and *The Sibyl*.

APPENDIX I

The oral sources of the narratives and the numbers by which they are referred to in the article

1—Loppi.	Elvi Ketonen KRK 59:55.
2—Perniö.	G. E. Hjorth 9. 1890.
3—Puumala.	Mauno Kuusitie KRK 80:9.
4—Pielavesi.	Armas Nissinen KRK 107:348.
5—Kokemäki.	Frans Leino KRK 28:1.

6—Sääksmäki.	Karoliina Tähtinen KRK 68:7.
7—Kauhava.	Matti Jussila 459. 1937.
8—Jalasjärvi.	L. Ojala KRK 186:196.
9—Kaavi.	Kerttu Savolainen KT 159:6. 1936.
10—Rääkkylä.	Tahvo Koskelo KRK 160.3.
11—Pielavesi.	Eino Pulkkinen KRK 112:451.
12—Puumala.	Mauno Kuusitie KT 231:44. 1939.
13—Kuopio.	Eino Kemppainen 402. 1936.
14—Kaavi.	Sirkka Tiilikainen (Hämeenlinnan alakouluseminaari) 9907. 1939.
15—Nokia.	A. Railonsala 2619. 1939.
16—Vihti.	Fanny Eström. KT 228:175. 1939.
17—Paattinen.	K. V. Kaukovalta KT 4:8. 1936.
18—Ähtäri.	Anna Oikari KT 28:197. 1937.
19—Karstula.	A. Rautiainen 1295. 1939.
20—Kuolemajärvi.	Ulla Mannonen 10517. 1939.
21—Vampula.	P. Hongisto 1020. 1937.
22—Viitasaari.	Kusti Heimonen KT 230:806. 1939.
23—Hongonjoki.	Rauni Karsikko (Satakuntalainen Osakunta) 1148. 1939.
24—Askola.	J. Tyyskä 203. 1888.
25—Kolari.	Hanna Keränen KRK 246:46.
26—Kangasniemi.	Kalle Viinikainen KRK 89:110.
27—Savo(?).	L. Niiranen 5. 1888.
28—Kuusamo.	Uuno Kallunki. KRK 236:11.
29—Noormarkku.	F. Lindgren b/56. 1892.
30—Keltto.	L. V. Pälkkönen a/19. 1891.
31—Ylivieska.	Vilhelm Vilpula 199. 1938.
32—Suonenjoki.	Eero Kansanen 23. 1938.
33—Keuruu.	Arvo Etelämäki 6. 1938.
34—Kalanti.	Selma Saarnio 602. 1938.
35—Jämsä.	Kalle Nieminen 3903. 1938.
36—Vihti.	Kaarlo Ranta 307. 1936.
37—Orimattila.	A. Järvinen KRK 58:145.
38—Nousiainen.	F. Leivo 2293. 1937.
39—Valkeasaari.	Ulla Mannonen 11181. 1949.
40—Joroinen.	Viljo Salminen KRK 86:68.
41—Artjärvi.	K. E. Uino 36. 1889.
42—Hollola.	Hilma Jokela 8. 1938.
43—Ilmajoki.	Eino Hakala KRK 176:43.
44—Koivisto.	Ulla Mannonen 47. 1936.
45—Joroinen.	A. Kinnunen 144. 1886.
46—Hollola.	A. Ali-Heikkilä 11.
47—Orimattila.	A. Järvinen 204. 1937.

48—Kuorevesi.   Hilja Soimamäki 12. 1938.
49—Luopioinen.   Hilda Virtanen 32. 1938.
50—Jalasjärvi.   L. Ojala KRK 186:197.
51—Utajärvi.   Kustaa Pentti KRK 217:192.
52—Kestilä.   Sigrid Lämsä KRK 213:56.
53—Askainen.   Jalmari Jaatinen b/158. 1915.
54—Sysmä.   E. J. Ekman 2093. 1937.
55—Suoniemi.   E. Järventausta 1623. 1939.
56—Vehmaa.   Onni Mäkinen KT 225:375. 1939.
57—Kärsämäki.   E. Keränen 139. 1883.
58—Mouhijärvi.   E. Järventausta 1625. 1939.

The order follows genre distinctions according to the catalogue of the Archives.

APPENDIX 2

The elements of the legend of the Wandering Jew in Finland

I. The Sin

    a. The suffering of Jesus
       1. carried the cross
       2. was hanged on the cross
       3. was persecuted
       4. wanders in the world

    b. The entrance of the Cobbler
       1. Jesus asked to rest on the stairs of his house
       2. Jesus asked for help with carrying the cross
       3. Jesus asked the Cobbler specifically to help him carry the cross

    c. The motivations for the reaction of the Cobbler
       1. the wicked character of cobblers generally
       2. his richness, his Jewishness
       3. enmity towards Jesus
       4. hardness of his heart
       5. fear for the excitement of the hateful masses

    d. The Cobbler's activity before the reaction
       1. he put on one shoe
       2. made Pilate's shoes

      3. he was carrying a child in his bosom
      4. carried a sack on his back
      5. came back from the field

  e. The reaction of the Cobbler
      1. an uttering
      2. blasphemy
      3. denial of help
      4. throwing away
      5. kick

II. The Punishment

  f. Jesus' verdict
      1. uttering
      2. act

  g. The motivation for the fulfillment of the curse
      1. the urge to wander
      2. bad conscience
      3. burning earth
      4. madness
      5. burning soul

  h. The description of the fulfillment of the curse
      1. carried his tools
      2. sighed
      3. wearing one shoe
      4. turned back the child

APPENDIX 3

The chaining of the elements in the various versions of the legend of the Wandering Jew in Finland.

The versions are identified by the numbers mentioned in Appendix 1, the elements by the signs allotted to them in Appendix 2. The numbers within the table signify the order of the elements in the legend.

	a_1	a_2	a_3	a_4	b_1	b_2	b_3	c_1	c_2	c_3	c_4	c_5	d_1	d_2	d_3	d_4	d_5	e_1	e_2	e_3	e_4	e_5	f_1	f_2	g_1	g_2	g_3	g_4	g_5	h_1	h_2	h_3	h_4
1	2										1										3			4									
2				1																	2		3										
3	1				2													4			3		5		6								
4	1					2																		3									
5		1						2											3				4										
6	1				2																3		4										
7	1				2													3					4										
8	1				3				2	4									6		5		7				8						
9	1																		2					3						4			
10	1				2																3		4										
11	1				2																3							4			5		
12	1				2																3		4										

APPENDIX 3 (Continued)

	h4	h3	h2	h1	g5	g4	g3	g2	g1	f2	f1	e5	e4	e3	e2	e1	d5	d4	d3	d2	d1	c5	c4	c3	c2	c1	b3	b2	b1	a4	a3	a2	a1
13								3																	3				2				1
14														2													1						1
15										4			3																2				1
16											6			5		4	1											3					2
17														1																			
18											3				1																		2
19		6									5		4								3								2				1
20											4		3																2				1
21											3				2																	1	
22											6	4	3			5													2				1
23											4		3																2				1
24													3																2				1
25											4																		2		1		
26														2													1	2					
27										4				3																			1
28											4		3																2				1

APPENDIX 3 (Continued)

	a_1	a_2	a_3	a_4	b_1	b_2	b_3	c_1	c_2	c_3	c_4	c_5	d_1	d_2	d_3	d_4	d_5	e_1	e_2	e_3	e_4	e_5	f_1	f_2	g_1	g_2	g_3	g_4	g_5	h_1	h_2	h_3	h_4
29				1	2									3	4			5					6										7
30	1				2	5												3					4						6				
31				1	2						3							4					5										
32	1				2		2								3			4		3	3		5										
33	1																						4										
34	1	1			2													4	2				5										
35												3											3										
36	1				2													4			3		5										5
37	1				2									1,4							5		4										
38	2				3																2		6										
39	3																			3			4	1									
40	1					2																	4										
41																				1			1										
42																								2									
43																								1									
44	2				3									1							4		5										

THE SWEDISH WANDERINGS
OF THE ETERNAL JEW

Bengt af Klintberg

Swedish folklorist Bengt af Klintberg examines the legend of the Wandering Jew as it is illuminated by folk beliefs. He utilizes both printed materials and archival records. The various Swedish folklore archives, like those of the Finnish Literary Society, offer a remarkable resource for students of the legend. From the array of source material, af Klintberg demonstrates how a migratory legend which did not originate in Sweden takes on local characteristics by becoming integrated into a preexisting folk belief and folk literary system.

The Wandering Jew is described in terms of attributes associated with a variety of figures from the local folklore repertoire, thus attaining a specifically Swedish oicotypal configuration. (Oicotype is a standard term in folkloristic parlance, coined by the Swedish folklorist Carl Wilhelm von Sydow, which refers to a special local or regional form of an item of folklore.) Af Klintberg widens the scope of the discussion with his survey of some of the illustrations found in the chapbook editions of the legend in Sweden. (For a later version of this essay in Swedish, which includes many additional texts, see Bengt af Klintberg, Harens Klagan *[Stockholm: Pan/Norstedts, 1978], pp. 22–47.)*

The legend of the Wandering Jew has also been collected from oral tradition in other Scandinavian countries. Erik Dal, in his "Ahasverus, den evige jøde, sagnet i Dansk og Tysk Folkedigtning," Fund og Forskning i det Kongelige Biblioteks Samlinger, *12 (1965): 31–42, deals predominantly with literary and printed versions of the legend. The article is co-authored with R. Edelmann who contributed the second section, "Sagnets oprindelse og baggrund" (Ibid., pp. 42–46), which deals with the historical and literary background for the emergence of the legend. Dal's other article on the subject is more specifically concerned with Danish material, and it concentrates on one folk-literary genre, the folksong, with comparisons to other genres particularly the chapbook. See E. Dal, "Ahasverus in Danemark; Volksbuch, Volkslieder und Verwandtes,"* Jahrbuch für Volksliederforschung, *9 (1964): 144–70. Eivind Heggenes in a short personal essay recalls having read a note on the appearance of the Wandering Jew in an American Mormon newspaper and also reproduces a belief account of the same figure collected by him from a Norwegian woman. See E. Heggenes, "Folksegna um Ahasverus, den Eviga Jøden,"* Syn og Segn, *44 (1938): 321–27.*

Among the Swedish popular beliefs the Eternal Jew holds a position which is in many respects unique. He has been known for around 300 years, a not very significant age considering the fact that most characters of Swedish folklore were already formed during pre-Christian times. Thus the prominent place he holds, especially in south Swedish folk tradition, is the result of a rapidly mounting interest—something of a vogue in popular beliefs. On the other hand, countless details show how completely he has been integrated in the pattern of Swedish folk beliefs about supernatural beings. This circumstance can be interpreted in two ways: either that a popular conception needs shorter time to spread than has usually been supposed, or that the fusion has been facilitated in this case because one could connect the Eternal Jew-complex with previously existing patterns. Probably in this case both interpretations are valid.

This paper will deal primarily with the Eternal Jew in Swedish popular beliefs. My account is based on about 150 records, most

Reprinted from *Papers of the Fourth World Congress of Jewish Studies*, Vol. II (Jerusalem, 1968), pp. 115–19.

of which are kept, unprinted, in Swedish folklore archives.[1] But
first of all, I shall briefly mention the printed sources which have
contributed to spreading the conception of the Eternal Jew. The
starting point will of course be the German broadsheet, dating to
1602, which presents the relation of Paulus von Eitzen, and where
the name Ahasuerus, the Jewish birth, and the shoemaking profession appeared together for the first time. It created the Scandinavian name for the Eternal Jew, the Shoemaker of Jerusalem. As
will be demonstrated later, this name has led to the consequence
that the shoemaking profession, far more than Jewish birth, has
been given a leading rôle in the popular beliefs. The broadsheet
was translated into Swedish for the first time in 1643 and then
came out in a stream of new editions, that did not stop until the
end of the 19th century. In the Royal Library of Stockholm there
are 43 editions of the broadsheet. They all seem to go back to a
somewhat more recent German print, dated "Reval 1614." In all
cases except six the story told by Paulus von Eitzen has been
published as the first of "Three Trustworthy Relations" (*Trenne
trovärdiga relationer*). The following two are an anti-Semitic account of the punishments that the twelve Jewish tribes must suffer
and an account of Pilate's death and his unquiet corpse. The older
Swedish broadsheets were usually printed in the bigger cities all
over the country, while the later ones are usually to be found in
southern Sweden. This is an indication of the importance of popular conceptions derived from the southern neighbor countries,
which created a basis for the increasing interest in the immortal
shoemaker. In the town of Jönköping in Småland, for example, at
least twelve editions were published between 1826 and 1857.

A German sequel of little literary value was also translated into
Swedish. It deals with Ahasuerus' further adventures in Germany
and his death, and it ends with his prophecy about the imminent
arrival of Judgment Day. In the Royal Library of Stockholm this
sequel has been kept in four prints, the two oldest ones from 1787.
Another two prints from Jönköping, of 1815 and 1818, have the
same contents but end with a sensational appendix, in which it is
told that the Shoemaker of Jerusalem was discovered among the
crowd at the Värnamo market, a well known market-place in
southern Sweden. His look and exotic dress are described in the

following words: He was of "a tall and strong figure, with a long beard and an ancient visage, carrying on his back a shoebox as shoemakers generally do. He was dressed in a long suit of intertwined horsehair, trousers and waistcoat of camel skin, and a headgear, reminiscent of a winter cap, made of tiger hide. This man seemed to be most distressed, folding his hands as if for prayer, and wandered anxiously around." Since he has dramatically revealed who he is, he starts a penitential sermon aimed against oaths, drunkenness and obscene songs. As a proof of the verity of his story the informant tells that he has not only seen and talked to the Shoemaker of Jerusalem, but also offered him snuff. Many details confirm that the story is one of those which were directly inspired by the relation of Paulus von Eitzen about two centuries before.

In southern Sweden a Danish song, written in the earlier half of the 18th century and translated into Swedish in 1833, was given great importance. It has been preserved only in five Swedish broadsheets and one complete record, except for around ten fragmentary records of our time. It has been treated thoroughly by Erik Dal,[2] and therefore I only mention that its influence on the south-western Swedish tradition has been considerable. The contents summarize the main features of the prose narrative. The text is not distinguished by any subtlety and did not improve through translation into Swedish, but it is effective and answers the purpose of satisfying a popular taste for sensations. It was still sung in some southern Swedish provinces fifty years ago.

A later Swedish song with the title "The Shoemaker of Jerusalem," preserved in four broadsheets, has, on the other hand, hardly influenced the folk tradition. This is not so strange, however; the contents are satirical, and the Eternal Jew has turned into a political wiseacre without any similarity to the tragic figure of the legend. The song has its main interest as a proof of the widespread popularity that the Shoemaker of Jerusalem enjoyed at that time.

Turning to the oral sources, one finds a creature far more fantastic than the Ahasuerus of the broadsheets, where a certain degree of realism was often attained. The tragic aura, which is due to symbolic interpretations, is not found in the folk beliefs. Here,

Ahasuerus is just a man suffering under a terrific punishment, who was looked upon with curiosity, pity and fright. Most of the traits in the popular beliefs have reached Sweden from Germany and Denmark, but some features seem to have been added in Sweden. The Eternal Jew in folk beliefs melted together with Ahasuerus from the broadsheets into a creature who by degrees became well known in the whole of southern Sweden. In central Sweden, the western province of Värmland became a center of the traditions far more than did the other parts, and from the vast districts of northern Sweden there are hardly any records at all.

The most widespread feature, related in countless records, concerns the appearance of the shoemaker. He carries his shoemaker's attribute, the bundle of lasts, on his back, and, like himself, it is quite overgrown with green moss. These two clear and graphic details, the bundle of lasts and the moss, have served as signs of recognition; they were what people looked for and thought they found on certain strange wanderers who passed on the roads. Their importance has been stressed in various ways. One record from Värmland tells that the lasts are becoming more and more heavy from the growing moss, and another record from the same province states that there is quite a mountain of moss covering the bundle of lasts. A third record, also from Värmland, has caught in an excellent way the shivering and expectant feeling that people had, thinking of the Shoemaker of Jerusalem: "I remember so well how the lads waited for the Shoemaker of Jerusalem to come, because there was a legend that you could hear from old folks that there should not be one place on earth where he had not been. He would not get peace before. And we also waited to see the moss on the bundle of lasts. He carried a big bundle of lasts on his back, and there were supposed to be mosses growing on it." A sparsely recorded southern Swedish belief, that has been known also in Germany[3] and Denmark,[4] claims that he could be recognized by his footsteps as well: the nails in his shoes left prints formed like crosses.

Despite many fantastic features, the folk beliefs often will show a strong realism. That the Eternal Jew does not age is a trait impossible quite to accept; like others he has to submit to aging. Therefore, several records tell that he gets younger every 100 years. This detail is found already in the account by Roger of Wendover from the 13th century about the doorkeeper Cartaphilus,[5] but it might well have arisen independently. The hundred years' interval is the ordinary stylistic method of describing a high age in popular narration. At the same time it explains why the Eternal Jew can sometimes be seen as an old man and sometimes as a man of about thirty years. In Värmland it is related: "If he gets too old, he grows young again to the age that he had at that time, about 30 years." In Småland one informant claims that he becomes a child once again every 100 years, but another that he is transformed every 100 years in the other direction becoming a little older than the century before. A common conception was that he passed a district once every 100 years. This opinion has created a legend, well known in Germany,[6] that can also be found in Skåne. It describes how the Eternal Jew tells about the appearance of the neighborhood at his last visit. On those places that are now cultivated, an immense beech forest was then growing. The farmers check his statement, which is shown to be true. In some places he was interpreted as a bad omen when he appeared, signifying, for instance, that doomsday was close at hand. In a record from Skåne he has been understood as an omen of war. In the same record the hundred years' interval reappears in an unexpected connection: he can lie dormant for a hundred years each time. "And I don't hold that for unbelievable," adds the informant.

This statement, however, is unique; the common belief is that he shall never get any rest. The restlessness, the compulsion to wander is strongly stressed in the Swedish records, and it can sometimes be described with an almost painful intensity, as in this record: "The Shoemaker of Jerusalem had to walk and walk always right to Judgement Day. And if he would sit down some time, there was always ringing in his ears: 'Get up and walk! Get up and walk!' "

But the folk tradition would not be real if, as it stressed the unquiet of the Eternal Jew, it did not work out rules for how he should get rest. According to a southern Swedish record he is only permitted to rest when he has reached a churchyard. He may stay there as long as it takes to read Our Father and the Blessing.

According to another informant, he is permitted to rest a moment on his staff each time he comes to a crossroad.

These records, however, are only to be looked upon as local explanations from a rich supply of Christian patterns. Quite the dominating belief is the notable conception that the Eternal Jew is allowed to rest only one night each year, Christmas night. But the only place where he could be seated was on a plow that had been left in the field under the sky. This belief is exemplified in around 20 records, a few of which also mention the harrow as a permitted resting-place. But the main characteristic of this belief is its warning function: the plow where the shoemaker is seated will thereafter be impossible to use, it will bring a bad harvest, from the furrows that it plows will grow nothing but weeds. The conception is given as a reason for putting the tools into the sheds in good time before Christmas. In some sparse records his function as a bugaboo has been enlarged to involve everything that has to do with the care of the implements. In such cases it is told that he runs as fast as the wind and everywhere looks for an opportunity to make mischief. All edged tools must be in their right places, therefore, and no implement left out in the fields after harvest.

This belief has also been recorded all over Denmark[7] and in Germany.[8] But in some places in both these countries a quite contrary conception has existed:[9] one ought to leave two harrows leaning towards each other in the field when the work of the week was over, so that the Eternal Jew could rest upon them. The question is how two so contradictory conceptions have been able to arise. The explanation is simple: the belief in the Eternal Jew is in neither case primary. What was important was to handle the farm implements in a practical way, to lean the harrows towards each other in the field to dry, and to put the plows under a roof before Christmas. The dominant rôle of the Eternal Jew among supernatural conceptions afterwards leads to the creation of a rule: by thinking of the Eternal Jew and his rest, one should not have any difficulties in remembering how to handle plow and harrow properly.

The belief that the Shoemaker of Jerusalem brings evil on those tools upon which he sits has reached so far up in Sweden as Södermanland, Närke and Västmanland, provinces where the legend of the Eternal Jew has not been recorded. A conception known in Denmark, for example, that everything touched by the Eternal Jew is struck by misfortune, is not known in Sweden. However, an isolated record from south-western Sweden might incidentally be mentioned as an example of how the Eternal Jew also acts in legends close to the anecdote. Here he is said to bring upon all he meets the curse that they have to carry on their work until sunset. In one farm he meets a farmer who is measuring linen cloth, and it does not run short until the evening, but in another farm the master is passing his urine and cannot stop until sunset.

What has been said up to now shows that the legend of the Eternal Jew has not the supreme position in Swedish popular beliefs that might be imagined from the wide distribution of the broadsheets. However, the contents of the legend are correctly told in about 40 records, mostly from places directly influenced by the prose narrative or the Danish song. A visual detail that is found in both these printed sources is that Ahasuerus is holding his smallest child on his arm when Jesus passes his house, and that has stayed in the memory of several informants. The moving description in the prose narrative of his pious behaviour in the church might be regarded as a background to three records, telling how he has been noticed standing in a Swedish church during the sermon, bowing each time Jesus' name was mentioned. The dramatic highpoint of the legend, the situation when Jesus stops in front of Ahasuerus' house to rest and is driven away, has not always been able to survive in Swedish popular tradition. In a dozen records the reason for the curse of the wandering Jew has faded to a vague explanation, e.g., that he "had sinned once," or that "he had done so much evil that he was sentenced by Our Lord to walk around the earth until doomsday," or that "Jesus had asked him for something and he did not care." Especially in western Sweden the motif has been replaced by some other that has either seemed more visual or has had a direct connection with his profession as a shoemaker. In about ten records Jesus asks the shoemaker to help him to carry the Cross, but the latter refuses. The change from the original motif might be explained as a demand in popular narrative style to strengthen the reciprocity between sin and punishment. Because the shoemaker has refused to carry the Cross he must carry his own bundle of lasts through eternity. The same tendency is found in another description of the scene outside the shoemaker's house: "He started mocking at Jesus and wished that the Cross were even heavier. From that day the shoemaker had to take the heavy bundle of lasts on his back and set out in the world." A fine example of popular reciprocity is given in the reply of Jesus in the following record: "If you do not allow a dying man to rest, then death shall not allow you to rest. You shall wander!" A feature that might remind one of the legend of Malchus[10] and has been kept in a German broadsheet on Ahasuerus[11] is also found in some western Swedish recordings. The Shoemaker of Jerusalem is said to have beaten Jesus on the back with a last, and therefore he will have to walk around carrying his lasts for all time. The motif is probably of an independent Swedish origin. It might be explained by the prominent place of the bundle of lasts in Swedish folk beliefs.

Another two records have spun an explanation on the fact that he is a shoemaker. One of them runs as follows: "Jesus had come to him and asked him to repair his shoes. But the Shoemaker had refused, since he thought he would get no money for his work. As a punishment for this unwillingness to help the Saviour he was doomed never to find any peace but to walk around the earth without shoes on his feet until the end of time." The other one builds even more freely upon the same theme. The Shoemaker had made a pair of high fisher boots for Peter, that were not water-tight, and in anger Peter punished him with a curse that he should walk around with his tools till doomsday. Finally one can find a connection with the profession of shoemaking in a single record from Värmland, according to which he carries all his worn pairs of shoes on his back.

The legend received its most remarkable form in almost a dozen records scattered over southern Sweden. As in the following record from Skåne the thrashing sound of certain migrant birds in the air has been interpreted as the Shoemaker of Jerusalem: "In the autumn the cranes come flying. My mother told me that when you heard the sound of them you said: 'That is the Shoemaker of Jerusalem.' He would come flying in the air, and sometimes you could hear the lasts clattering. In the Saviour's time he had done some injury and was doomed to be a flying spirit who never got peace."

The most common other interpretation in the same area is that the sound comes from Odin and his hunt, breaking forth over the autumn sky. This conception is spread over Europe under several names: the wild huntsman, the wild hunt, the army of the dead, and others.[12] In order to understand how the old Nordic god Odin and the wandering Shoemaker of Jerusalem could have been mixed up, one has to know how both of them have been conceived of in recent Swedish folklore. A group of legends is told about Odin concerning his pursuit of the female wood-spirit, and certain sounds in the air are considered to be him and his hunt. This has meant that people could conceive of him as in the following record from Småland: "Odin was a king in old times, and he wanted to do nothing, but only hunt. So he got as a punishment from Our Lord that he should hunt for eternity." Like Odin, the Shoemaker of Jerusalem has come to be assigned to a category of supernatural flying beings, that, unblessed and restless, move around, waiting for redemption on Judgement Day. An informant from Halland tells: "The hunt of Odin, that is the Shoemaker of Jerusalem. He did not want to help the Saviour. One shall not stand listening when one hears the hunt of Odin." In another record from the same province it is clearly demonstrated how the confusion could have developed: "The hunt of Odin shall move around in the air until Judgement Day. It was someone who hunted on a Sunday, and that became his punishment. The Shoemaker of Jerusalem was sewing on a Sunday, and that is why he must walk until Judgement Day." It may be noticed that the province where the record was made has most strictly preserved an orthodox Protestantism that stressed the sanctity of Sunday.

Besides the widespread conception of the hunt of Odin, some western Swedish provinces have interpreted the sound of flying wings as a big harrow that went over the sky, the so called hunger-harrow. In one single record about this belief one will find a reminiscence of the Shoemaker of Jerusalem—a name, found in the same Old Testament book as is the biblical Ahasuerus. The phenomenon is called the harrow of Haman,[13] and Haman is said to be a Jewish farmer from the time of Christ, who was in such a hurry to harrow that he had no time to listen to the preaching of Christ. Therefore he must continue harrowing until Judgement Day.

Finally, one might note some other single records, illustrating in various ways how the Eternal Jew has been changed into a dangerous supernatural being that roams about, awaiting the redemption of Judgement Day. A woman of Skåne tells how she, accompanied by her son, once met a little old man with glowing, red, staring eyes. The boy had greeted him with a "good evening," and soon afterwards had been seriously ill. The old man was the Shoemaker of Jerusalem. The situation is identical with hundreds of Swedish descriptions of how a meeting with a supernatural being, e.g., a ghost, a fairy or a water spirit, is followed by illness. Another record from the same province tells that a young woman should lift her skirts in order to make the Eternal Jew disappear. The magic protection that comes from the uncovering of oneself is otherwise especially known in connection with dangerous supernatural beings like ghosts, milkhares, etc. One other record from Skåne contains a situation that at first sight does not seem extraordinary. An acquaintance of the informant is out in the forest. "Then he met someone, who had a big bundle on his back, and everything was mossy, the man as well as the bundle. And when he asked him what he was walking for, he said that he walked for the grace and mercy of God until Judgement Day." The exchange of words is the same as in a widespread Swedish legend where a person meets the waterspirit, the fairies or other supernatural beings, who tell that they wait for redemption on Judgement Day. It is more than a coincidence that all these three examples come from Skåne, the southernmost province of Sweden. There, the belief in the Shoemaker of Jerusalem reached such a degree that it burst the bounds confining him to the legend. He became a frightening, unblessed being, flying or wandering, whom one was ready to meet everywhere.

There should also be mentioned a couple of locally distributed sayings connected with the Shoemaker of Jerusalem. In the province of Södermanland, 'Shoemaker of Jerusalem' is a nickname for a slow and dilatory person, and in Småland one asks a person who has gone astray or been away for a long time if he has been in the company of the Shoemaker of Jerusalem.

In conclusion, it can be established that the image of the Eternal Jew in Swedish folk beliefs has arisen through an interaction of printed sources (above all, of course, the German broadsheet of 1602) with popular conceptions (of which almost all derived from the south). His Scandinavian name has dictated that great importance has been given to his shoemaking profession, and the shoemaker's attribute, the bundle of lasts, has been an active element in the creation of new variants of the legend. The main reason that he has been able to integrate so rapidly into Swedish popular beliefs is the already existing traditions about supernatural beings, condemned to be unblessed until Doomsday. In the first place this applies to the hunt of Odin, in a wider sense to all sprites of nature. This has also meant that the Eternal Jew has been provided with certain supernatural features that are very far from the contents of the broadsheets.

NOTES

1. The material consists of 147 records, distributed as follows: Folklivsarkivet, Lund, 36; Varbergs museums arkiv, Varberg, 1; Västsvenska folkminnesarkivet, Gothenburg, 63; Nordiska museet, Stockholm, 7; Landsmåls- och folkminnesarkivet, Uppsala, 24; printed records, 16. Among the printed records the following ones might especially be mentioned: *Folkminnen och Folktankar* (periodical) vol. 18, p. 169: vol. 19, p. 186; vol. 20, p. 182; vol. 23, p. 204; and R. Nilsson & C. M. Bergstrand, *Folktro och folksed på Värmlandsnäs* 3 (1962), pp. 221–22.

2. E. Dal, "Ahasverus in Dänemark," *Jahrbuch für Volksliedforschung* 9 (1964).

3. F. Sieber, *Sächsische Sagen* (1926), p. 123.

4. H. F. Feilberg, *Bidrag til en Ordbog over Jyske Almuesmål* 2, p. 40.

5. L. Neubaur, *Die Sage vom Ewigen Juden* (1884), p. 8.

6. Neubaur, pp. 28–29.

7. Feilberg, p. 40.

8. K. Müllenhof, *Sagen, Märchen und Lieder der Herzogtümer Schleswig* (Holstein und Lauenburg, 1845), p. 547.

9. Denmark: Feilberg, p. 40; Germany: A. Kuhn, *Sagen, Gebräuche und Märchen aus Westfalen* 2 (1859), p. 32; A. Kuhn & W. Schwarz,

Norddeutsche Sagen, Märchen und Gebräuche (1848), p. 451; E. L. Roch-holz, *Deutscher Glaube und Brauch* etc. 2 (1867), p. 55; O. Schell, *Bergische Sagen* (1897), p. 46; L. Strackerjan, *Aberglaube und Sagen aus dem Herzog-tum Oldenburg* (1909) 1, p. 452, and 2, p. 55; A. Wuttke, *Der deutsche Volksaberglaube der Gegenwart* (1900), p. 476.

10. Neubaur, pp. 4–5.
11. Neubaur, p. 19.
12. Cf. Lutz Röhrich, "Die Frauenjagdsage," *Proceedings of the IVth International Congress for Folk-Narrative Research in Athens 1964* (Athens, 1965), pp. 408–423.
13. Like Ahasuerus, the name of Haman is taken from the Book of Esther, in which Haman is the chief minister of the Persian King Ahasuerus.

Illustrations

The illustrations of the Swedish broadsheets are interesting in many respects. One can find, for example, how the older ones generally did not strive to give the Eternal Jew characteristic Jewish features, while in the more recent ones those features are sometimes strongly emphasized. Further, the illustrations show how a broadsheet printer proceeded to publish a picture. Since he lived in a time when the word "copyright" was not yet invented, he chose an older illustration and had a wood-carving made, as similar to the original as possible. Afterwards, his illustration might be used by another printer in the same way. The result is that there exist long series of pictures, where the imitations more and more lose the realistic character of the original and grow crudely stylized instead.

As was remarked by Professor Lutz Röhrich in the discussion after the paper, there is an interesting conformity between the development of the Eternal Jew in folk traditions and in the broadsheet illustrations. In both he is originally depicted with the realism of the historical legend, and in both he gradually turns into a fantastic creature. The historic figure becomes demonic, and the pictures show a being that has almost lost its human features.

Swedish Broadsheet Illustrations of the Eternal Jew

Sweden, 18th century, after 17th-century German illustration.

Tryckt Åhr 1734.

Anti-Semitic broadsheet, 1734.

Nyköping, Sweden, 1774, 1787.

Trenne Trowärdige
RELATIONER,
Then första:
Om en Jude och Skomakare af Jerusalem, then oddelige Ahasverus benämd.
Then Andra:
Om thet Straff hwart slägte ibland Judarna i synnerhet lida måste.
Then Tredje:
Om Pilati Död och oroliga döda kropp.

Tryckt i Norrköping år 1776.

Norrköping, 1776.

Sådan skapnad hade denna Mannen under sin jordiska wandring.

Örebro, 1787.

darna i synnerhet lida måste.
Den Tredje:
Om Pilati död och oroliga döda kropp.

Gefle, 1793, 1798.

Swedish Broadsheet Illustrations of the Eternal Jew

iſonnerhet lida måſte,
ſamt
om Pilati död och oroliga döda kropp

Malmö 1832.
Tryckt i Berlingſka Boktryckeriet.

Malmö, 1832, 1833.

Stockholm, Elméns och Granbergs Tryckeri, 1823

Stockholm, 1823; Jönköping, 1826, 1833.

Lund.

Lund, 1833, 1834.

Om Pilati död och oroliga döda kropp.

Om det ſtraff hwart Slägte ibland Judarne
i ſonnerhet lida måſte.

Om Pilati död och oroliga döda kropp.

Jönköping, 1833

Norrköping, tryckte hos Chr. Törnequiſt, 1845.

Stockholm, 1829.

Jönköping, 1833–57.

Norrköping, 1845.

WODAN, THE WILD HUNTSMAN, AND THE WANDERING JEW

Karl Blind

Studies of the Wandering Jew generally tend to be descriptive and historical rather than analytic or interpretive. Nevertheless, there is a small group of essays which, from various theoretical perspectives, speculate about the possible meaning or significance of the legend. The critical question is whether or not the Wandering Jew is a representation of some deeper layer of meaning. Is he an allegorical figure? Is he a symbol? If so, of what? Depending upon the particular theoretical bias of the investigator, there are different answers to these questions.

One central approach to the interpretation of myth and other forms of folk narrative which was widely practiced in the latter half of the nineteenth century had a heavy philological bent. For the scholars of this school, the language of the texts and especially proper names were typically construed as valuable clues leading to an understanding of the underlying or original meaning of a narrative. The method consisted principally of meticulous comparative study of cognate or similar texts from neighboring cultural areas. Through this comparison, hypothetical origins as well as possible lines of influence and transmission were reconstructed. Modern texts were usually treated as survivals or transformations of elements which could be traced to older archaic religions and belief systems. The philological school of myth tended to concen-

trate upon the Indo-European tradition, especially the German (Teutonic) material.

Karl Blind discusses the Wandering Jew from the philological-mythological perspective. Accordingly, he attempts to show how the legend is a transformation of the earlier Teutonic mythical figure of the god Wodan and the later related figure of the Wild Huntsman. Whereas af Klintberg's essay was concerned with demonstrating how old forms fit into new environments, Blind's interest is rather in seeking to discover the old forms underlying modern texts. For a short note in the same vein proposing an alternative origin, see Albert J. Edmunds, "The Wandering Jew: His Probable Buddhist Origin," Notes and Queries, NS 7 (Jan. 18, 1913): 47. It is interesting that the association of the Wandering Jew with both Wodan and the Buddha was suggested much earlier, e.g., by Ernst Ludwig Rochholz, in his Schweizersagen aus dem Aargau (Aarau, 1856), II, pp. 307–308.

I

If the science of comparative mythology had no other use, it would still be valuable as a means of overthrowing prejudice and dispersing the dark clouds of an antiquated bigotry. In this sense it may, even in our so-called enlightened age, not be out of place to show how the tale of the "Wandering Jew," with whose image so many ideas of religious odiousness are connected, has, after all, mainly arisen from the gradual transfiguration of a heathen divine form, not lacking in grandeur of conception, which originally and properly belongs to the creed of our own Germanic forefathers.

Of similar curious transfigurations for the worse, more than one can be proved. I need only refer to the popular custom, still prevailing in several parts of Germany and the Scandinavian North, of the so-called "Burning of Judas" about Easter time. It is instructive to trace out the upgrowth of this much-relished ceremony, which seems to have naturally originated from Christianity, whilst in truth it can be clearly fathered back to a perver-

Reprinted from *Gentleman's Magazine*, 249 (1880): 32–48.

sion of an early heathen idea, in which undoubtedly some crude philosophical views of cosmogony had once been embodied. A few indications will render this apparent.

Among the Pagan Teutonic tribes, as amongst most ancient nations, the Universe was thought to have been slowly and gradually evolved from an aboriginal state of Chaos, out of which there came first a race of Giants, called *Jötun* in the Germanic North; and then only a race of Gods. The Gods had to wage war against the Giants, and finally vanquished them. In all likelihood, the Titans represented torpid, barren Nature; the Gods, the powers of Life, which struggle into shapely form. It is an idea of Evolution, only in anthropomorphic symbolism, such as mankind everywhere has been fond of in its attempts at guessing the great riddle of the world.

Now, a custom once existed, without doubt, in accordance with the semi-dramatic bent of all early religions, of celebrating this divine victory over the uncouth *Jötun* by a festival, when a giant doll was carried round in Guy Fawkes manner, to be finally burnt. To this day there are traces of this heathen rite, but unfortunately mixed up now with a great deal of religious acrimony, owing to that misunderstanding of obsolete words which plays so large a part in the metamorphosis of myths. The rite is still performed, as it unquestionably was of yore, in Spring—about Easter, which is named after the German Goddess of Spring, Eostre, or Ostara—that is to say, at a time of year when torpid Nature awakes into shapely forms. The doll is still burnt; only, it is called "Judas." These *"Judas*-fires" evidently have their origin in the *Jötun-*, or giant-, burning. The transition from one word to the other was an easy one. In some places the people, misled by a further transmogrification of ideas and words, run about, wildly shouting:—"Burn the old Jew! Burn the old Jew!"

The *Jötun*, in fact, has been converted into a Judas, and then into a Jew. And so a Pagan superstition serves, in what is called a Christian age of the religion of love, for the maintenance of an unjust prejudice against an inoffensive class of fellow-citizens.

Similar pranks of religious animosity have been played with the name of a Germanic elf-spirit, who seems to be a diminished dwarf form of Wodan, or Odin, the great God with the Broad

Hat. His broad hat symbolizes the canopy of heaven. The elf-spirit is therefore naturally called by a diminutive expression, *Hütchen*, Little Hat, or Hattikin. At the same time, a general name for serviceable elfin spirits is in Germany *Gütchen*, Goody-ones—a name which originally may also have arisen from that of Wodan, who in a Longobardic form is called Gwodan, in a Frankish form Godan; whence the Godesberg, near Bonn.

The *Gütchen*, or *Gütel*, are supposed in the folk-tales to be fond of playing with children. For this reason, playthings are left about the house for the elfin visitors, so that they may amuse themselves, and be less constantly about the children; the parents not quite liking a constant intercourse. This seems all very harmless so far as it goes, though not in accordance with common sense. But, unfortunately, when mothers or nurses found that children's sleep was often disturbed, they began to bear a grudge to the spirits; and then a slight change in the name of the elfin took place. From *Hütchen*, *Gütchen*, or *Gütel*, they were converted into *Jüdchen*, and *Jüdel*—little Jews! Then stories arose of the "little Jews" vexing the helpless children, of inflicting red pustules upon their rosy faces, even of burning them. Frolicsome house-gnomes of the heathen Teutonic religion suddenly became demoniacal spirits of an "accursed race," and the flame of fanaticism was lustily fed.

We all know, alas! what deeds such fanaticism is capable of doing. The history of the Middle Ages bears fearful witness to the inhuman character of this religious animosity. A single quotation may suffice. It is taken from Matthaeus Parisiensis, a writer who also records for the first time the story of the "Wandering Jew."

Many people in England—the author in question writes in his "Historia Major"—who were about (in the reign of Richard I, in 1190) to make the voyage to Jerusalem, resolved first to rise against the Jews.[1] All Jews that were found in their houses at Norwich were massacred by the Crusaders. So, also, those at Stamford and at St. Edmunds. At York, five hundred Jews, not counting the little children and the women, locked themselves up in the Tower with the consent of the governor and the castellan, from fear of an intended rising of the populace. On the Jews offering a sum of money as a ransom for safety, the people rejected the proposition. Then one of the Israelites, learned in the law, advised his coreligionists that it would be better to die for their law than to fall into the hands of the enemy. Upon this, each Jew in the Tower provided himself with a sharp knife to cut the neck of his wife, of his sons and daughters: then, throwing down the blood-dripping heads upon the Christians, the survivors set fire to the citadel, burning themselves and the remnant of the corpses together with the King's Palace. On their part, the inhabitants and the soldiers burnt down all the houses of the Jews, dividing their treasure among themselves.

So Matthaeus Parisiensis, who also mentions the tale of the Wandering Jew—a tale illustrated in our time by Gustave Doré in a manner calculated to leave no doubt upon the beholder that Ahasverus expiates the cruelty he is said to have shown to Jesus when the latter was bearing his cross to Golgotha. Yet, like the Judas-fires and the *Jüdel* tale, the story of the restless Ahasverus is also moulded upon a figure of the heathen Germanic creed!

II

This point has been made out by eminent authorities in Teutonic mythology. In the following pages I intend supplementing and grouping together the scattered evidence, adding here and there some fresh points and suggestions.

By way of comparison, it will be useful first to bring to recollection that legends about men living on for ever are to be found among various nations of the East. Biblical personages, like Enoch and Elias, have thus been used in Oriental folk-lore for the purpose of a myth symbolizing eternal existence. Similar ideas are personified in fabulous accounts founded on the epic "Schahnameh" of the Persian poet Firdusi, as well as legends of Mohammedan Arabs.

It is not to be denied that these Oriental fictions may, in some cases, have served to influence European folk-tales. The Crusades, indeed, brought about a great intermixture of thought between the East and the West. At the same time, we find on Western soil such strongly marked typical figures of Teutonic fancy—bearing so thoroughly, in their characteristics and their attributes, a likeness to the forms of the decayed creed of the Germanic heathens—that we cannot but believe them to be entirely of native growth, and to have served even as moulds in which some legends of apparently Christian origin were cast.

Thus, in Germany, there is the tale of the "Eternal Huntsman," in some parts of the country called Hakelbernd, or Hakelberg—evidently a mythic creation dating from the time of the Asa religion of our forefathers. There is a tale of the "Eternal Waggoner," Hotemann, chiefly to be met with among the descendants of the Nether Saxons, who, among all the tribes of Germany proper, held out longest in their Wodan worship against the conquering and Christianising policy of the Frankish emperor Karl the Great. There is, further, the curious tale of a "Flying Seafarer," which Richard Wagner, who has treated so many subjects of national mythology, has used for a well-known operatic text. To the same cycle of myths is attributed the tale of the *Ewige Jude*, or "Eternal Jew."

The thesis is, that the Wandering Jew has been evolved, as regards the main component parts of his individuality in Germany, from the figure of the Wild Huntsman, who himself is probably a later mask of the chief Teutonic deity Wodan, or Odin, after the latter had been disposed from his high status through the spread of Christianity. In proof of this thesis it can certainly be shown—

1. That there are German Tales of the Wild Huntsman, accounting for his forced peregrinations, *in which no Jew whatever is mentioned*, though an alleged insult offered to Christ forms a part of the myth.

2. That these same tales repose on an essentially heathen basis; so much so, that the Wild Huntsman who restlessly wanders about as an expiation for some insult committed against Christ, is actually *identified with a horse-flesh-eating race*, as the ancient Germans and Scandinavians are known to have been.

3. That in various German tales the "Eternal Huntsman" and the "Eternal Jew" are said *to be the same person*.

4. That several chief attributes of the Wild Huntsman and the Wandering Jew are the same, and that, to all appearance, there has

been even a similar word-transmutation, as in the case of *Jötun* into Judas, and of *Gütchen* into *Jüdchen*.

III

Before approaching the German myth of the Wandering Jew, it will be well to cast a glance at the character of the God upon whom his figure is now assumed to have been modelled.

Odin or Wodan, the Spirit of the Universe, was conceived by our forefathers as a great Wanderer. His very name describes him as the All-pervading. *Watan* in Old High German, *wadan* in Old Saxon, and *vadha*, in Old Norse, are of the same root as the Latin *vadere* and (with the introduction of a nasal sound) the German *wandern*—to go, to permeate, to wander about. Wodan is the Breath of the World; his voice is in the rushing wind. Restlessly he travels through all lands. The Sanskrit *wâta*, which etymologically belongs to the same root, signifies the wind; and the wind, in that early Aryan tongue, is also called "the Ever Travelling."

Hence several of the many names under which Odin was known represent him as being for ever on the move. In the poetic Edda he is called Gangradr; Gangleri (still preserved in the Scottish "gangrel," that is, a stroller); and Wegtam—all meaning the Wayfarer.[2] In one of the Eddic songs, in which he appears incarnated as Grimnir, he wears a blue mantle—a symbolic representation of the sky, of which he is the lord, and along which he incessantly travels. In the prose Edda, where his image is reflected, in the "Incantation of Gylfi," under the guise of a man who makes enquiries about all things in the Heavenly Hall of Asgard, he assumes a name meaning "The Wayfarer." He there says that he "comes from a pathless distance," and asks "for a night's lodging"—exactly as, in later times, we find the Wandering Jew saying, and asking for, the same.

In the Icelandic Heimskringla (the "World Circle") the semi-historical, semi-mythical Odin, whose realm lay near the Black Sea, and who ruled in company with twelve temple-priests, called *Diar* (that is, Gods, or divines), again appears as a great migratory warrior. He was "often away for years, wandering through many lands." The story of this powerful captain in war, who led the Germanic hosts from Asia or Asa-land, through Gardariki (Russia) and Saxon-land (Germany) to the Scandinavian North, is inextricably mixed up with the story of the Odin of mythology. But it is noteworthy that a restless, peregrinatory spirit—that spirit which, later on, made the Teutonic tribes overrun all Europe, and even the North of Africa—is also the characteristic of the warlike leader of the Icelandic hero-chronicle.

Saxo calls Odin the *viator indefessus*—the Indefatigable Wanderer. The Northern sagas are full of the records of his many journeys. In the Ragnar Lodbrog Saga, however, we see Odin already changed into a grey-headed pilgrim, with long beard, broad hat, and nail-clad shoes, pointing out the paths to Rome. The broad hat everywhere characterizes the great God in Teutonic lands. It signifies the cloud region—the headdress, as it were, of the earth. In many Germanic tales, the once powerful ruler of the world wears a motley mantle of many colours pieced together. This seemingly undignified garment is but another symbolic rendering of the spotted sky.

Now, the motley, many-coloured mantle, as well as the enormous broad hat and the heavy shoes of the Wandering Wodan, recur, on the one hand, in the curious shirt of St. Christophorus, and, on the other, in two of the chief attributes of the Wandering Jew. The coincidence is so striking, that Gotthard Heidegger already declared, at a time when the science of mythology was little developed yet, that "the great Christophorus and the Wandering Jew go together." At present, little doubt is entertained that, so far as the Church legend is concerned in Germanic countries, Christophorus carrying the Saviour over the water has replaced the older heathen tale of the giant Wate carrying Wieland over the water. Curiously enough, this tale has its prototype in a Krishna legend in India. Wate, as even his name shows, was only a Titanic counterpart of Wodan, who himself appears in the Asa religion also under the form of a water-god, or Neptune.

But before going into a comparison between the symbolical attributes of the errant Ahasverus and those of Germanic deities, the tale of the Wild Huntsman has to be looked at, for he is the link between Wodan and the Wandering Jew.

IV

This tale of the Wild Huntsman is found all over Germany, and in neighbouring countries where the German race has penetrated during the migrations, in an endless variety of forms. Wodan-Odin was the Psychopompos, the leader of the departed into Walhalla. The Wild Huntsman, who has taken his place, careers along the sky with his ghostly retinue. In the same way Freia, who in heathen times received a number of the dead in her heavenly abode,[3] is converted into a Wild Huntress, who hurries round at night with the unfortunate souls.

The names given in Germany to these spectral leaders of a nocturnal devilry bear a mark which cannot be mistaken. In German-Austria, the Wild Huntsman is called Wotn, Wut, or Wode; in Holstein, Mecklenburg, and Pomerania, Wod. The name corresponds to that of the Wild Huntsman in Sweden, where it is Oden. In the same way a female leader of the Wild Chase meets us as Frau Wode, Gode, or Gauden; again, as Frick, Berchta, Holla, Hera, Herka, or, biblically changed, Herodias; all the former names, with the apparent exception of the latter, being but appellatives of the same heathen goddess. To the seemingly biblical name of Herodias, in some places a male Herodis corresponds. But I hold that a Hera, Odin's wife, could without difficulty be formed into a Herodias. And an Oden, who was a *Heer-Vater* (Father of the Armed Hosts), and who afterwards became a leader of the *Wilde Heer*, was as easily disguised into a Herodis.

In some Westphalian tales, the Great Wanderer, World-Runner, and Wild Huntsman appears as "Rodes." Undoubtedly, this is a corruption from Rodso, or Hruodso—the Glorious—one of the appellatives of the great God who still goes about, in German Christmas mummeries, as Knecht Ruprecht; that is, Hruodperaht, or Resplendent-in-Glory. From "Rodes" the name is, in other Westphalian tales, also changed into Herodes.

Beda relates that March, among the Anglo-Saxons, was called Rhedmonath, because they sacrificed in that month to their goddess Rheda. In a rimed chronicle of Appenzell, in Switzerland—where the old German names of the calendar months have tenaciously kept their grounds—March still appears as "Redimonat."

So also we find "Retmonat" in Chorion's *Ehrenkranz der teutschen Sprach*, published at Strassburg in 1644. Rheda, in Old High German, would be Hruoda; and a female name of that kind is, indeed, preserved in old documents. It fully corresponds to Wodan's appellative Hruodso. Now, from Hruoda, too, the transition to Herodias was easy. As to Oden having been in Germany—even as in the Scandinavian North—a current form of the God's name, besides that of Wodan, there cannot be any doubt. It is testified to by the name of the Oden-Wald, or Oden's Forest, in Southern Germany. And there, again, we meet with the Wild Huntsman as the "Rodensteiner," reminding us of the North German "Rodes." The chain of mythological evidence is thus complete.

Hakelbernd is a further name of the Wild Huntsman in northwestern Germany. Grimm identifies it as Hakol-berand—that is, the bearer or wearer of the *hökull*, the mantle or armour; in other words—Wodan with the Mantle. From "Hakelbernd" the name has, here and there, been changed into a Squire Hackelberg. In the neighborhood of Hildesheim, this spectral leader of a wild chase is said to make his great world-journey "every seven years." Seven is a sacred number in Teutonic mythology, as in that of many other nations. The Edda is full of allusions to the mystic number; so are the German *Märchen*. When Hackelberg chases, he can be heard for many miles "rattling with his shoes." This same wandering spook has an oak forest and a mountain that are named after him[4]—a remarkable coincidence with the South German tale of the forest-haunting and hill-enchanted Wandering Jew, of whom I shall have to say more by-and-by. The shoes also play a considerable part in the myth of Ahasverus.

V

At winter solstice time, the chief Teutonic deities were supposed to go or ride about in stately procession. Hence the Wild Huntsman chases in the woods chiefly in the nights during Advent time. In Southern Germany, besides the names mentioned, he also bears the appellation of the Giant Huntsman—the great God having become a Titan; of the Hunter Ruprecht—i.e., of Wodan-

Hruodperaht; of the Hunter Hans—probably not from the German form of Johannes, but from *Ans* or *As*, that is, God; and of the Fiery Huntsman. The latter designation is quite in consonance with the original character of the Asa Creed—a Fire Religion, as distinguished from the Vana or Water Cult. Yet, in other Swabian localities the Wild Huntsman, very curiously, is called the "Neck." By this name we are openly led back, in my opinion, to that remarkable Vana religion, which was once essentially the creed of the Swabian or Suevian race, at the time when it dwelt near the shores of the Baltic and of the German Ocean. Neck is a water-spirit. It is, in many Teutonic languages, but another form of Nix; and Odin, as Nikor or Nikudr, was a father of the Nixes or Nikses, and a Ruler of the Sea, like Poseidon, the Zeus of the Sea.

A further Swabian name of the Wild Huntsman is the Little World Hunter—or *Welts-Jägerle*, the Swabians being extremely fond of caressing diminutives. By soft mispronunciation this name is sometimes changed into *Weltsch-Jägerle*, when, by dropping the "t," the idea arises that the spectre is a Welsh (or foreign) Hunter! It is noteworthy that, in most of these tales, he rides on a grey or white horse. It is the white or grey horse of Odin—again the symbol of the sky.

Strangely enough, a Swabian tale says that the horse of the Wild Huntsman, or Neck, "has been fetched from the sea"—an extraordinary idea among an inland-dwelling people, whose largest sheet of water is the Lake of Constance. Evidently, the sea-born stallion is a recollection from the time, long gone by, when the Swabian tribe dwelt near the sea-shore. In the same South German tale it is said, by way of explaining the colour of the steed of the Wild Hunter, that "a grey horse is a noble animal, because it has the colour of Heaven; in Hell, therefore, there are only black steeds." So the Wild Huntsman, after all, is not of hellish extraction! In truth, he is but a travestied God.

Primitive races have often looked upon the sky as a cloud sea or heavenly ocean. Hence the apparent contradiction between the maritime origin and the celestial characteristics of the horse of the Wild Huntsman is no contradiction at all. In the Swabian tale he rides with his steed "through the air, over the earth, and through the water"—a conception quite Eddic in tone. He is therefore sometimes called the Rider, or the Roarer—a good designation for a Storm-God. And he has a broad-brimmed hat, like Wodan, which, when left on the ground, nobody can raise, for it then becomes like a stone. The lowering cloud cannot be raised by the hand of man.

Again, we hear the Wild Huntsman spoken of in Southern Germany as the *Schimmel-Reiter*, the Rider on the White Horse. It is the well-known colour of Wodan-Odin's steed. Now and then the Wild Hunter, however, stalks about on foot, with a hammer hanging at his side by a leather strap. With this hammer he knocks in the forest. The God of Thunder, whose symbol the hammer was, seems here to be mixed up with the figure of Wodan. As to the Wild Chase being Wodan's Host of the Departed Spirits, this fact comes out also in the name of *Wute's Heer*—Wodan's Army. The Wute's Heer—sometimes pronounced Muotes Heer—is occasionally abbreviated into " 's Wuotas"; softer, "s' Muotas." Or it is made into a *Wüthendes Heer*, a Raging Host—another easy transition, even etymologically speaking; for *Wuth* (that is, all-pervading spirit and passion, or rage) comes from the same root as the name of Wodan.

The Wild Chase is said to career along the Milky Way. It is Wodan's or Freia's well-known path. Germanic warriors, who boasted of Divine descent—as, for instance, Orry, the conqueror of the Isle of Man—therefore asserted that they had come from the Milky Way. A large fish is said to fly in front of the Wild Chase. It seems to me to point to Odin's character as a chief water-deity, or to that early Vana-cult which, after a struggle mentioned in the Edda, was merged in the Asa Religion—when the Water-, Sun-, and Love-Goddess Freyja, together with her nearest relations, was taken over into Asgard as a hostage. The Germanic race, too, has its wave-born Aphrodite.

Saxo describes Odin as riding on a white horse, covered with a white shield. In German tales of the sixteenth century, Berchtold—the male form of Berchta, that is, of Freia, the consort of Wodan—appears at the head of the Wild Chase, dressed in white, on a white horse, the pack of dogs being even of white colour. It is still the typification of the sky with which the celestial rulers are originally identical, as has been proved from Vedic, Greek, and Norse names of gods.

This white or grey horse (*Schimmel*, or *Grau-Schimmel*) again occurs in a Saxon tale of the Meissen district, which describes Hans Jagenteufel—the *Ans, As*, or God who has been "devilled" into a ghostly huntsman—as careering through the forest in a long grey coat, on a grey horse. Thus he roves and raves about until the crack of doom. The New Faith, in fact, could not do without this degraded form of the Old Faith. It positively wanted it as a foil and counterfoil—as something to be kept in the background; to be continually abjured; and yet to be believed in with a shudder, lest the zeal of the faithful should grow weak, if all danger of the return of the old "devilry" were removed. At the same time, however, the Wild Huntsman and his retinue were often represented as being decapitated forms, carrying their heads under the arm. The new religion struck at the head of the old creed, exhibiting it only as a horrid example.

VI

But it is time to return to that restless son of Israel who is also used as such a horrid example.

Perhaps one of the clearest proofs of the phantom figure of the Wandering Jew having been grafted upon that of the great Wanderer and World-Hunter, Wodan, is to be found in a tale of the Harz Mountains. There it is said that the Wild Huntsman careers "over the seven mountain-towns every seven years." The reason given for his ceaseless wanderings is, that "he would not allow our Lord Jesus Christ to quench his thirst at a river, nor at a water-trough for cattle, from both of which he drove him away, telling him that he ought to drink from a horse-pond." For this reason the Wild Huntsman must wander about for ever, and feed upon horse-flesh. And whoever calls out after him, when his ghostly chase comes by, will see the Wild Huntsman turn round, and be compelled by him to eat horse-flesh too.

No allusion whatever is made, in this tale, to a Jew, though the name of Christ is pressed into it in a way very like the Ahasverus legend. We seem to get here a mythic rendering of the struggle between the old Germanic faith and the Christian religion. The "horse-pond" and the "horse-flesh" are, to all appearance, typical references to our horse-worshipping,[5] horse-sacrificing, horse-flesh-eating forefathers, who came to Britain under the leadership of Hengist and Horsa. To call out wantonly after the Eternal Huntsman entails the danger of being forced by him to eat horse-flesh—that is, to return to the old creed. The holy supper of the Teutonic tribes consisted of horse-flesh and mead. When Christianity came in, the eating of horse-flesh was abolished as a heathen custom. But at German witches' banquets—in other words, at secret festive ceremonies in which the pagan traditions were still kept up—there continued for a long time a custom of drinking from horse-shoes. In order fully to understand this custom, it ought to be remembered that both Odin and the horse which he gave as a gift to Sigurd were called Grani, which certainly means "him with the mane." (The Goths called their long locks *grans*. In the Nether German "Reynard the Fox," the bristles over the mouths of animals are designated by the same word. The beard of corn-ears is still called *Grannen* in German.)

I have no doubt that Germanic deities were at one time adored in the shape of animals, even as among nations so advanced in culture as the Hindoo and the Egyptians. Well may Odin-Wodan therefore have once been worshipped as a long-maned horse, or Grani; and this would all the more explain the high veneration in which the presages by the horse were held.

Thus the Harz tale of the horse-flesh-eating Wild Hunter and his septennial wanderings is a manifest link between the heathen mythology and the Christianised Ahasverus legend. A further link is to be found in a folk-tale of Southern Germany.

At Röthenberg, and other places in Swabia, as well as in the Black Forest, in Baden, people say that the "Everlasting Hunter" (*der ewige Jäger*) is the same person as the "Everlasting Jew" (*der ewige Jude*).[6] Both expressions are actually used there as identical. Of the Everlasting Jew it is fabled that he possesses a groat in his pocket, which never fails him, howsoever often he may spend it. This peculiarity strongly reminds us of similar "wishing things," or exhaustless treasures, of the great Germanic god, one of whose names was Oski, or Wunsch, that is, Wish.

Again, there goes a tale at Bretten, in Baden, that a forest in that neighbourhood is haunted by the Wandering Jew. It is a curious abode for a migrating son of Israel. The representative of a race which is nowhere held to have any romantic attachment to the woods, such as the Teutonic nations are known to feel, is thus localized in a manner perfectly fitting the wraith of the Storm-god, who has been transmuted into a Leader of the Wild Chase.

Besides Wodan, lingering recollections of another heathen deity seem to have contributed to the formation of the figure of the Wandering Jew. The heavy shoes of the latter are said, in some tales, to be "made up of a hundred pieces—the very masterpiece of a cobbler's painstaking cleverness." This strongly brings to recollection the colossal shoe of a Germanic god who represents the eternal Imperishableness of Nature—namely, of the Eddic Vidar. It was considered a religious duty for all men in the North to collect, during their lifetime, for sacrificial purposes, as it were, the leather stripes which they cut off from the parts of the shoes where the heels and the toes are.[7] In this manner an immense shoe was to be gradually formed for Vidar, so that, when at the End of All Things he has to battle with the wolf Fenrir, he should be well protected in trying with his foot to open the jaws of that monstrous beast.

Vidar is the symbol of an everlasting force. After the great overthrow of Gods and men, when the world is renewed, he still lives. Vidar's name means the Renewer—him who makes the world again; from Gothic, *vithra*; German, *wieder*. Ahasverus, the Everlasting, with his many-pieced heavy shoes, is at all events a curious counterpart of Vidar.

Why the name of "Ahasverus," which is that of Persian and Median kings, should have been chosen for the Wandering Jew, who, significantly enough, is said to have been a shoemaker, has baffled the interpreters of the myth. The name may have arisen from a learned whim; indeed, among the common German people, it does not occur. In our folk-tales the mythical figure is only known as the *Ewige Jude*, and, as before shown, is often looked upon as identical with the *Ewige Jäger*. Of Vidar with the Shoe no trace has apparently been preserved in Germany. This, however, is no proof that a corresponding deity may not once have been believed in amongst us. A great deal of German mythology has been lost by the disfavour of time. Yet, unexpected finds—as, for instance, in the case of the Merseburg Spell-song, or the discovery of the name "Friga-Holda" in a Latin document of the Gothic epoch of Spain—have repeatedly shown how much identity there was between the creed of the Scandinavian and the German Teutons.

If an "As-vidar" (God Vidar) has once been believed in in Germany, it would not require too great an effort of the imagination to assume that by a lengthening of the word "As"[8] and by a contraction of "Vidar," the name might have been changed into Ahasver. *Wieder*, in some German dialects, is contracted into *wie'r* or *we'r*. An *As-wer*, or *Ahasver*, could thus be easily formed. I throw out this hint as the merest indication of a possibility. The thesis of a gradual engrafting of the image of the Wandering Jew upon the form of a German deity does not want that support. It fully stands by itself.

VII

There is another name of the Wandering Jew which is held to have possibly an affinity with the Teutonic circle of gods. In a Latinised form it occurs, in Boulanger's *Historia Sui Temporis*, as "Buttadeus."

"Butta" is, by some writers on Germanic mythology, assumed to point to Wodan—to be only another pronunciation of the same name, by the law of letter-change. And indeed we find, in Germanic tales, the wife of the great God Perchta or Bertha—which is one of the cognomens of Freia-Holda—called *Pudel-Mutter*; and various ghost-like apparitions in German villages designated as *Dorf-Pudel*. Originally, this has, no doubt, nothing to do with the spectral dog in *Faust*. Remembering the present meaning of *Pudel* (poodle) in German, the word *Pudel-Mutter* looks like a tremendous and most laughable descent from a divine status. But the fall is not greater—to give but one instance out of a thousand—than that from *Cœur du Roi* to Cowderoy, when the cow takes the precedence of the king.

We have seen Odin changed, in a northern saga, into a pilgrim pointing out the paths to Rome. No wonder we should meet with a mythical figure, in Swiss tales, called "The Pilgrim from Rome," who is dressed in corresponding garments, and who has the broad hat, the large mantle, and the heavy iron-sheeted shoes common to the Germanic deities mentioned, as well as to the "Wandering Jew"—*without, however, bearing that latter name.*

Yet close by the locality where this tale is current in Switzerland, we find the same figure again called the *Ewige Jude*—namely, in parishes where there are Jewish communities, as well as in the Frick valley, which is mainly inhabited by Roman Catholics. To all evidence, religious antipathy has coloured the myth in these latter localities. The Wanderer, or grey-headed, broad-hatted pilgrim, was converted into a Jew, for the sake of pointing a moral and adorning a tale of bigotry.

The gradual transition from the heathen Germanic circle of ideas to the Christian legend is provable in many other ways. On Swiss and German soil, in places of close proximity, the same phantom form is alternately called the Eternal Hunter and the Eternal Jew, as well as the Pilgrim from Rome, or the Wandering Pilate. In the last-mentioned form, he is assigned a local habitation in the Pilatus Mountain of Switzerland. It is a well-known process of Germanic mythology to "enmountain," if I may say so, the deposed heathen gods, to charm them away into hills and underground caves, where they are converted into kings and emperors, often with a retinue of twelve men, corresponding to the duodecimal number of the deities.

A forest-haunting or hill-enchanted Jew has clearly no meaning. But if the *Jude* was originally a Wodan, Godan, or Gudan—and, indeed, there is a Frankish form of the God's appellation, from which the Godesberg, near Bonn, has its name—then the mystery is at once dissolved. Godan may, by softer pronunciation, have been changed into a *Jude* or Jew—even as the "*Gütchen*," the German spirit forms, were converted into *Jüdchen,* or little Jews.

Where the Wanderer is known, in the Aargau, as the *Ewige Jude,* it is related that in the inn where he asks for a night's lodging he does not go to bed, but walks about, without rest, in his room during the whole night, and then leaves in the morning. He once stated that, when for the first time he came to that Rhenish corner where Basel stands at present, there was nothing but a dark forest of black fir. On his second journey he found there a large copse of thorn-bushes; on his third, a town, rent by an earthquake. If—he added—he comes the same way a fourth time, one would have to go for miles and miles, in order to find even as much as little twigs for making a besom.

The immense age and everlastingness of the Wanderer are fully indicated in this description.

At Bern, he is said to have, on one occasion, left his staff and his shoes. In a "History of the Jews in Switzerland" (Basle, 1768), the Zurich clergyman, Ulrich, reports that in the Government Library at Berne a precious relic is preserved, namely, the aforesaid staff and a pair of shoes of the "Eternal, Immortal Jew"; the shoes being "uncommonly large and made of a hundred snips—a shoemaker's masterpiece, because patched together with the utmost labour, diligence, and cleverness out of so many shreds of leather." Evidently some impostor—who, however, kept to the floating ideas of the old Germanic myth, which had grown into a Christian legend—had thought fit, in order to maintain his assumed character, to present the town of Bern, as it were, with a diminished facsimile of Vidar's shoe.

At Ulm, also, the Wandering Jew is said to have left a pair of his shoes. This persistent connection of a decayed divine figure with shoes and the cobbler's craft comes out in a number of tales about the Wild Huntsman. In Northern Germany, one of the many forms of the *Ewig-Jäger* is called Schlorf-Hacker—a ghastly figure in rattling shoes or slippers that jumps pick-a-back upon men's shoulders.[9] In Glarus, the departed spirits of the Wild Chase are actually called "Shoemakers," as if they had been contributors to Vidar's shoe. A full explanation of this symbolism—for it can be nothing else—is still wanting. But the importance of the shoe, both in the Germanic creed and in the Ahasverus legend, is undeniable, and it clearly forms a thread of connection between the two circles of mythology.

VIII

When the real meaning of a myth is lost, popular fancy always tries to construct some new explanation. Even at a seat of English learning, the old Germanic Yule-tide custom of the Boar's Head Dinner—originally a holy supper of the heathen Teutons—is interpreted now as a festive commemoration of the miraculous escape of an Oxford student from the tusks of a bristly quadruped. Nothing can be made out more clearly than that the banquet in question is the remnant of a sacrificial ceremony once held in honour of Fro, or Freyr, the God of Light, whose symbol and sacred animal was the sun-boar, and who was pre-eminently worshipped at winter solstice.[10] But how few there are, even amongst the most learned, who know this simple fact, or who have ever been startled by the palpable impossibility of the modernizing explanation of the Boar's Head Dinner!

We cannot wonder, therefore, that the restless chasing of the Wild Huntsman—though he still bears here and there the name of Wotn, or Wodan, and though he be replaced in other districts by a Wild Huntress, who is called after one of the names of Wodan's consort—should be explained now as the expiation of the crime of hunting on Sunday, committed by some nobleman or squire in defiance of the orders of the Church. The details of this Christianising explanation vary in every locality. Men are always ready to explain, offhand, that which they do not understand in the least. Yet the great heathen Germanic traits of the Wild Chase are preserved without change in places lying far asunder. In the same way there has been a Boar's Head Dinner, until a comparatively recent time, in more places than one in England; and at Court there is still, at Christmas, a diminished survival of the custom. But only at Oxford the impossible story of the student is told.

So, also, there are different tales accounting for the peregrinations of that mythical figure which is variously known as the horse-flesh-eating Eternal Hunter who insulted Christ, as the Pilgrim from Rome, as Pilatus the Wanderer, as the Hill-enchanted and Forest-haunting Jew, as Ahasver, Buttadeus, and so forth. But again, the chief characteristics of the Restless Wanderer remain everywhere the same; and in not a few districts this form is inextricably mixed up with that of the Wild Huntsman, who also dwells in a hill and haunts a forest, and whose Wodan or Godan name may in Germany have facilitated the transition to a *Jude*.

When we keep these things in mind, we shall see how useful it is to study the creed of our forefathers as a means of dispelling the dark shadows of present bigotry. Such fuller knowledge of a collapsed circle of ideas which often show so remarkable a contact with the Vedic religion, enables us to enjoy, as a weird poetical conception, that which otherwise would only strike us as the superstition of a contemptible religious fanaticism. For all times to come, a Great Breath, a *Mahan Atma*, will rustle through the leaves, rage across hill and dale, and stir river and sea with mighty motion. In so far, there will never be a lack of an Eternal Wanderer. If we understand the myth in this natural sense, a curse will be removed; a feeling of relief will be created in bosoms yet heavily burdened with prejudices; and evidence will have been furnished that a grain of sense, however overlaid with absurdities, is often to be found in cruel fancies in which the human mind seems to have gone most wildly astray.

NOTES

1. "Eodem anno, multi per Angliam Hierosolymam properantes, prius in Judaeos insurgere decreverunt." (London editon of *Historia Major*, of 1571; p. 211.)

2. See *Wafthrûdnismâl; Grimnismâl; Vegtamskvidha*, and *Gylfaginnîng*.

3. "Freyja is the noblest of the Goddesses. She has the dwelling in Heaven which is called Folkwang; and when she goes to battle, one half of the fallen belong to her, and the other half to Odin." (*Gylfi's Incantation*; 24.)

4. Müller-Schambach's *Niedersächsische Sagen*.

5. Tacitus' *Germania*, x.:—"They are also in the habit of interrogating the voice and flight of birds; and it is their peculiar custom to take counsel by means of presages and monitions from horses. In their woods and groves, white horses, not to be put to any work for mortal man, are kept at public cost. Attached to the sacred car they are accompanied, on foot, by the priest and the king, or by some other head of the community, who observe their neighing and snorting. No other kind of augury

enjoys greater confidence, not only among the people, but also among the chieftains and the priests. These, indeed, look upon themselves as ministers of the Gods, but upon the horses as beings initiated into the divine will.''

In the second Lay of Gudrun, in the Edda, a consultation of the horse is also mentioned. It refers to the death of Sigurd:—

Weeping I went	to talk to Grani;
With wetted cheek	I prayed the steed to tell,
Then Grani his head	bowed down in the grass;
Well knew the steed	that his master was dead.

6. *Deutsche Sagen, Sitten und Gebräuche aus Schwaben*. Von Prof. Ernst Meier.

7. In ancient times, Germanic shoes appear, sandal-like, to have been open at the heel and the toe; which, from a sanitary point of view, was certainly the better arrangement.

8. The Osning mountain, Osnabrück, the "Oanswald" figure formed by Bavarian reapers from the last sheaf, and many names like Oswald, Osbrecht, etc., testify to the Asa name having been also that of German Gods.

9. Kuhn's *Norddeutsche Sagen*.

10. See *The Boar's Head Dinner at Oxford, and a Germanic Sun-God*, by Karl Blind, in *The Gentleman's Magazine* for January 1877.

THE WANDERING JEW IN THE CLINIC

A STUDY IN NEUROTIC PATHOLOGY

Henry Meige

In contrast with historical and mythological approaches to the Wandering Jew are a number of critical essays which fall under the general rubric of psychology. Within the framework of psychology, one can find great diversity of interpretation. The following three essays offer quite distinct readings of the Wandering Jew, and at the same time they reflect something of the historical development of clinical psychology.

The first of these essays by Dr. Henry Meige is based upon observations made at the famous clinic located at Salpêtrière. This clinic directed by Charcot is also renowned for having influenced Sigmund Freud, who spent some time there as a young physician. The selection reprinted below in translation is the introduction to a short monograph, Le Juif-errant à la Salpêtrière: Etudes sur certains nevropathes, *published in 1893. Meige's hypothesis is that the legend reflects an actual medical condition which he was able to diagnose from examining a number of Jewish patients who had voluntarily come to the clinic for treatment. The alleged nervous disease supposedly manifested itself in an irresistible urge to wander. The bulk of the monograph consists of documented life histories complete with detailed notations describing body movements and minutiae of motor behavior. There are even pictures of the patients.*

> *The seemingly scientific case histories are then essentially compared with versions of the legend, and Meige concludes that the case histories and legend are related. Meige contends that the legend expresses psychological pathology. With this view, the legend is not a symbolic representation, but a literal reflection of mental aberration. Jews have a neurotic tendency to wander; therefore we have the legend of the Wandering Jew.*

Of all popular legends, the Wandering Jew is, without doubt, one of the most universally disseminated. The mysterious figure of the *Eternal Roamer* has always charmed the common people. Moreover, novelists, poets, scholars, and painters have studied, commented upon, and reproduced his immutable and gripping traits in thousands of forms. Who does not know the famous lament reprinted each year under a penny etching from Epinal?

Yet, this famous Jew, this bearded traveler, whom nothing could restrain in his interminable peregrinations, was not noticed by most physicians. Of what interest could he be to them?

However, in one of his Tuesday lessons at the Salpêtrière,[1] Professor Charcot told the story of a man by the name of Klein, a Hungarian Israelite.[2] "I introduce him to you as *a true descendant of Ahasverus or Cartophilus*, as you would say. The fact is that, like the compulsive (neurotic) travelers of whom I have already spoken, he is constantly driven by an irresistible need to move on, to travel, without being able to settle down anywhere. That is why he has been crisscrossing Europe for three years in search of the fortune which he has not yet encountered."

This is not an isolated case. We have come to recognize several similar examples among the cosmopolitan Israelites who stop at the Salpêtrière. It is always the same story; it is always more or less the same face. Each year we see some poor, miserably dressed devils arriving at the clinic. Their emaciated faces, with deep and sad creases, disappear beneath huge unkempt beards. In a lament-

Reprinted from *Le Juif-errant à la Salpêtrière* (Paris, 1893), pp. 5–8. We are again indebted to folklorist Lee Benzinger for translating this essay from French into English.

able tone, they tell a story filled with painful peripeteia, and if one did not interrupt them, one would probably never hear the end.

Born far away, in the direction of Poland or in the depths of Germany, they have been accompanied since childhood by misery and illness. They fled their native land in order to escape from this or that, but nowhere have they found work which they consider suitable nor the remedy which they seek. And after leagues and leagues traveled on foot, in the wind and rain, in the cold and the most atrocious deprivation, they land at the Salpêtrière, attracted by its renown.

How did they live during these long journeys? Rarely from their work; they do not know how to, or cannot, work. Public charity and, especially, Jewish philanthropic societies have, from one city to another, taken care of their most pressing needs. Besides, they are satisfied with little, being deprived of everything.

Almost all of these Israelites are chronic neurotics, enumerating their pains and dwelling obsessively on the reading of notes about sensations which they have carefully analyzed and recorded: tenacious headaches, digestive problems, persistent insomnia, erratic aches of the limbs or back, etc. Several of them, clearly hysterics, have classic attacks, followed sometimes by hemiplegia and hemiasthesia, which appear or disappear as the result of an emotion or trauma. In addition, all show signs of a special mental state. They are constantly obsessed by the need to travel, to go from city to city, from hospital to hospital, in search of a new treatment, an unfindable remedy. They try all the recommended medications, avid for novelty, but they soon reject them, inventing a frivolous pretext for not continuing, and, with the reappearing impulse, they flee one fine day, drawn by a new mirage of a distant cure.

Let us not forget that they are Jews, and that it is a characteristic of their race to move with extreme ease. At home nowhere, and at home everywhere, the Israelites never hesitate to leave their homes for an important business affair and, particularly if they are ill, to go in search of an effective remedy. Constantly alert for new things, and always quickly informed thanks to their cosmopolitan connections, one sees them coming from all corners of the earth in order to consult reputable physicians. If one of them has been cured, all will know it, and each will be ready to try the same remedy.

In addition, being Israelites, they are particularly susceptible to all sorts of manifestations of nervous disorders. The great frequency of nervous disorders in the Jewish race is a remarkable thing. Whether it is a question of epilepsy, hysteria, neurotic symptoms, or mental illnesses, the proportion of Jews is always considerable. Mr. Charcot returned to this point many times, and his experience in this matter is based on hundreds of cases.[3]

The first Israelite traveler[4] he encountered was a rug merchant who came from Bukhara to Paris fifteen years ago. He appeared one fine morning in a strange costume consisting of a long black tunic pulled in at the waist by a belt with a turquoise-encrusted silver buckle. The long coils of hair, cut in a peculiar fashion, were covered by a Persian cap. He did not know a word of French, and it is by means of a letter in Hebrew, which he presented, that his religion and nationality became known.

It was difficult to make him explain his illness. He complained especially of genital impotence, and this distressed him greatly. But one can assume that his treatment was effective and that, back in his native country, he praised it lavishly, for not a year passed since that time that Mr. Charcot did not see Israelites from the same country come to him complaining of the same symptoms. Their costume has undergone some changes, and they dress more or less according to the current fashion, but they retain their haircut and their little cap which they hide under a top hat.

At the Salpêtrière, one can always see an exotic Jew in treatment. Sometimes he comes from Russia or Hungary, sometimes from Turkey or Armenia. Many come from Odessa and some from India. One of them, a poor rabbi from Tetouan, came for several months to have his sclerosis treated. He arrived punctually every day, accompanied by his daughter and dressed in his Moroccan costume, which is well known in the service.[5]

We shall always remember one incident during a journey to Tunisia and Tripoli that we had the good fortune of making with Mr. Charcot. To his great astonishment, several Israelites stopped him in the streets of Sousse, Tripoli, and Malta. They were former patients who had crossed the Mediterranean to come to him in Paris, seeking a cure for their neuroses.

One must therefore attribute the influx of a large part of our travelers to the ease with which Israelites are able to move about, but it would not be fair to ascribe their truly surprising peregrinations solely to this characteristic of their race. These people are first of all profoundly psychopathic; clinical observations attest to this. In addition, they are subjected to irresistible impulses which entice them into perpetual vagabondage. Their obsession is not absurd in itself; nothing is more legitimate than to go in search of a lucrative job or an effective remedy. What is no longer reasonable is never to be able to continue an occupation undertaken or a treatment initiated, to be always seeking *something else and somewhere else*. What is pathological is not to be able to resist this need to keep moving, which nothing justifies and which may even be detrimental.

Well! Aside from the interesting aspects which these cases present from a neuropathological point of view, we detect a curious analogy between the histories of these patients and that of the legendary character who seems to synthesize them: the *Wandering Jew*. And we have been led to believe that the latter could well be nothing but a *sort of prototype of the psychopathic Israelite peregrinating around the world*.

NOTES

1. Charcot, *Leçons du Mardi*, 19 fev. 1889, pp. 347 ff.
2. [Trans. note: Before the establishment of the independent state of Israel in 1948, Jews of all nationalities were often referred to as Israelites.]
3. In the near future, Dr. Dutil will publish a study on the pathology of Jews where the question will be treated in full. There one will see the preceding assertions developed and verified.
4. Oral communication.
5. [Trans. note: The author is no doubt referring to the military service. The Zouaves—soldiers in the French infantry in North Africa—dressed in wide pantaloons and caps of the tribe where the first Zouaves were recruited.]

AHASVER
A MYTHIC IMAGE
OF THE JEW

E. Isaac-Edersheim

Some years after his visit to Charcot's clinic, Freud outlined a controversial theory of parent-child relationships which he termed the Oedipus complex. According to this notion, there is a rivalry between sons and fathers which may include unconscious expressions of hate and aggression. In this essay by Isaac-Edersheim, Freud's Oedipal theory is applied to the legend of the Wandering Jew (as part of a three part study on Messiah, the Golem, and Ahasuerus). In essence, the Christian son (Jesus) is opposed to the Jewish father (Ahasuerus). The figure of the Jew thus provides a suitable, guilt-free target for Oedipal wishes. (God is thus the father one can love while the Wandering Jew is the father one can despise and abuse.)

The essay was obviously written during the Nazi era, and its daring analysis of supposed Christian father-hatred as an explanation for anti-Semitism is all the more remarkable. In this interpretation, the Wandering Jew is a symbolic expression of a psychopathological condition, but the condition is Christian, not Jewish. For further consideration of possible Oedipal elements in the Christian holy family, see Alan Dundes, "The Hero Pattern and the Life of Jesus," in Interpreting Folklore *(Bloomington, 1980), pp. 223–61.*

Despite the many attempts to interpret the legend of the Wandering Jew, one does not find anything very surprising. Many authors have given up in the face of it.[1] Some others who have critically analyzed this material see the explanation in something which is no explanation at all: i.e., the legend of the Wandering Jew has originated in the mind of a single individual and hence is a product of fantasy created by the author of a popular prose romance.[2]

Of course, such an explanation is absolutely inadequate, for it is clearly apparent that the Wandering Jew, just like the Golem and the Messiah, belongs to those figures into which the popular mind has projected its repressed wishes. It may well be that the author of a popular prose romance has also incorporated a few individual ideas (which are in any case dependent upon the psyche and, as such, must correspond to those common human wishes from which they initially derived). Nevertheless, in the story of the Wandering Jew we find the residue of feelings from many generations, which is already apparent in that this legend has enjoyed such enormous circulation and attention, thus answering something which is deeply hidden yet indestructible. And it is also apparent from this that one encounters everywhere analogies, Christian and heathen, which share common elements or motifs with this myth.[3]

The most widespread interpretation is that Ahasver is a symbol of the Jewish people, who have sinned against Christ and who since then wander about, scattered among nations, and cannot die. From Schudt[4] to Killen, one encounters this explanation.

Naturally, this explanation is correct. The correspondence which we sense between the legendary figure of the Wandering Jew and a certain image of the Jewish people, familiar to us from

Reprinted from the *Internationale Zeitschrift für Psychoanalyse*, 26 (1941): 286–315. (Only pp. 303–15 are presented in translation here.) We are indebted to anthropologist Uli Linke for translating this essay from the German.

numerous tendentious writings and popular fantasies, is too striking to be ignored. The image of a symbolic figure in which the
characteristics of a people are reflected is very popular. One thinks
of John Bull, the Dutch Maiden, *Marianne*, Uncle Sam, etc.

Without doubt, some have projected many features of the Jewish people onto the Wandering Jew. They have sought an explanation for this wandering, eternal people and have been content
to have it in the just punishment and atonement for the crime
committed against Christ. They have been satisfied with this testimony for Christianity which simultaneously triumphed over Judaism.

For us, however, this cannot be a solution. With it, we do not
get to the core of the myth. All puzzles remain unresolved. Why
this punishment, and why this offense? What deeper meaning does
the myth have, and by what psychic forces and wishes was it
formed? And above all, can we trace back and comprehend the
mysterious, irresistible figure of the Wandering Jew?

We all feel that there is something alive within us. Within ourselves, there is an association which merges with the person and
the story of the Wandering Jew, an association which corresponds
to an inner force and meaning. Despite the inadequacy of the
material, it does not let authors, whether literary or scientific, rest.
It also does not let us rest, so that we must dare to attempt to
conquer and comprehend the material.

We have thus far discovered that the Wandering Jew is a symbol
for the Jewish people, something which the use of language and
conceptions of his figure confirm and which, in some way, we
have known all along. We have discovered parallels with several
heathen and Christian figures: Malchus, John, Cartaphilus,
Wodan, Judas. We may assume with some certainty that the legend has more or less consciously adopted some of their themes or
developed from corresponding motifs.

From this, it apparently follows that all attempts to derive or
explain Ahasver by means of other figures must fail from the
outset, and there remains only the one possibility: to find the
explanation within the material itself.

From the associations within ourselves, from the curious pop-

ularity of this figure which so very much occupied the Christian
world of the Middle Ages and which still today has preserved its
symbolic significance, and above all, from its story, its foreign
appearance, its puzzling force, we will, with the aid of the psychoanalytic method, strive to analyze the core around which the
story has been constructed, a core from which feelings and wishes
have created and reshaped the well-known figure.

We may assume that the Wandering Jew was not an insignificant figure. It had to be a powerful figure to capture and inspire
the imagination of many generations. A nameless, countless
crowd of people had slandered, passed sentence upon, and crucified Christ. Who then is this powerful opponent, this Antichrist,
who was never forgiven for this one offense—to have driven Jesus
away from his own threshold—but who was instead placed under
such a dreadful curse?

This indeed has aroused the curiosity of many authors, for this
curse stands in striking opposition to the patience, the kind forgiveness, which history attributes to Jesus.[5] Schudt, the author of
Jüdische Merkwürdigkeiten (1714), has even drawn on this observation as proof for his theory that the Ahasver legend is based upon
individual, worthless fantasy, since one could not acknowledge
something which stands in such contradiction to Christian teaching and tradition.

In literary works, authors have also attempted to come to terms
with this strange contradiction. Some have let the curse come
from a voice in heaven rather than from Jesus himself (Goethe,
Schubart, Arnim); others have so much increased the severity of
Ahasver's offense that they thereby created a crime which justified
and made comprehensible such a heavy penalty. Gutzkow refers
to the "heartless pushing person," Bruch "the evil principle in
humanity," Stern the "ambitious mercenary spirit" who chased
away Christ because he was afraid that he would ruin his business,
and Wedekind "the worshipper of outward success."

How is this to be explained? The reason must lie in the belief
that the Wandering Jew was not just any unwitting sinner, one
among many, but the powerful opponent of Christ, the hated one,
who had to be defeated. Not a simple man, but a superhuman
figure, who had to be degraded. Perhaps one finds a trace, a hint,

of this in the local legends mentioned earlier, which bring the Wandering Jew into association with certain natural phenomena (i.e., the creation of lakes, the existence of exceptionally large rocks). There one can perhaps see creation myths as they exist in countless numbers in other countries, especially in the Orient, deeply rooted in folk fantasy, transmitted by tradition, later reworked, and always reformulated anew. Here, then, the unconscious knowledge of the Wandering Jew as a superhuman figure bursts forth into local tradition. In the intensity of this degradation, one recognizes the feelings of hatred, of respect, and, perhaps also, of never completely repressed love[6] for the originally powerful authority figure. Who was it? In light of the inaccessible material and the indeterminate figure, we will have to search for the secret of his origin in his story—that is, in the only thing which we know about him—in his offense and his punishment.

What significance does the punishment have? From psychoanalysis, we know that the *jus talionis*, "the law of retaliation," rules in the unconscious—"eye for an eye, tooth for a tooth," one of the most often cited and most contested phrases from the Old Testament. Again and again this phrase has been taken out of its historical and psychological context in order to prove the low morality and thirst for revenge (in contrast to Christian love) of the Jewish people. Even without the aid of psychoanalysis, it becomes clear that the immense importance and extreme disgust which have been attached to this passage merely prove that the concern is with something which deeply moves humanity and which wrings its heart. The Christian precepts of forgiveness and charity do not correspond to the unconscious inclinations, and they were therefore the source of these intense and never-ending discussions about this much reviled biblical quotation. A curious incongruity exists in this world. In theory, retaliation and cruelty are considered so vile that even the inner inclination and wish for revenge must be repressed. In practice, the violation of this Christian principle, extending even beyond the "law of retaliation," has never been greatly restricted.

According, then, to the "law of retaliation," we must recognize in Ahasver, whose punishment is to wander about for eternity, someone who once drove away, rejected, or perhaps killed another.[7] In the legend, as it is told to us, one finds a trace of this, a survival of the originally important event: Ahasver pushed Christ off his threshold.

Where do we find the explanation for this forced wandering, for the significance of this curse? In the legend of Cain, the most ancient wanderer. Once we understand the story of Cain, then we will also understand more about Ahasver's offense and punishment:

> Genesis IV:12: But the Lord spoke (to Cain): "When you till the ground, it will no longer yield its crops for you. A vagabond and a fugitive you shall be on the earth."
>
> 13: Then Cain said to the Lord: "Too great is my offense that it could be forgiven."
>
> 14: "Today you are driving me from the land, and I will be hidden from your presence; A vagabond and a fugitive I shall be on the earth, and whoever finds me will kill me."
>
> 15: But the Lord said to him: "Not so, if anyone kills Cain, he will suffer vengeance seven times over." Then the Lord put a mark on Cain so that whoever found him would not kill him.

In order to understand the story of Cain, the nature of his offense, his punishment, and the mark of Cain, we have to know the significance of murder and the position of the murderer among ancient and primitive peoples. A murder, even the killing of an enemy, is and was among the primitives a serious matter which one could not simply ignore. It could have serious consequences which one had to anticipate and influence as much as possible in one's own favor.

The returning, triumphant warrior was and is among all tribes taboo, untouchable, subject to numerous restrictions. He has to live in isolation for a period of time because he is dangerous and brings disaster to everyone who comes near him. After many rituals of repentance and purification, he can then finally return to the community.

The incentive for all these measures is not moral aversion to, or condemnation of, murder, but instead it springs first from fear of the soul of the murdered individual. The countless ceremonies and performances which the murderer has to observe have the function of imploring the soul of the dead to be reconciled to him.

The overpowering fear of demons which very much oppresses and aggravates the life of primitives also dominates their relationship with the dead and especially with those who have been murdered. All the peculiar taboos which the living, especially the murderer, must observe after a blood relative's death, or after a military expedition, can be explained largely by the fear of the ghosts of the dead, the demons into which the dead are transformed and who are a constant threat to the survivors.[8]

Now we perhaps understand that among many ancient peoples and primitive tribes the murderer was not driven away because of moral considerations or for reasons of punishment—that was added later—but rather his presence was a danger for the entire tribe. He was taboo, untouchable. Everybody who came near him was contaminated and thus threatened by the greatest dangers.[9]

Therefore, even if, in the biblical narrative, morality and the sense of the sacredness of human life determine deed and punishment, we may assume that the theme of Cain's wandering goes back to the ancient taboo of the murderer. In this context, the mark on Cain's forehead might have been a warning, a sign that an untouchable was approaching who, according to the very meaning of the word, could not be killed. In the Bible, the mark of Cain was explicitly made a sign for the protection of his life but not, as we may assume according to our argument, a sign of shame and punishment.[10]

A further development of this thought leads to the idea of immortality. If no one may kill Cain, he must live forever. Here we see the parallel to Ahasver, the cursed one, whose restlessness, like Cain's, is eternal; he can neither die nor be killed.

This idea of eternity or immortality has gone through a curious development. The ostracism, which was once considered as an actual protection, became a moral punishment. There, of course, different psychological motives and factors of development began to merge. It was primarily a different attitude toward murder in general. One no longer viewed it exclusively as an action against which one had to seek protection for utilitarian reasons, since contact with the murderer had fatal consequences for everyone, but rather as an action which had to be condemned and punished for moral reasons. Moreover, there was the added problem of death. In the past, as today, everyone faced death with diverging feelings. On the one hand, immortality was a desideratum, a reward, as revealed by the story of the Apostle John; on the other hand, it became a curse, as in the case of Cain and Ahasver.

The longing for immortality must be the result of the fear of death, and it is therefore understandable that one tended to interpret immortality as a reward. Yet deep inside, man sensed that this could not be the right approach toward mastering his fear of death, that to remain on earth forever would be more of a punishment than a reward. It is thus all the more understandable that the reward was transferred to heaven, whereas immortality on earth became a punishment. All things considered, it must be a consolation to be able to project to the outside world thoughts about dying and death, thoughts of murder, whether repressed or not, thoughts about immortality and eternity, and thereby make the attempt to come to terms with them.

Thus in the case of both figures, Cain and Ahasver, the restless wandering and inability to die constitute a consistent idea. Now we shall seek to discover whether we can also find a consistent idea concealed in their misdeed.

Cain murdered his brother Abel because God rejected his offering and accepted the one offered by Abel. He slew his brother out of rage and jealousy.[11] It is clear that this fratricide, like some others, is really directed against the father. In the biblical narrative, we sense the presence of Yahveh (who takes the place of the father; one forgets that another father, Adam, even exists). And it is the father—Yahveh—whom Cain wants to hurt. Of course, this does not preclude that the brother, the rival, can also be the object of hatred and jealousy. On the deepest level of consciousness, however, it is the brother, as Rank explained in detail in *Das Inzestmotiv*, who is always a substitute for the loved and feared father.[12] We can trace this development in myth and fairy tale.[13]

The myth has created consistent character traits and destinies in our two very distant and different figures: the wild murderer Cain kills his gentle brother Abel (we do not read anything about these characteristics in the Bible; however, popular fantasy has fixed the characters in this and in no other way in our imagination); the sinner Ahasver chases away the gentle, suffering Christ.

When we now examine Ahasver's actions and the retribution according to the *jus talionis*, then we may well assume that the offense attributed to him cannot be the original one, just as Ahasver cannot be the original figure. Both offense and perpetrator stand for a more serious crime, for a greater evildoer; both are degraded, faded. Striking and chasing away point to the more serious crimes: murder and expulsion.[14] In the vague but powerful Ahasver figure, we recognize the demoted yet never defeated adversary and predecessor of Christ; in him we recognize the eternal god Yahveh once more.

We can thus integrate the relationship between Ahasver and Jesus into the long sequence of mythological (once real) events which include the brother-brother and son-father antagonism, with the expulsion and murder of the elders by the younger generation, or the reverse. This should mean: sons see in the father the rival for the favor of the mother, the authority which governs and impedes their lives. That is why the sons have sometimes overcome the respect and the love which also grows and driven away or killed the father. Yet the sons themselves become older, become themselves fathers, and within them grows the fear of revenge, heightened by the jealousy of the younger generation which has life still ahead of it and will take their place. For this reason, one often finds the story of the father who has his newborn child killed or exposed so that in the course of things the retaliation may not be fulfilled. Yet, when the son escapes this fate, he usually returns to his parental home as an adolescent and, consciously or unconsciously, kills his father and usurps his position (Zeus,[15] Osiris,[16] Oedipus, Parsifal, and all other examples which Rank explains in *Das Inzestmotiv* and *Der Mythus von der Geburt des Helden*).

Thus the primal event (reconstructed by Freud in *Totem und Tabu*), which always has to repeat itself, is, after its repression, forever projected anew in myth and legend, in gods and mortals. What we are told about Uranos, Kronos and Zeus, about Seth and Osiris, and countless other godly figures, with variations which depend upon the amount of repression and guilt, we see recur in the story of Jesus and Yahveh, in the degraded figure of Ahasver.

We thus see how, in the world of gods, in this collective world of fantasy, the generations mutually fight and displace one another. The myth tells how, over and over again, new gods rise up, are driven away, fade, and make way for new, triumphant generations.

Yet, from the history of religions, and from myths and legends, we can establish that the old gods do not release their worshippers without further ado. One does not break away with impunity from an authority, who for us was the highest. One is not a triumphant rebel without being haunted by fear and guilt at the same time.

We know from the religious history of ancient peoples that one often tried to escape these difficulties by still showing the old, defeated gods some sort of respect to be on the safe side; one still created for them a modest little place, albeit in the shadow of the new, triumphant god. When monotheism prevailed, this was no longer possible. The strictest monotheism, as propagated by the prophet, permitted no compromise. Folk belief, however, is exceedingly tenacious, difficult to influence and eradicate. Even after the victory of Christianity, superstition did not cease to exist. We meet the old gods again in popular superstition, distorted, but not totally unrecognizable. The evil spirits and demons are the shadows of the old gods (cf. Wodan and the Wild Huntsman). When misery increased, when illness and shortages threatened, then one often turned to the old gods, trying to appease them, to bribe them, so that they would let go of their victim. In this way, one can retrieve the old heathen, as well as the Oriental and Greek, gods.[17]

When one has become fairly absorbed in what the old gods, the old authority, meant to humanity, with what feelings of doubt, fear, and awe one stood face to face with them, then we can begin to grasp the power which Yahveh, the God of the Jewish people and the Old Testament, still retained after the revolution of Christianity. The single, eternal God disappeared, yet He remained. Despite the fact that the revolution had gained victory through Jesus' uprising, God the Father remained even for Christendom the highest, to whom—in the end—all love and respect had to flow. But what kind of god was this? Was he the sole god of the

Old Testament, which also remained the Bible for Christians? Or was he a new god? (A so-called god of love in contrast to the notorious god of vengeance.)

In light of this confusion of perceptions, it was no wonder that ambivalent feelings were felt towards the Jewish god, feelings of hatred and contempt and, at the same time, of love and respect, because he was also their own god, the father of Jesus, and the father of everyone. This ambivalence was too dangerous and too difficult. The feelings of hatred and aggression were projected outward; they created Ahasver.[18]

Now we also comprehend why this legend was so exceptionally popular and inspiring, although not inspiring enough to cause the creation of a work of art worthy of this figure or able to solve its mystery. We understand, too, why this figure is so vague; it had to be unrecognizable in its degradation and, above all, the single god could only continue to exist outside of space, time, and form.[19]

The religious turbulence of the Reformation projected onto the Wandering Jew the old problems of increasing feelings of doubt and aggression and awareness of sin, which have again become a burning issue today. In Ahasver, Judaism was condemned and Christianity confirmed. He was a twofold witness of the offense and the deserved punishment of the Jews as well as of the reality of Christ, of his life and suffering, and of the affirmation of Christianity.

In the course of history, his figure has transformed and changed to a point past recognition. Layer upon layer was added, often completely concealing the original figure, often with the original reemerging. Yet, despite all these layers, all these additions and new interpretations, again and again one will discover this myth of the father-god as the original core.

Within the Wandering Jew wanders the father-god rejected by the young generation, the symbol of the intergenerational struggle, who continues to remain alive yet had to be humiliated in the attempt to dominate him, to forget him.

Within him further wanders Cain, the eternal murderer and rebel.

Within him wanders the murderer of primitive times, pursued by the ghost of his victim, a danger thereby to every member of the tribe, a regression to a primitive stage when murder was automatically punished by taboo, which could strike anyone who came in contact with him, including his murderers. In the Wandering Jew wanders the Jewish people.

NOTES

1. See, for instance, *Religion in Geschichte und Gegenwart*: "The legend is to be understood as myth, as the framing of an idea. Which idea, however, lies at the bottom of this myth cannot be determined, despite the countless attempts at interpretation and poetic revisions, in which even Goethe himself participated."

Baring-Gould, in *Curious Myths of the Middle Ages* (London, 1888), states: "But no myth is wholly without foundation, and there must be some substantial verity upon which this vast superstructure of legend has been raised. What that is, I am unable to discover."

2. For example, the *Enzyklopädie für Theologie und Kirche* writes: "Then, that we are here not dealing with a gradual reformulation undertaken by the folk but rather with an invention by a single individual becomes apparent, among other things, in the sudden appearance of the narrative." We find approximately the same idea in F. Helbig's *Die Sage vom Ewigen Juden* (1874), p. 51: "It thus almost seems as if our legend itself is an invention of the Christian priests, just as its first rendition also stems from a monk, perhaps created with the intent to sweep aside the emerging doubts about the actual existence of Christ by means of the presentation of a witness still alive."

3. Most of the authors have also sensed this, more or less consciously, and are of the opinion that here it is a matter of a myth and of an ancient fantasy, deeply rooted in the past, even if they have been unable to follow its traces any further.

Compare the previously cited conclusion of the article "Der Ewige Jude," in *Religion in Geschichte und Gegenwart*, and W. Zirus: "The Wandering Jew is, as we noted above, a literary product. That which the folk ascribe to him in terms of mythical features has been adapted later from the old legendary figures"; a combination of contradictory convictions. [Ed. note: The citation comes from Zirus, *Der ewige Jude in der Dichtung* (Leipzig, 1928), p. 81.]

4. "This Wandering Jew is in essence not a single person but the

whole of the Jewish people, who, after the crucifixion of Christ, wandered scattered throughout the world, and who, according to the Witness of Christ, shall remain until Judgment Day." The *Encyclopaedia Judaica* observes, "The point of the legend doubtless turns against the Jewish people's tenacity for life." And see also the *Jewish Encyclopedia*: "The figure of the doomed sinner forced to wander without the hope of rest in death till the millennium impressed itself upon the popular imagination and then passed into literary art, mainly with reference to the seeming immortality of the wandering Jewish race." [Ed. note: Earlier in his essay, Isaac-Edersheim refers to Johann Jakob Schudt, *Jüdische Merkwürdigkeiten* (1714), and Alice Killen, "L'Évolution de la légende du Juif errant," *Revue de Littérature Comparée* (1925).]

5. See also Grasse, *Die Sage vom Ewigen Juden* (Dresden, 1844), p. 29, "Most suspicious seems the circumstance that, in the very case of this man, our Savior should have made an exception to his infinite patience, particularly since he was nailed to the cross and prayed for his tormentors and spoke: 'Father, forgive them for they know not what they do' (Luke 23 and 24)."

6. In this context, I shall note the curious phenomenon that this ambivalent emotional orientation is perhaps also expressed in the following: the Buttadeus mentioned earlier, who is brought into association with Ahasver or who is perhaps identical with him, and whose name means "the one who beats God," appears in Italy also under the name "Servo di Dio," in Spanish as "Servo di Dios."

7. The legend of the Gypsies' origin furnishes typical proof of this. Of course, one has always wondered how this strange, nomadic existence is to be explained, and one has construed the answer according to the 'law of retaliation' in the following manner: When Mary went to Egypt with the baby Jesus, she begged the ancestors of the Gypsies for hospitality. They are said to have denied her request and forced her to move on. As a form of punishment, Gypsies and their descendants must keep wandering forever.

8. In *Totem und Tabu* (chapter 2, "Das Tabu und die Ambivalenz der Gefühlsregnungen"), Freud explains the psychological origin of this anxiety. With the concept "fear of demons," nothing is yet explained, since it is not a real but a psychic anxiety. A taboo, Freud explains, emerges where a forbidden action comes into conflict with unconscious human inclinations; this means in our case that the prohibition to kill someone comes into conflict with the generally unconscious wish to kill, which probably everyone has once harbored against his fellows and especially against those who are closest to him ("The taboo is an ancient prohibition, imposed externally (by an authority) and directed against the strongest human desires. The desire to breach it persists in the unconscious; human beings who obey the taboo have an ambivalent orientation toward the object of the taboo.") The fear of demons is thereby

explained as the outward projection of hostile feelings against the deceased, who have now become hostile ghosts and threaten the mourner with disaster and bad luck.

9. See Frazer, "The Mark of Cain," *Folklore in the Old Testament*: "The reason alleged here for banishing the murderer from the camp probably gives the key to all the similar restrictions laid on murderers and among the primitive peoples; the seclusion of their persons from society is dictated by no moral aversion to their crime; it springs from prudential motives, which resolve themselves into a simple dread of the dangerous ghost, by which the homicide is supposed to be pursued and haunted."

10. Frazer, however, proffers still other, somewhat diverging hypotheses: "Thus the mark of Cain may have been a mode of disguising a homicide or of rendering him so repulsive or formidable in appearance that his victim's ghost would either not know him or at least give him a wide berth."

11. Genesis IV, 3: In the course of time Cain brought some of the fruits of the soil as an offering to the Lord. Gen. IV, 4: But Abel brought fat portions from some of his firstborn of his flock. The Lord looked with favor on Abel and his offering. Gen. IV, 5: But on Cain and his offering he did not look with favor. So Cain was very angry, and his face was downcast. Gen. IV, 6: There the Lord said to Cain, "Why are you angry? Why is your face downcast?. . ."

12. Rank traces this hatred and the rivalry back to the wish for incest such as exists between children and parents. The relationship between brothers and sisters is only a transference of the original bond between parents and children: ". . . and already point out that the sexual inclinations of siblings with its negative consequences (fraternal hatred and jealousy), just as we learned to understand it in the inner life of the individual as a second, less offensive level of the parental incest, so even in the history of development it is merely the necessary consequence of the original, but soon prohibited, marriage between parents and children . . ." (p. 416).

Rank also explains the hostility between Cain and Abel or between Cain and Yahveh in terms of this wish for incest, in connection with which he makes reference to various old legends. (We also find them in Ben Gorion, *Die Sagen der Juden*, pp. 95 ff.) Rank also cites modern literary creations in which a conflict takes place between two brothers over one woman, who is their sister, sometimes a twin sister, or in which Cain's love for his mother Eve is central (pp. 556, 557).

13. See also Rank, "Das Brudermärchen," in *Beiträge zur Mythenforschung* (1922).

14. This is also evident in Ahasver. It is not without significance that he chases Jesus off his threshold just as Jesus is on his way to be crucified.

Yet Jesus does not kill Ahasver for this as a form of retaliation; instead, we go back to the old primitive time when the murderer was declared taboo and thus had to wander about.

15. Uranus is emasculated and driven away by his son Cronus. For fear that the same could be done to him by his children, Cronus swallows them all immediately after their birth. His wife eventually substitutes a rock for the newborn child. This rescued child is Zeus, who for his part kills Cronus and becomes the highest god.

16. The story of Seth and Osiris is a brother-myth, and thus belongs to those myths which, as Rank explains, represent another level and substitute for the original father-son rivalry. Seth kills Osiris out of hate and jealousy, cuts him into pieces, and throws him into the Nile. He is rescued from there by his sister and lover Isis, who brings him back to life with the aid of other gods.

17. Heine felt drawn to these defeated gods (because, as he himself explains, he always stood on the side of the oppressed), and, in addition to the poem "Die Götter Griechenlands," he dedicated to this theme two interesting essays: "Götter im Exil" and "Elementargeister." With his great literary and intuitive-psychological talent, he creates an image of the mysterious, of the unreal and yet inescapable appeal (cf. the Lorelei motif) which still emanates from those old gods, who, even as the living dead, arrange their meetings and hostly festivities from which issues a tremendous splendor which at once entices and repels, while inexorably pushing everyone into destruction who cannot withdraw from it. In "Götter im Exil," Heine writes, "Here again, I speak about the transformation into demons which the Graeco-Roman gods suffered when Christianity attained supremacy in the world." Popular belief ascribed to those gods a truly real yet hopeless existence, in this opinion being in complete agreement with the teachings of the Church. The latter did by no means declare the old gods to be chimera, such as the philosophers had done, to be products of falsehood and error; instead it rather took them for evil demons, who tumbled from their height of power through the victory of Christ, who now continued their activities on earth in the darkness of old temple ruins or magical forests, and who tempted weak Christians who thereby lost their way, with their enticing devilish tricks, with lust and beauty, and especially with dance and song. Compare also the poem "Die Götter Griechenlands":

> No, nevermore, those are no clouds.
> Those they are themselves, the gods of Hellas,
> Who once ruled the world with joy,
> But now, thrust aside and deceased,
> Move about as monstrous ghosts
> In the midnight sky.

18. In his book *Der eigene und der fremde Gott* (Vienna, 1923), pp. 74 ff., Th. Reik demonstrated that the figure of Judas must be understood in the same manner as the counterpart of Jesus. The peoples who adopted Christianity were more burdened the more time passed by feelings of repentance and guilt because of the revolution which had taken place against the father. Their aggressions found an outlet in the figure of Judas who took the sins upon himself and allowed Jesus to become the Savior. With this perspective also the relationship between Ahasver and Jesus is to be understood as a parallel to the one between Judas and Jesus.

19. W. Zirus, whose books I have repeatedly cited, in *Der Ewige Jude in der Dichtung*, p. 151, offers an excellent characterization of Ahasver, without, however, reaching an explanation of the very accurately understood peculiarity of this figure.

"The figure of the Wandering Jew is not grounded in reality; he has no historical name; his eternal life is not fixed by space or time. Bound by no tradition, he floats in mystical darkness which becomes especially apparent in comparison with the clearly outlined figure of Christ, his only counterpart. When observed realistically, even the logic of his curse is relatively weak; Ahasver's hard-heartedness against Christ is not sufficiently motivated in the traditional narrative. Esthetically, this could have led to the vagueness, dogmatically, also to the interpretation which opposed the church. Even worse, the figure lacked inner growth through various stages. Christ goes a long way to his goal; we see him as he grows from a boy to a teacher; he becomes a martyr and eventually triumphs as a transfigured one. Even Faust has his fluctuating development, even Prometheus, but Ahasver is a fixed figure. A single event is told about him, and then he wanders without change. He is rooted in eternity rather than in reality; his life passes, far from human relationships, without climax or end. He does not appear to be a person; his shadowy, endless existence rather induces aversion."

AHASVER,
THE ETERNAL WANDERER
PSYCHOLOGICAL ASPECTS

S. Hurwitz

From Freudian beginnings a number of competing psychological schools arose. Among these, Jungian theory is perhaps the best known. The theory has been widely applied to myth and other forms of folk narrative. Perhaps the most striking and controversial concept in Jungian theory involves the archetype, which is allegedly part of what Jung terms the collective unconscious. One archetype, for example, is the "shadow," which represents the dark, or negative, side of the human psyche.

In this essay, S. Hurwitz applies Jungian depth psychology to the legend of the Wandering Jew. Hurwitz discusses the earlier essay by Isaac-Edersheim, but he does not even mention the Oedipal reading of the legend proposed there. (Jungians are much less interested in sexual interpretations than are Freudians.)

The idea that the Wandering Jew might be related to biblical Cain and other wandering figures in various cultures was suggested by Jung himself in Wandlungen und Symbole der Libido, *first published in 1912. At that time, Jung went so far as to offer a solar interpretation of the legend of the Wandering Jew. He claims "the wish-fulfillment idea of the legend is very clear. The mystic material for it is the immutable model of the Sun's course. The Sun sets periodically, but does not die." See* Psychology of the Unconscious *(New York, 1925), pp. 216–17.*

*Jung's interpretation can be contrasted with the earlier suggestion
of Wesselofsky that "It's easy to see how the Wandering Jew can
be associated with the phases of the moon. They both seem to be
dying, and, yet, they are both always rejuvenated." In support of
his thesis, Wesselofsky cited a Ukrainian text which includes the
following: "Every four weeks the moon is reborn, and, therewith,
the Jews who crucified Christ and kept watch over the Lord's
tomb in Jerusalem are also reborn. These Jews are still standing
there, and when they are asked by passers-by, 'When were you
born?' they answer, 'Yesterday,' 'When will you die?' 'Tomorrow.'" See A. Wesselofsky, "Der ewige Jude,"* Archiv für
Slavische Philologie, *5 (1881): 401. For another Ukrainian
example of the Wandering Jew-moon linkage, consider the following text recorded in Galicia in the 1880s: "There was such a Jew:
when they were torturing Christ and were already taking him to
be crucified, Christ came up with his cross and wanted to lean
awhile against the Jew's house and to rest, but he cried: 'Go
hence! Go hence!' Christ turned around and said to him: 'I shall
go, but you too must go, and roam the earth until the Last Judgment.' So he is still wandering. He has recently been seen, people
say, up our way. But it is hard to recognize him, because when
the moon is old he is very, very old, and when the moon is young
he turns young again." For this text and translation of the text
cited by Wesselofsky, see Avrahm Yarmolinsky, "The Wandering Jew: A Contribution Toward the Slavonic Bibliography of
the Legend,"* in Studies in Jewish Bibliography and Related
Subjects in Memory of Abraham Solomon Freidus (1867–
1923) *(New York, 1929), pp. 327–28.*

*Jung's comments on the Wandering Jew were not limited to his
solar interpretation. In an essay on Wotan first published in 1936,
Jung mentioned the legend in passing: "Wotan is a restless wanderer who creates restlessness and stirs up strife, now here now
there, or works magic. He was soon changed into the devil by
Christianity and only lived on in fast flickering-out local tradition
as a ghostly hunter who was seen with his retinue on stormy
nights. But the role of the restless wanderer was taken over in the
Middle Ages by Ahasuerus, the Wandering Jew, which is not a
Jewish but a Christian legend. In other words, the motif of the*

wanderer who has not accepted Christ, was projected on to the Jews, just as we always rediscover our own psychic contents, which have become unconscious, in other people." See C. G. Jung, Essays on Contemporary Events *(London, 1947), p. 3.*

There has been no lack of attempts to interpret the figure of the Wandering Jew. However, most of the attempts at interpretation are not of a psychological nature but are rather more historical or literary. Only in recent times have several psychologists concerned themselves with this subject matter. But just like almost all the historians and literary critics, they have also been taken in by the temptation to identify the figure of Ahasver with the whole of the Jewish people, a tendency which has prevailed since Schudt (1714: 488 ff.).

Modern and psychoanalytically oriented authors have repeatedly made an attempt to present the Wandering Jew as a decidedly Jewish myth which contains a reflection of Jewish character. Isaac-Edersheim (1941) and later Graber (1958) have held this view. But what both of these authors have failed to notice is the essential fact *that the Ahasver myth is not a Jewish myth at all.* Neither in the Biblical nor the Talmudic-Rabbinic writings, nor in the prose literature of the Aggada or the Midrash, nor the immensely rich scripts of the kabbalah can such a figure be attested even by way of intimation. And on those very few occasions when Jewish authors have treated the material (H. Heine, A. Goldfaden, E. Fleg, D. Pinsker, E. Zangwill, and others), it can be proven without difficulty that they took the material from secondary Christian sources. On these occasions, by the way, a certain transformation of the *mythologem* [mythological theme] was able to assert itself insofar as the negative features of Ahasver vanished throughout, and the Wandering Jew became a positive symbol.[1] In Jewish literary tradition, the Jewish concept of the *'am 'olam,* 'the eternal people,' most closely approximates the figure of Ahasver. This

Reprinted from *Analytische Psychologie,* 6 (1975): 450–71. (Only pp. 459–71 are presented in translation here.) We are indebted again to anthropologist Uli Linke for translating this portion of the essay for this volume.

concept, however, does not refer so much to the existence of a single individual as to the totality of the people of Israel. Also, the eternal existence in this context is by no means to be understood as the punishment for an offense, but rather as a divine promise, even a duty: to serve Yahveh as "a people of priests and as a holy people." Even the various prophetic promises about an 'olam haba, a forthcoming eternal era of salvation and bliss which will supersede the present era—the 'olam haze—of sin and disaster, do not correspond to those conceptions which are expressed in connection with the Ahasver myth.

Although both of the authors mentioned above have repeatedly pointed to the decidedly mythic character of Ahasver, they have done so without drawing any psychological conclusions from this observation. Throughout, they even identify themselves with the all too simplistic rational explanation that Ahasver is a sort of allegory or reflection of the Jewish people, which wanders through history without home or roots and which will only come to rest at a point in the distant future. Perhaps unconsciously it was implied that "at the end of all time," i.e., at Jesus' return, which especially in the Middle Ages was expected soon, the Jewish people would acknowledge Christ and would thereby be redeemed. Up to the present day, this interpretive attempt has remained the most generally recognized reading of the myth, so we must briefly analyze it.

Isaac-Edersheim (1941) has for the first time attempted to offer a psychoanalytic interpretation of the problem, even if it is not free of completely arbitrary speculations and internal contradictions. Following Grässe (1844) and Helbig (1874), he has primarily pointed to the mythic character of the hero. On the other hand, he correctly notes that one "without doubt projects many features of the Jewish people onto the Wandering Jew." In a somewhat forced fashion, he attempts to identify Ahasver with Yahveh, as the opponent of Christ, an attempt in which he does not succeed satisfactorily. Though Isaac-Edersheim rejects all projections, in the conclusion of his discussion he comes back to his initial statement: "Within the Wandering Jew wanders the Jewish people."

Graber (1958) has adopted Isaac-Edersheim's train of thought and has sought to develop it further. In this case, he has advanced an original hypothesis which, from a psychological standpoint, is interesting. He advocates the view that the Jewish people, as a collectivity as well as every individual Jew insofar as he lives in Galuth (the Diaspora), carries inside himself an Ahasverian base structure and that the myth of Ahasver reflects these Jewish character traits. According to Graber, these Ahasverian aspects of the Jew are expressed through an "inner restlessness and drive to move." Graber attempts to attribute the cause of this inner turmoil and restlessness to the historically conditioned inner conflict between the originally nomadic and later sedentary way of life of the Jewish people, which Israel experienced during the land acquisition at Canaan. Given this perspective, one could see within the Jewish people as a collectivity, but also within every single present-day Jew, a "tendency toward nomadism, a life in a foreign country and among a foreign population." Jewish psychology would thus be characterized by a continuous inner conflict between two mutually opposed tendencies. On the one hand, it would come to renewed attempts at "assimilation, integration, identification with the foreigners," in this way amounting to a virtual "denial of the characteristic Jewish nature." On the other hand, one could discern the ancient drive toward nomadism and, therewith, an "escape from sedentarization." In this sense, the soul of the Jew, insofar as he lived in the Diaspora, would be characterized by an inner struggle between the longing for the lost native country and the self-denial in a foreign land. In this conflict, the Ahasverian destiny would in the end prevail: *the Jew is forced to wander from within.* The following discussion will explain the various reasons why Graber's hypothesis is untenable, as impressive as it may seem initially, especially from a psychological point of view.

Above all, it seems to me that Graber has to a certain degree understood the facts of the case historically correctly, but he has interpreted them completely wrong. First, it must be said that one can hardly speak of a completely nomadic way of life for the Ḥabiru tribes, except perhaps during the brief, mythical, early era of the patriarchs. And even then, prior to the acquisition of land, these people led only a seminomadic existence, since they had become livestock farmers relatively early.

Further, it must be said that the opposing tendencies toward
assimilation and toward preservation of independent characteristics are in no way typical of the character of the Jewish people.
They are rather the expression of a psychology which is by no
means valid only for Jews. It applies likewise to all those primarily
Mediterranean and certain Indo-European peoples who in their
early history invaded foreign areas of cultivation, either from the
steppes of inner Asia and Arabia or from migratory movements
of other sorts, became sedentary, and more or less by force assim-
ilated the native population. By the way, such migrations existed
long before the influx of the Hebrew tribes into Canaan. At a later
time, from the desert, Semitic as well as Indo-European peoples
repeatedly invaded areas of cultivation, where they became sedentary. To these belong not only the Achaeans, Iranians, Scythians,
Hittites, etc., but also, at a later time, the Dorians and Etruscans,
the latter, as everybody knows, becoming the real carriers of culture in the Roman empire. Very similar is the case of those tribes
which, at the time of the Dorian migration—which was not much
later than the acquisition of land in Canaan—invaded Greece from
the steppes of Asia and drove away the native population to the
Aegean Islands and to the mainland of Asia Minor. Especially in
modern times, there has been no lack of attempts to demonstrate
the Etruscan character of the Romans up to the present day. Yet,
in my opinion, this is a matter of highly conjectural speculation
which historically as well as psychologically stands on unsup-
ported foundations. In any case, insofar as one actually believes in
a structural influence through migration, one would have to assume it equally for most Mediterranean peoples and even for most
central European peoples. Besides, with such migrations it is the
general rule that the invading tribal units adopt the often more
advanced culture of the conquered native population. However,
this has only limited application in the case of the Hebraic tribes,
since the Canaanite religion, with its worship of nature and its
matriarchal orientation, could only to a limited degree prove itself
superior to the more patriarchal Hebraic culture, with its strict
monotheistic Yahveh cult. Based on these considerations, one can
justly agree with the view put forth by Cornioley (1941), who

perceives the opposing behavior between nomadic and sedentary life-styles as the expression of a common human problem.

Graber's hypotheses collapse above all because they are based on completely false historical presuppositions. Even those who have but a rather narrow range of knowledge of Western history, and specifically of the history of the Jewish people, can furnish proof without difficulty that almost all Jewish migratory movements, starting with the Babylonian captivity throughout the whole of the Middle Ages to modern times, *can never be explained on the basis of inner causes*. The numerous migrations of the Jews were entirely the result of forcible mass expulsion, which resulted from the infamous accusations concerning the desecration of eucharistic wafers, ritual murders, and the poisoning of wells. To give only a few examples, in Germany, the forced expulsion took place around 1012, in England about 1290, in Hungary in 1360, in France in 1394, and in Bohemia in 1542. A classic example of this is the Iberian Peninsula, where in 1492 in Spain and in 1498 in Portugal more than 300,000 Jews were forcibly expelled insofar as they did not submit to baptism even though they had been settled there for more than 1500 years. Was it in this case also the "Ahasverian character" which drove these people to poverty, suffering, and despair? To postulate this would border on cynicism.

From this perspective, one can assert with certainty that Graber, with his hypothesis about the Ahasverian-nomadic character of the Jews, succumbed to the dangers of psychologism. His theory does not hold up either from a historical or from a psychological point of view.

Neither the explanations of Isaac-Edersheim nor the hypotheses of Graber are capable of satisfying even slightly a psychological orientation. To be sure, both authors emphasize the mythical character of their hero, but they do so without drawing any psychological conclusions whatsoever from this fact. But it is exactly here, in my opinion, that the starting point lies from which one could gain a psychological understanding of the Ahasver myth.

Specifically, if the case of Ahasver—as we have already established—is not concerned with a Jewish myth, i.e., a genuine creation by a layer of the collective soul of the Jewish people, then

we must ask ourselves, where did this myth begin? In all this, it is
particularly striking that the figure of Ahasver, much in contrast
to certain other related mythical figures such as Faust or Tannhäuser, appears relatively colorless and vague. For this reason, Zirus
(1928) has tried to present the figure of Ahasverus as a sort of
"literary creation." But this very vagueness might have been an
additional reason why this figure attracted numerous projections.
Thus, we cannot avoid drawing upon later legendary and mythical material, besides the original myth, for purposes of interpretation.

When we trace the individual elements which underlie the different Ahasver narratives, we can distinguish three principal
sources: Christian, Jewish, and heathen-Germanic. The Christian
motifs mainly go back to a figure mentioned in the synoptic gospels, the immortal John, who on occasion emerges as a completely
mythical figure. Moreover, the eternal John presents the positive
aspects of that figure whose negative opposing force is Ahasver.

At the same time, certain connections of Ahasver to the Antichrist should not be overlooked. To be sure, Ahasver is not
exactly identified with the Antichrist, but in the Christian tradition there exist certain oppositions: Christ is about to meet his
death in Golgotha and thereby is to find his peace; Ahasver is
condemned never to be able to die. Leschnitzer (1962) has pointed
out that at the time of Paulus von Eitzen, that is, at the composition of the German chapbooks, in the so-called Protestant theology, the "blissful death" meant for Christians the highest
expectation of happiness. The inability to die means, from this
perspective, the greatest curse that can befall a human being. Just
as at the return of Christ, according to the legend, the Antichrist
will find his death and therewith his redemption, so also Ahasver
will then be redeemed. Besides, the expectation of this deliverance
at the "Last Judgment" shows how much—psychologically
speaking—the whole problem has been repressed from consciousness and pushed into the unconscious.

The Jewish characteristics emerge, above all, in the Cainlike
character of Ahasver. Cain is a human being who places himself
outside of human and divine laws, who as a result of his wicked
deed has become a vagrant and a fugitive. Even Cain is in a certain

sense a Buttadeus, who in his brother Abel has struck God himself. Despite all that, Cain also has some positive features: as a farmer and a founder of cities, he is an actual carrier of culture. In the Apocalypse of Moses, he is referred to as *Adiophotos*, "the one without light," "the dark one," but at the same time as *Diaphotos*, "the enlightened." In the apocryphal book *The Life of Adam and Eve*, Cain is referred to as the "son with light." According to a Midrash, the mark of Cain did not consist of a flaming sign but of a horn (Midrash Ber. Rabba 22,11). The horned Cain thereby takes on a sunlike quality. On certain images imprinted on coins, the sun-hero Jupiter-Ammon is similarly equipped with horns. The intrinsic relationship between horns and rays is evident in the Hebraic use of language, where the word *qeren*, the plural *quarnaim*, is in a like manner employed for "horns" as well as "rays." In Exodus 34:29, it is said about Moses that the skin of his face shone during his meeting with God. Similarly, it is written in a Midrash: during the hour when God was occupied with the writing of the *Torah*, a ray of light emanating from the holy script passed over to Moses, and his face began to radiate (Midrash Megalle Amuqot 91c). As is well known, Aquila and the Vulgate have described Moses as having horns, since in this passage they erroneously translated the Hebrew word for "rays" as "horns."

Another connection to the Jewish scriptures is evident in Ahasver's relationship to Elijah and Enoch. About both it is reported that they did not die but were removed from earth to meet with God alive. According to the Epistle of John, Enoch and Elijah will appear on the Day of Judgment and testify against the Antichrist (Apocalypse of John, 11:3). Within the body of mythical ideas of numerous peoples, it is stated that their sun-heroes will return at the end of the present era. In Judaism, it was Moses, Enoch, and Elijah to whom the Midrash refers as the returning figures (Midrash Deut. Rabba 3). In Christianity, it was Christ and Elijah, the latter of whom was identified with the Apostle John early on (Mark, 9:12; Matthew, 11:14). An Islamic-Sufi parallel speaks of the immortal Chadhir and his companion Dhulqarnain (Jung, 1952:323). The latter is the "two-horned": namely, Alexander the Great equipped with horns, that is, rays. As Ahasver is referred to as the "eternally young one," so is Chadhir also the "eternally

young one." And like Ahasver, so is Chadhir also a "never tiring
wanderer." According to Tabari, who is cited by C. G. Jung
(1952:322), Chadhir, together with Dhulqarnain, discovered the
secret river of life in the Far East and drank from it, after which
both of them became immortal.

Perhaps the most significant parallel to Ahasver appears to lie,
however, in heathen-Germanic mythology. To this domain belongs above all Ahasver's relationship to Wotan.[2] Like Ahasver,
Wotan is also a restless wanderer (see Saxo Grammaticus, *Gesta
Danorum*, 1886). His nature as a continuously roving and wandering god is expressed in numerous legendary narratives in which
Wotan appears first as a beggar, then as an unknown singer or
strange guest. These aspects are shown by his various names:
Vegtamr, "the one who knows the way," *Gangleri,* "the one tired
of walking," or *Ganggratr*, "the one who gives advice while wandering from place to place" (Ninck, 1935:73 ff.).

Like Ahasver, Wotan also is described as a grey-haired old man,
with a coarse long coat and a hat, pulled far down. It is said about
him that he wears a wide-brimmed hat, which "draws a long
shadow over his forehead." Therefore, he is sometimes also called
Sidhoeter, which means "the one with a wide-brimmed hat" (Höfler, 1934:36; Menzel, 1885:166 ff.).

The close relationship between Ahasver and Wotan, however,
is made especially explicit in those later folk traditions in which
Pontius Pilate, who is a related figure, appears. Like Ahasver,
Pilate can find neither rest nor peace because of his condemnation
of Christ; he flees from God and man, from country to country.
According to one version, he is called to Rome to account for his
execution of Christ. There he commits suicide, but the waves of
the Tiber into which his corpse is thrown refuse to accept him.
According to another legend, during his aimless travels through
numerous countries, he also comes to Switzerland, where he is
sighted in different regions. He flees to Lucerne, but everywhere
people shout at him: "See there judge Pilate!" He comes to the
mountain called Fräkmünt, which is later named Pilate after him,
and he wants to drown himself in the small, mountain lake at the
foot of the peak. He suddenly meets Ahasver, who strangles him
and throws his corpse into the lake, where it sinks. Since that

time, the lake is cursed. During some nights, it is lashed by sudden storms. It is maintained that once a year Pilate shows himself there in his official uniform as a Roman judge. Whoever meets him must soon die.

But especially in the Mt. Pilate region, the legend of Wotan and his wild army has always remained alive; one may even say that Mt. Pilate has become the true Wotan's mountain. In his *Pilati Montis Historia*, Capeller tells how the "raging army" has been repeatedly seen on the mountain. The Lucerne city scribe Renward Cysat tells in the sixteenth century that the mountain "is loaded with evil spirits." For this reason, no one dared to climb it in the past. Also, as reported by Cysat, "there are still other ghosts in these wild, tall Alps. Several can only be heard and seen by night, such as the riding ones but also those who apparently take the shape of several persons who one knew during their lifetime. Some come up the mountain and through the forest, riding and running to the Pilate Lake" (Cysat, 1935:73). In this manner, in the literature of legends, Mt. Pilate became the mountain of Wotan, Pilate, and Ahasver. And just as in Germanic legend Wotan is the god of the storm, so in France Ahasver's appearance is linked to storms, thunderstorms, famine, and epidemics.

The motif of the Wandering Jew, however, is found not only in the heathen-Germanic culture. In the literature of Sumer, Buddhism, Judaism, Christianity, and Islam, it can likewise be attested as an explicitly archetypal motif. In Sumerian-Babylonian mythology, particularly in the Gilgamesh Epic, we find perhaps the most well-known of these figures who during their lifetime were granted immortality (de Liagre Böhl, 1960:80; Heidel, 1949:74; Meissner, 1902:9; Schott, 1958). This epic was originally based on a Sumerian song cycle which was discovered in the library of the Assyrian King Assurbanipal by Layard, Rassam, and Smith. Various Akkadian fragments and pieces in Hittite, Assyrian, and Greek were found later.

During his nocturnal sea journey to see his ancestor Utnapishtim, who had survived the Great Flood and thereby has become immortal, the hero meets the goddess Siduri, who initially dissuades him from his undertaking. Then at his insistence she refers him to Utnapishtim's navigator Urshanabi, who is prepared to undertake the journey with Gilgamesh across the water of death to the islands of the souls. After Utnapishtim has told his life story, he advises Gilgamesh to get the herb of life, the one which "makes the old young again," which grows at the bottom of the sea. Gilgamesh succeeds in this, but then the herb of life is stolen from him by a snake. Thereafter, Gilgamesh and Urshanabi return to the human world.

In the text, it is unclear why Gilgamesh may no longer return to Utnapishtim and why Urshanabi is sentenced to be forever banned from the islands of the souls. It is likely that Gilgamesh's offense is less severe. That is supported by Utnapishtim's detailed account of the winning of his immortality and the advice about how Gilgamesh can win the herb of life. Hence Urshanabi's offense appears to be disproportionately greater. Most authors such as Gressmann (1926:181), Ungnad (1921:111), and Heidel (1949:74) are of the opinion that Urshanabi's offense consists in bringing a mortal to the region of the souls. In connection with this, we must above all make mention of the Greek myth of Charon; Charon is also persuaded to bring the mortal Hercules to Hades, as punishment for which he is chained to the rocks of Hades for a whole year (Roscher, 1884:186).

In any case, the nocturnal journey across the ocean is for neither Gilgamesh nor Urshanabi a repeatable event. Jensen (1906:47 ff.)—who is cited by C. G. Jung (1952:334, n. 46)—has noted that Urshanabi remains forever banned and that he became the actual prototype of the Wandering Jew. According to my opinion, however, it rather concerns a related archetypal image. In contrast to other related myths, the Christian Ahasver myth presents a certain progression. For Christ's statement "You will wait until I return" presupposes that Christ will return and redeem Ahasver. The folk legend especially has placed this motif in the foreground: at the end of all time, when Christ returns, Ahasver shall meet Him, and, after he has atoned for his offense by a lifelong period of wandering and is reconciled with Him, he will find a peaceful death. In Buddhism, it is Pindola[3] who is sentenced to eternal life because of his disobedience against Buddha (Burnouf, 1876:556). The Cain motif of the Bible has already been noted. A similar figure is also mentioned in Islam; it concerns al-Samiri, the one who leads the people astray. According to the twentieth sura of the *Koran*, he is cursed by Moses upon his return from Mount Sinai because, during Moses' absence, he made the golden calf, a role which the Bible assigns to Aaron. Since that time, he wanders lonely and abandoned up to the end of his life. Arabic legends also tell about Zerib, a grandson of Elijah, who on God's command must wait until the return of Christ (Zirus, 1928:26). Whenever this archetypal motif of the Eternal Wanderer appears, the wanderer nearly always carries a burden of guilt. In Germany, it is above all the Wild Huntsman who resides in the Black Forest. Like Ahasver, he is the harbinger of storms and bad weather. In France, he became the *chasseur maudit*, who hunts in the woods of Fontainebleau, brought into association with St. Hubert, the patron saint of hunters. The Wild Huntsman is a similar figure who lives in the forest of Windsor. At a later time, it was the legends of Tannhäuser and the Flying Dutchman which placed the motif of the offense and its redemption in the foreground.

In my opinion, all these figures represent only variations of the same archetypal motif of the Eternal Wanderer wherein, in particular, the relationship of the Ahasver motif to Wotan stands in the foreground. Following C. G. Jung, Wotan represents the "instinctual-emotional as well as the intuitive-inspirational side of the unconscious of the Germanic peoples" (Jung, 1952:323; 1956:17). Ahasver shares with Wotan emotionality, unpredictability, and driving power. On the other hand, he completely lacks the intuitive-inspirational side. But even at that he is an often iridescent and dual personality which has now a positive, now a negative character: on the one hand, he is cruel and without feeling; on the other hand, he is gentle, wise, and ready to help. Morpurgo reports how he escorts two children who were surprised by a snowstorm safely back to their home (1891:15 ff.). On the other hand, he strangles Pilate as well as the thief Barabbas without hesitation. He also lets Salome, whom he forced to dance for him, drown in the waters of the Danube at a later time (Plancy, 1866). Without doubt, Ahasver, just like Wotan, is concerned with a split, earthy side of the Western Christian human being. This side was initially projected onto the heathen (Malchus-Cartaphilos-motif). After the gradual Christianization period dur-

ing the time of the Crusades, the Jew became more and more the
carrier of such projections (Buttadeus-Ahasver motif). These projections in particular are an expression of the fact that the Western
soul adopted Christianity only superficially and identified itself
onesidedly with the spiritual aspect, while the chthonic side was
repressed. Besides, that the Jew was in a special way admirably
suited for such shadowy projections is understandable enough
from his historical destiny; it was above all the external homelessness, but also the rejection of Christ as a figure of salvation, which
accommodated such projections, almost suggested them.

   The fact that Ahasver is not a Jewish but an explicitly Western
Christian myth suggests that *the Eternal Wanderer Ahasver corresponds to the latent heathen and Jewish side present in the Western
Christian unconscious.* Naturally, this archetypal figure never became conscious; it was in part projected and in part simply lived,
without reflection. How much the negative side of Ahasver lived
may be amply documented by the Crusades, during which not
only was the whole of the Jewish population of the Rhineland
massacred, but also the whole of the Islamic and Jewish population of Jerusalem was eliminated. On the other hand, it should
also be mentioned that during this time the positive side of Ahasver lived as well: human kindness and readiness to help were
practically realized in the erection of numerous pilgrim's hospitals
and hospices, whereby in particular the various spiritual knightly
orders distinguished themselves.

   So we can say that Ahasver has the essence of a genuine myth,
or more precisely, a *mythologem.* This is supported not only by its
primitive features but above all by the wide dissemination of the
motif. In his restlessness and drive to move, in his kindness and
readiness to help, but also in his cruelty and lack of feeling, Ahasver is not at all a reflection of the Jewish people or of the individual
Jew as has been generally assumed up until now, but rather he is
a symbol of unredeemed Western Christian man who has not
integrated his shadow side and has not yet found his balance.

   The myth of the Wandering Jew and its history is dealt with in
the first section of this paper. Reference is made to the sources of
the various motifs on which the myth is based.[4] In the second

section, an attempt is made to interpret the myth along psychological lines. In discussing psychoanalytic interpretations, it is especially Graber's (1958) theory of the Jew as the "restless wanderer" which is refuted. Parallels to myths in the religious history of Judaism, Christianity, Islam, and Buddhism are shown. The close ties with the Wotan myth are illustrated and emphasized. Based on this, it becomes apparent that the latent heathen and Jewish traits in the unconscious of man in Christian Western civilization have found expression in the figure of Ahasver.

NOTES

1. Acher, M. (Birnbaum, M.) in an unpublished, so-called Ahasver poem. Ahasver is experienced as the double of the poet.
2. According to my knowledge, three authors have independently and simultaneously pointed to the relationship of Ahasver to Wotan: K. Blind, *Wotan, der wilde Jäger und der wandernde Jude* (1880); F. Mauthner, *Der neue Ahasver* (Dresden, 1882); Ch. Schoebel, *La Légende du Juif errant* (Paris, 1877).
3. In the *Acoka Avadana*, it says that Pindola transgressed a commandment of Buddha, and therefore he was forever denied entrance to Nirvana.
4. [Ed. note: The first portion of this essay was not reprinted here.]

BIBLIOGRAPHY

Burnouf, E., *Introduction à l'histoire du bouddhisme indien*. Paris, 1876.
Cornioley, H., "Der Ewige Jude." *Der Psychologe* 1, no. 3 (1941): 89 ff.
Cysat, R., in M. Ninck, *Wodan und germanischer Schicksalsglaube* (Jena, 1935), p. 73 [evil spirits].
de Liagre Bohl, F. M. Th., in *Lexikon für Theologie und Geschichte* 4 (1960): 80 [Gilgamesh epic].
Graber, G. H., "Ahasver und die Judenfrage." *Der Psychologe* 1, no. 8 (1958): 303 ff and 1, no. 9 (1958): 358 ff.
Grässe, J. Th., *Die Sage vom Ewigen Juden*. Dresden, 1844.
Gressman, H., *Altorientalische Texte zum Alten Testament*. Berlin, 1926.
Heidel, A., *The Gilgamesh Epic and Old Testament Parallels*. Chicago, 1949.

Höfler, D., *Kultische Geheimgebräuche der Germanen*. Frankfurt a.M.,
    1934.
Isaac-Edersheim, E., "Messias, Golem, Ahasver: Drei mythische Gestal-
    ten des Judentums." *Internationale Zeitschrift für Psychoanalyse* 26
    (1941): 286 ff.
Jensen, P., *Das Gilgamesh-epos in der Weltliteratur*. Strassburg, 1906.
Jung, C. G., *Symbole der Wandlung*. Zürich, 1952.
———, "Wotan," in *Aufsätze zur Zeitgeschichte* (Zürich, 1956), p. 17.
Leschnitzer, A., "Der Gestaltwandel Ahasvers," in *zwei Welten, Fest-
    schrift für S. Moses* (Tel Aviv, 1962), pp. 470 ff.
Meissner, B., "Ein altbabylonisches Fragment des Gilgameschepos."
    Mitteilungen der Vorderasiatischen Gesellschaft. Berlin, 1902.
Menzel, W., *Odin*. Stuttgart, 1885.
Morpurgo, S., *L'ebreo errante in Italia*. Florence, 1891.
Ninck, M., *Wodan und germanischer Schicksalsglaube*. Jena, 1935.
Plancy, G., *Légendes du Juif errant et des seize reines de Munster*. Paris, 1866.
Roscher, W. H., *Ausführliches Lexikon der griechischen und römischen My-
    thologie*, vol. 1. Leipzig, 1884–86.
Saxo Grammaticus, *Gesta Danorum*. 1886.
Schott, A., *Das Gilgamesch-Epos*. Neu übersetzt und mit Anmerkungen
    versehen. Tfl. X, Col. 28. Stuttgart, 1958.
Schudt, J. J., *Jüdische Merkwürdigkeiten*, vol. 4, pp. 488 ff. Frankfurt,
    1714.
Ungnad, A., *Die Religion der Babylonier und Assyrier*. Jena, 1921.
von Franz, M.-L., "Die Visionen des Niklaus von Flüe." *Studien aus dem
    C. G. Jung Institut* 9 (1959): 80.
Zirus, W., *Der Ewige Jude in der Dichtung*. Leipzig, 1928.

THE WANDERING JEW
THE ALIENATION
OF THE JEWISH IMAGE
IN CHRISTIAN CONSCIOUSNESS

Adolf L. Leschnitzer

Another approach to the Wandering Jew involves the history of ideas rather than the perception of the legend solely in terms of one particular theory of personality. In such a historical perspective, shifts in attitude may be examined in terms of their philosophical and political import. If the Wandering Jew reflects the Christian stereotypic notions of Jews, then, to the extent that stereotypes change through time, the functions of the legend may change accordingly.

In the following essay, Adolf Leschnitzer of the Free University of Berlin attempts to delineate what he considers a dramatic shift in the European image of the Jew in the nineteenth century. The idea that the Wandering Jew was a historical figure present at the Crucifixion, thereby functioning as a witness for Christian faith, changed to the notion of the Wandering Jew as a symbolic (some authors say "mythical") figure standing for the Jewish people in secularized terms. Schopenhauer's statement is representative: "Ahasuerus, the Wandering Jew, is nothing but the personification of the whole Jewish race. Since he has sinned grievously against the Saviour and World-Redeemer, he shall never be delivered from earthly existence and its burden and moreover shall wander homeless in foreign lands. This is just the flight *and fate of the small Jewish race which, strange to relate, was driven from its native land some two thousand years ago and has ever since existed and wandered homeless." See Arthur Schopen-*hauer, Parerga and Paralipomena: Short Philosophical Es-says, *Vol. II (Oxford, 1974), p. 261. This view often served as a charter for anti-Semitic sentiments. Schopenhauer himself goes on to recommend that Jews be converted to Christianity and/or that they be encouraged to marry gentiles. "Then," he continues, "in the course of a hundred years, there will be only a very few Jews left, and soon the ghost will be exorcized. Ahasuerus will be buried, and the chosen people will not know where their abode was. This desirable result, however, will be frustrated if the emancipation of the Jews is carried to the point of their obtaining political rights . . . " (Ibid., p. 264).*

Leschnitzer is much more concerned with the image of the Jew in the legend than with the legend per se. His discussion of the anti-Semitic component in perceptions of the Wandering Jew leads him inevitably to conclude with a brief reference to twentieth-century Nazi ideology.

The concept of the "Wandering Jew" or, in German, "Der Ewige Jude," the eternal, that is, the everlasting Jew, can be traced to a German chapbook entitled: *Kurze Beschreibung und Erzählung von einem Juden mit Namen Ahasver.* What do the two phrases "The Wandering Jew" and "Der Ewige Jude" mean?[1]

Generally, both English and German dictionaries give two meanings.[2] First, there is the medieval legendary figure of a man who treated Christ mockingly or with contempt on his way to the crucifixion and who is condemned to wander upon the earth until the return of Christ. Second, there is an obviously ironical variant of the first definition: a man who never settles down, a figure of a restlessly roving person.

Let us now consider popular usage: In Gottfried Keller's novella *Das Fähnlein der sieben Aufrechten* there is a passage that sheds clear light upon the use of the phrase in everyday language. A citizen

Reprinted from *Viator: Medieval and Renaissance Studies*, 2 (1971): 391–96.

of Zurich, around 1860, says the following in the course of a chat in an inn:

> Just as it is proper, at times, for a man to think of death in the midst of the best years of his life so, in an hour of reflection, he might concern himself with the inevitable end of his fatherland so that he might love it all the more devoutly in the present; for everything in this world is transitory and subject to change. Or have not far bigger nations than ours perished? Or do you wish one day to drag on an existence like that of the Eternal Jew who cannot die, bowing before all newly risen peoples, this man who stood at the grave of the Egyptians, the Greeks, and the Romans? No! A people that knows that one day it will no longer exist, makes all the more vital use of its days, lives all the longer and leaves behind it a glorious heritage; for it will not rest until it has fully developed the potentialities that are latent within it, like a diligent and provident man who sets his house in order before his inevitable demise. This, in my opinion, is the crux of the matter. Once a destiny of a people has been fulfilled, a few days more or less do not matter. New events wait impatiently on the threshold of their time.[3]

The concept of the Eternal Jew is clearly delineated here. Normally—and this is the underlying idea—a people is born, lives, achieves, and dies. Jewry, on the other hand, is something abnormal, as if it were a living corpse, a specter. It has survived the great peoples of ancient history and reaches into our time, a mystery, an enigma. Jewry lives on and on, although it has lived up to its destiny, has accomplished its task. For what purpose, one must ask, does it still live? But beyond all these considerations Keller's words conjure up a mythical image of compulsive force, the weird figure of the Eternal Wanderer who cannot die, forever dragging on an existence without aim or purpose.

What is the relation between the meaning of the phrase as I have just developed it and the definitions of the dictionaries? The second, the ironic meaning, "A person who never settles down," or "figure of a restlessly roving person" is not relevant. The first definition seems to be appropriate, but one is struck by the fact that there is absolutely no reference to the cause of the eternal wandering nor is there any reference to Christ. This may be accidental. Since all reference to Christ, however, seems to be omitted in very many, probably most, mentions of the Eternal Jew in the nineteenth century, one gains the impression that this is the rule rather than the exception.

Is it possible that in nineteenth-century Germany a third meaning may have developed, which has not yet received lexical definition, namely that of a mythical figure not unlike the Flying Dutchman or the Wild Huntsman ("Der wilde Jaeger")? Be that as it may, this figure, whether called the Wandering Jew, the Eternal Jew, or Ahasverus, has been considered ancient, precisely because he is a mythical character, as ancient as the Jewish diaspora itself. If he has been considered somewhat younger, then, at best, it is as a figure of late Antiquity or of medieval times. These assumptions are wrong. The figure is actually much younger and was not yet known in the sixteenth century. The first edition of the German chapbook *Brief Description and Story of a Jew named Ahasverus*, from which the first meaning given by the dictionaries stems, was published in 1602.

The figure has no genuine precursors. A figure such as the Christian penitent Kartaphilus in the thirteenth century writings of Roger of Wendover and Matthew of Paris, which may have been known to the writer of the chapbook, lacks all the essential characteristics of the figure of Ahasverus: he does not wander around, he is no Jew, to mention only two deviations.

But is our first impression really all wrong? Does not this early modern figure perhaps still present certain medieval traits? To answer this question we must keep in view how diaspora Jewry looked to people in the Middle Ages. We must arrive at the basic characteristics of the image that has remained the same throughout the centuries despite certain nuances and shadings and which, to a certain extent, is still in effect, particularly among Roman Catholics.

We can summarize this Jewish image in Christian consciousness, as known since the days of Saint Augustine, in the following manner: First, the Jews have lost their claim to being the Chosen People, but on the Day of Judgment or shortly before it they will be converted and will gain entry into the Kingdom of Heaven. Second, as punishment for having killed Christ and for refusal to believe in him, the Jews have been scattered and, through their writings, bear witness to the fact that the Christians did not invent their prophecies concerning Christ.

The first dictum dates from early Christian times and can be traced to Saint Paul: Branches—the converted Gentiles—have been cut from the wild olive tree—paganism—and have been grafted upon the cultivated olive tree—the true faith; the old branches—the Jews—have been cut off because they did not believe in Christ; but they will surely be grafted back; after the full number of Gentiles has come in, all Israel will gain salvation; the Israelites had to become enemies for the sake of the Gentiles, but for the sake of their forefathers they are beloved of God; God's grace and call are irrevocable.

This teaching is, above all, perhaps the strongest neutralization of anti-Judaism in Christian thinking that has ever occurred. *Populus Israel*, once the Chosen People, will in the fullness of time be chosen again and will belong to the *populus christianus*. The history of the world from Creation to the Day of Judgment is conceived of as an all-embracing continuum, one in which Israel plays a significant part.

The second teaching, developed later and retained by Saint Augustine, about the Jews bearing witness through their Scriptures, gained meaning only with the ever increasing allegorical exegesis of those very Scriptures on the part of the Christians. In effect this obviously rendered the Old Testament nothing but a prelude to the New.

Both teachings resulted in an image of the diaspora Jews who had to live on so that at the end of time the salvation of all mankind might become a reality. This explains the self-imposed restraint on the part of the Christian majority which perhaps partly accounts for the very existence of Jewish communities in medieval Europe.

Quite opposed to the concept embodied in the Eternal Jew, *Jewish* existence according to medieval concepts was, therefore, neither enigmatic nor meaningless. Jewry was a living community that, though it had gone astray, would one day find the right path and become the keystone of the edifice of the Christian church. This was the meaning of the Jewish diaspora, this was the reason why Jewry had to survive up to the end of all time.

Far from being a "living corpse," a weird, meaningless spectral being, to whom all that was left was to wait until it was allowed to go to its eternal rest, Jewry was a living community meaningfully fitting into the course of universal history as an indispensable entity. Its survival up to the end of history and its final conversion in the last moment of history, or shortly before it, was a condition sine qua non for the salvation of mankind, the second advent of the Lord, and the dawn of a new day, of the Kingdom of Heaven.

The medieval image of the Jew was the result of partial neutralization of anti-Judaism. It is true, the Jew continued to be an alien, did not belong to the majority group, was an outsider. There was a vague feeling, however, which for many centuries never ceased to exist: even if he was an alien, he would, or rather could, not remain so forever.

To summarize: It was beyond doubt that the Lord would return at the end of all time; and the conversion of the Jews, their incorporation into the *corpus christianum*, likewise taking place at the end of all time, was hardly less certain than the second advent of the Lord. Jews might be discriminated against, humiliated, persecuted, expelled. They might be considered the pariahs of Christendom, the most wretched, lowest people of this world. But they were part of this world. They belonged to it. Their survival was indispensable for the salvation of mankind.

It is already apparent why the mythical figure of the nineteenth century is mysterious, leads an existence devoid of meaning, and lacks all relation to Christ. In the mind of the people for whom our citizen of Zurich speaks there are only *gentes* left. The concept of the *populus christianus* which has already partially absorbed and which is to absorb the *gentes* still more, has vanished. It has become as nonexistent as the concept of a *populus Israel*. The Jews, too, are only a *gens* or, more properly, were one once upon a time like the peoples of Antiquity. However, the disappearance of those eschatological considerations which were connected with the concepts of *populus Israel* and of *populus christianus* results in much more than the mere mysteriousness and senselessness of the Eternal Jew's existence. The uninterrupted rise and fall of peoples, of the *gentes*, becomes an endless repetition, likewise lacking all sense and purpose for want of any kind of all-embracing universal historical conception.

This total disappearance of eschatological considerations was, a long time before, preceded by a partial one in the chapbook of 1602. The story of Ahasverus has a decidedly theological meaning if it is read in the light of certain theological teachings of its time. In early Protestant theology the eschatology of the end of the world was theoretically still retained but, practically speaking, lost its importance when compared with the eschatology of the individual, that is, the fate of the individual after death.[4] It is for this reason that Lutheran care of the soul was concerned primarily with blissful dying. The soul is judged directly after death, and believers are immediately granted perfect and eternal bliss by God and by Christ.[5] The chapbook is based on the assumption of the validity of this conception. The fate of Ahasverus, to whom the portal leading to bliss was forever closed, must have seemed the most horrible punishment conceivable to people who were versed in Lutheran ways of thinking.

But we must keep in mind that eternal life is generally regarded as a reward and not as punishment. The thought processes that were basic for an understanding of the chapbook were so subtle, so sophisticated that they were far beyond the capacity of the average reader to understand. As a result, later reprints or versions of the book, a great many of which appeared in the course of a century and a half, contained appendices depicting countless blood-curdling details of the punishment to be meted out to each of the Jewish tribes.

The chapbook documents the beginning of the disappearance in early modern times of eschatological concepts—a process that had to result in an intensification of the alienation of the Jewish image in Christian consciousness. A quarter of a millennium after the appearance of the chapbook, in the nineteenth century, Ahasverus underwent a metamorphosis and became the mythical figure of the Eternal Jew whose spectral image is completely isolated from everything that is Christian.

The mythical figure of the Eternal Jew as it appears in nineteenth-century colloquial German is a product of a mode of thinking that has become progressively secularized. Those people who conceived of the Eternal Jew in the same way as Keller described him in 1860 were not prone to indulge in eschatological considerations, regardless of whether these concerned the end of all human history or the salvation of the individual's soul. For decades, the mythical figure is referred to, but in a tone of ever increasing animosity and hatred. In the Keller passage that has been cited, the alienation is still neutralized because in the Switzerland of the 1860s, in a country where the emancipation of the Jews was just having a rather belated start, compassion and condescension were probably often extended to the underprivileged group. In the last third of the nineteenth century the mythical figure that was isolated because it had been detached from all Christian concepts was incorporated into a newly evolving mythology, the mythology of so-called "modern" anti-Semitism. Thus the figure, having been devoid of meaning for some time, gained a new meaning but, unfortunately, one that portended evil.

That consciousness, in which the alienation of the Jewish image now began to grow apace, was no longer a Christian one but rather un-Christian, or even anti-Christian. It had just become a fad in the German literature of those days to contrast shining, glorified and idealized German hero-types with dark, sinister Jewish villains.[6] Soon demagogic, anti-Semitic agitators began to conjure up the fantastic figure of a Jewish demon of darkness as a contrast to the Germanic Siegfried- or Baldur-type. They equated this demon with the eternal enemy of the Nordic race, the Eternal Jew. The victor in this mortal combat had to be the glorified Nordic type. This was the core of the new anti-Semitic mythology which began nationalistic and ended up by being racist. It soon gave rise to a new misshapen concept of universal history: the goal of history was no longer the Kingdom of Heaven, the realm of the world to come. Now the goal was, after the triumph of the allegedly noblest of races over all its sinister antagonists, the Nordic-Germanic *Reich* of this world in which there was room neither for Jews nor for Christianity.

NOTES

1. Some of the ideas that are set forth in this paper, but not the conclusion, also appear in my article "Der Gestaltwandel Ahasvers," in:

In zwei Welten; Siegfried Moses zum 75. Geburtstag. (Tel Aviv 1962) 470–505. Of the older literature on the subject, L. Neubaur, *Die Sage vom Ewigen Juden* (Leipzig 1884) is still indispensable. Recently, the problem of origin and career of the legend has been dealt by G. K. Anderson, *The Legend of the Wandering Jew* (Providence 1965); S. Baron, *A Social and Religious History of the Jews* 11 (New York 1967) 180–182, 374–375 (nn. 80–81).

2. See for instance *The Concise Oxford Dictionary of Current English*, ed. 3 (Oxford 1934) 1390; and *Deutsches Wörterbuch von Jacob und Wilhelm Grimm*, ed. Moritz Heyne (Leipzig 1877) 4.2.2353.

3. Gottfried Keller, *Gesammelte Werke*, 6 (Berlin 1889) 277.

4. Paul Althaus, in *Religion in Geschichte und Gegenwart* 2, ed. 2; (Tübingen 1928) "Die Erwartung des Reiches verkümmert, das Denken ist ganz auf das Anliegen der persoenlichen Heilsgewissheit gesammelt. Die endgeschichtliche Eschatologie wird theoretisch behauptet, verliert aber den Ton... Die Hoffnung ist in der Hauptsache individualistisch und jenseitig eingestellt."

5. Althaus: "Der Tod hat den Ernst des letzten Kampfes mit dem Satan, der endgueltigen Entscheidung. Daher gilt die Seelsorge auf lutherischem Boden ueberwiegend dem *seligen Sterben*. Die Seele erlebt das Gericht unmittelbar nach dem Tode."

6. Ernst Kohn-Bramstedt, *Aristocracy and the Middle Classes in Germany; Social Types in German Literature* (London 1937) 133–149.

THE WANDERING JEW
AS SACRED EXECUTIONER

Hyam Maccoby

One of the standard theories of folk narrative is the myth-ritual approach. According to this theory, all myths are considered to be the spoken counterparts of rites. Much of the myth-ritual scholarship is devoted to reconstructing the presumed original ritual which gave rise to a particular myth. The theory has also been applied to folktales and legends. Some of the hypothetical ritual reconstructions proposed seem quite forced and farfetched, but in the following essay by Hyam Maccoby we find a brilliant and insightful application of this theory. Not only does he place the legend of the Wandering Jew in a new, broader perspective, but he is able to illuminate the continuing importance of the legend in the modern world.

Maccoby first articulated his new interpretation of the Wandering Jew in an article published in 1972. Later, he expanded his notion of the Sacred Executioner into a full-length explanatory paradigm through which he attempted to find meaning in a whole series of narratives. We have elected to include both his initial essay as well as a selection from the later book where he further develops his reading of the Wandering Jew.

The legend of the Wandering Jew began as an insignificant anecdote. Gradually, however, the story acquired accretions which

Reprinted from *The Jewish Quarterly*, 20, No. 1 *(1972): 3–8;* and from *The Sacred Executioner: Human Sacrifice and the Legacy of Guilt* (London, 1982), pp. 166–73.

gave it significance and mythic status; and, in its full-blown form, the story is the re-incarnation of a very ancient archetype.

The legend is known to have developed out of a medieval (13th century) tale, or rather "tall story," about a man called Cartaphilus, who was neither a wanderer nor a Jew. However, some of the main features of the later story are already present in this first version. Cartaphilus was a Roman, Pilate's doorkeeper. He struck Jesus, on his way to his Crucifixion, and told him to hurry; Jesus answered, "I go, and you will wait for me until I return." By these words Jesus conferred on Cartaphilus the curse of immortality; an immortality of remorse, since Cartaphilus became a devout Christian. Cartaphilus was not a wanderer, for he lived through the centuries in Armenia. The German name for the Wandering Jew is *"der ewige Jude"*—"the Eternal Jew"—and this name is more faithful to the earliest version of the story than our "Wandering Jew" or the French *"le juif errant."* The gift of immortality remained, however, as an essential ingredient of the fully-developed story.

In the next century, the figure appears in Italy under the name of Johannes Buttadeus ("John-who-struck-God"). He has now become a Jew, instead of a Roman, and has become a Wanderer; part of his curse being that he is always restless and cannot remain in one place for long.

However, it was not until the beginning of the 17th century that the Wandering Jew legend really achieved popular success. His name has changed to "Ahasuerus." The legend now proliferates all over Europe. Sightings of the Wandering Jew are reported in much the same way as flying saucers are reported nowadays. Ahasuerus was once a shoe-maker by trade, a native of Jerusalem. He is now a convinced and repentant Christian, but must expiate the curse pronounced on him by Christ; he must live and wander until the Second Coming. The name "Ahasuerus" is rather a strange choice. The Biblical Ahasuerus was not a Jew but a Persian king, probably to be identified with Xerxes. But we may guess that this name was chosen because it was not too Christian and not too Jewish. Names like Simon or Matthew (or even John, the original but rejected choice), though Hebrew in origin, had too Christian a ring, while names like Solomon or Moses had acquired villainous or comic Jewish associations inappropriate to a noble penitent. An Old Testament name like Ahasuerus would sound vaguely Jewish to people not too well acquainted with the Old Testament story, just as Shakespeare's choice of the non-Jewish names Tubal and Chus, from the Old Testament, seemed appropriate enough for his Jewish characters in *The Merchant of Venice*. But "Ahasuerus," with its kingly associations, would also sound dignified.

Thus, even in the 17th-century-folk-tale version, the Wandering Jew is a dignified figure. The description of him as tall and stately, with a grave, sad expression, reinforced this impression of dignity. Later, in the elaborations of Romantic literature, this dignity becomes greater still, since the Wandering Jew is credited with supernatural knowledge and mystic powers. We may ask the question: "How was it that, in the 17th century, at the time of the greatest degradation and humiliation of the Jewish people, a folk-tale grew to popularity in which a Jew is represented as a noble, dignified and even awesome figure?" This was the time when, after centuries of anti-Jewish legislation, designed to expel the Jews from every honourable, dignified employment, they were at their lowest point. They were continually harassed and moved on from place to place; there was in fact a large-scale migration of Jews to Eastern countries. They were in sober truth Wandering Jews at this time, and this historical fact has been adduced to explain the growth of the Wandering Jew legend. But it does not account for the dignity of the Wandering Jew, which is so much at variance with the Jew's position of humiliation and with the figure of the Jew in other Christian folk-tales such as the Jew's Beautiful Daughter story, which reached literary status about this time in Marlowe's *Jew of Malta* and Shakespeare's *The Merchant of Venice*.

In the Wandering Jew legend we have an unexpected aspect of the Christian image of the Jew; an aspect which reflects a need of Christians to build up their image of the Jew as well as to break it down. It is as if the very success of the Christians in humiliating the Jew in the world of reality has led to a need for a more reverential image in the world of fantasy. As long as Christians feared the Jews, regarding them as figures of established power, they resorted to the weapons of ridicule and vilification. But when it became clear that the Jews were defeated and had become harmless objects of contempt, it became necessary to restore some of the lost awesomeness. The Wandering Jew represents both the defeat of the Jews and the restoration of their dignity.

The Jews and "the Second Coming"

We must remember that the aim of the Christians was never merely to beat down the Jews. If this had been so, the Jews could have been annihilated, like the Albigenses. One of the strongest beliefs of medieval Christians was that the Second Coming of Christ could not take place until the Jews were converted to Christianity. (Marvell's "till the conversion of the Jews" means simply "till the millennium.") The Jews, therefore, had to be preserved; otherwise the Second Coming could not take place. This was the point of the Disputations which were held periodically to convert the Jews. When Luther reformed the Christian religion, one of his first thoughts was that now at last the Jews could be converted. When medieval Church dignitaries, such as St. Bernard of Clairvaux, intervened with the raging mob to save the remnants of Jewish communities, their chief argument was not humanitarian but that the Jews were necessary for the Second Coming. This belief was not merely an outcome of St. Paul's pronouncement (Romans XI, 25) that the Jews would be converted in the last days. The matter goes much deeper than the interpretation of an isolated text. The Jews were never put on the same footing as the other heretics. They were the representatives of the Old Religion, against which Christianity had rebelled, and there was a feeling of bad conscience about them. The Jews were Father-figures, and rebellion against the father is never a straightforward expression of hatred. There is the residual feeling of love, the desire for approval, the desire to gain, after all, the father's blessing. Even the accusations against the Jews were an attempt by Christians to convince themselves that the Jews, despite all their appearance of indifference, really did believe in Christ. Why did the Jews steal the Communion wafer and stick pins in it, thus making it bleed, unless they believed, after all, that the wafer was the body of Christ?

The Wandering Jew aroused such passionate interest because he was a witness to the truth of Christianity—a witness sorely needed in the millennial excitements and conflicts of the 17th century. Only a Jew could give Christianity its final confirmation. The Wandering Jew was the very Jew whom centuries of Christian persecution had been designed to produce; dispossessed and beaten into humility and repentance, but retaining enough of the dignity of the Father to give his blessing and his clinching testimony to Christianity.

But the Wandering Jew also has a more universal significance. This Christian Jew-image is a relatively recent manifestation of a very ancient theme. It is interesting to compare the Wandering Jew with some figures of ancient mythology in order to discover what he means apart from the context of the Jewish-Christian conflict.

The essence of the Wandering Jew is that he is someone who has sinned deeply and is, therefore, condemned to punishment. But his punishment is an ambivalent one; from some angles it can even be regarded as a reward. He is cursed with eternal life; but this is also the reward of heroes, such as Arthur, or Frederick Barbarossa, or the Biblical Elijah. Indeed, the Wandering Jew derives directly some of his characteristics from the Christian hero, John, the favourite disciple of Jesus, who was also told by Jesus "Tarry till I come" (John XXI, 22), and whose name is attached to some versions of the Wandering Jew ("John Butta-deus" and the Spanish "Juan Espera en Deo"). Even the condemnation to wandering cannot be regarded as wholly a curse. To wander is more interesting than to stay at home. The Wandering Jew visits all lands, meets with exciting adventures and acquires strange knowledge. He has the romantic aura of such wandering heroes as Hercules, Dionysus, Odysseus and the Hebrew Patriarchs. He is one of those mythical figures who express the stay-at-home agriculturist's yearning for the lost freedom of the era of nomadism.

If the punishment of the Wandering Jew is equivocal, we are forced to the conclusion that there is something equivocal about his crime too. What is this crime which is also a heroic act, so that its punishment is also a reward?

One of the most interesting ancient analogues of the Wandering Jew legend is the Biblical story of Cain. In this story, Cain, after committing his terrible crime, is condemned to be a wanderer: "A fugitive and a vagabond shalt thou be in the earth." Instead of being condemned to death, Cain is condemned to life, and in order to ensure that his life should not be a short one, God "set a mark on Cain, lest any finding him should kill him." Yet we are then told that Cain "builded a city," and that his descendants were the founders of the arts. Jubal was "the father of all such as handle the harp and organ," and Tubal-Cain was "an instructor of every artificer in brass and iron." If, as modern scholars think, Cain was the eponymcus ancestor of the Kenite (Rechabite) tribe (a fact which the Biblical narrative purposely obscures), his descendants were a highly-respected Arab clan of nomadic smiths who adopted Judaism but retained their own tent-dwelling, ascetic way of life, for which the Prophet Jeremiah commended them (Jer. XXXV). The wandering life which was decreed for Cain as a punishment eventually became a sign of sanctity. The whole story is permeated by the ambivalence which we noted in the Wandering Jew story. Cain's crime and punishment are terrible; but in the outcome, he is shielded from death, acquires special gifts and talents, contributes in a distinguished way to civilization and becomes a holy person.

It may be objected that the Wandering Jew's crime of jostling Jesus on his way to crucifixion is too trivial to be compared with Cain's fratricide. In the original story of the Roman Cartaphilus the crime was indeed relatively trivial; but as soon as the sinner became not a Roman but a Jew, the significance and seriousness of the story were transformed. The crime became a symbol of the deicide of which the whole Jewish people was held to be guilty. Christian writers of the early Church, looking for allegorical meanings in the Old Testament stories, saw both Cain's murder of Abel and Joseph's betrayal by his brothers as foreshadowings of Jesus's betrayal and murder by his brothers, the Jews. So the crime of Cain and that of the Wandering Jew are not, after all, dissimilar.

In the wider field of mythology, the story of Oedipus presents some parallels with that of the Wandering Jew and Cain. Oedipus, having discovered that he has killed his father and married his mother, administers his own punishment. He blinds himself, and sets off on wanderings, which eventually lead him to Athens. He has acquired the gift of prophecy; he announces the place and time of his own death, and that his bones will bring prosperity to Athens. Though the gift of a charmed life is lacking in the story, we have the wandering, the special gifts and the eventual sanctity. There is the characteristic ambivalence, the feeling that the awesomeness of the crime confers heroic status.

Cain and Adam

There is an even more interesting parallel between the story of Cain and that of Adam (Edmund Leach, in *Genesis as Myth*, has suggested with some plausibility that they are variants of the same story). Adam, as a result of his crime, is thrust out from his true Home. The ground (as for Cain) becomes cursed for him. And yet his crime brings him gifts; he has acquired "the knowledge of good and evil." Without his crime he would have remained an innocent child; now he has grown up. The gift of immortality comes into the story too, for if Adam had sinned even further and eaten the Tree of Life, he would have become immortal. As it is, the punishment of death pronounced for eating of the Tree of Knowledge (Gen. III, 3) is not carried out. The crime of the sinner has made him into a hero; God Himself says, "The man is become as one of us." The theory that Adam's sin brought death into the world is late, and is in contradiction to Gen. III, 22.

The Hebrew story of Adam (which has been much distorted and misrepresented by Christian exegesis, especially in connection with the doctrine of Original Sin) is a profound parable of the human condition. It is primarily about the acquisition of knowledge and the guilt associated with this. The Wandering Jew story, however, like that of Cain, is primarily about violence; but the "violence" story has its "knowledge" aspect too, the idea that guilt and knowledge are intermixed, that a terrible crime of violence enables the criminal to break through to a higher state of awareness. "Knowledge through sin" is the common denominator of all these stories; though in some of them knowledge arises as a by-product of the sin, while in others the acquisition of forbidden knowledge is itself the sin. The Adam story is of the latter type; others of this type are the stories of Prometheus, and of Faust. Another example is Teiresias, who was punished because he found out too much about sex; blinded, like Oedipus, he acquired the gift of prophecy and prolonged life. The Adam story too, according to some interpreters, is concerned with the acquisition of sexual knowledge (see especially Theodore Reik's *Myth and Ritual*).

It was primarily the "knowledge" aspect of the Wandering Jew which interested Romantic writers such as Shelley (see *Queen Mab* and *Hellas*). Shelley saw the Wandering Jew as one of those rebels against authority, such as Adam, Prometheus and Faust, who defy the tyranny of God in order to acquire independent status and knowledge. The Wandering Jew certainly has this aspect, and from this point of view, he can be regarded, like Adam, as a symbol of mankind in general. Every man is a Wanderer, who has been ejected from the warmth of the Eden of childhood because of the sin of curiosity and desire for independence. But his punishment is his reward. The world of adulthood brings hardship, unrest, a life prolonged in agony, but it also brings responsibility, freedom, skill, sense of achievement, adventure and morality. This is the theme of the stories of Adam, Prometheus and Faust. (In the case of Adam, there is a great difference between the Adam of Judaism and the Adam of Christianity, the knowledge-guilt association being so much stronger in Christianity that the heroic aspect of Adam's sin is virtually obliterated).

The Christian-Jewish Conflict

The Romantic universalization of the Wandering Jew story, however, is not entirely satisfactory as an interpretation. This rendering omits the specific content of the story; the Jewishness of the Wandering Jew, the flavour of the Christian-Jewish conflict and the wider significances of that conflict. Shelley used the Wandering Jew as part of his attack on Christianity—or rather on organized Christianity, for Shelley, like other Romantics, was really re-asserting the antinomian essence of Christianity. Shelley, in fact, placed the Wandering Jew on the Cross; but that is not his place. He is the Crucifier, not the Crucified. (Coleridge's Ancient Mariner, based partly on the Wandering Jew and partly on Cain, retains more of the essence of their characters, since the Ancient Mariner is guilty of a genuine crime of violence.) Shelley wished to abolish Sin altogether from the story. The Wandering Jew is for him, like Prometheus and even Satan, not a sinner at all but a pure-souled revolutionary. But this is to by-pass the main point of the Wandering Jew story, which is that it is concerned with the problem of guilt. It is a Christian story, and it expresses the Christian method of dealing with the sense of guilt.

The role of the Jews was to take the blame for the Crucifixion. The Christian method of dealing with guilt is by the sacrifice of Jesus, who by suffering torture and death, rolls away the burden of sin from mankind, or at least from those who identify themselves with the sacrifice. This, of course, is a very old, perhaps the oldest, method of coping with the problem of guilt; the only thing new about Christianity is the unwillingness of the devotees to admit exactly what they are doing, though they come very close to it at times. The drawback of human sacrifice, as a purge of guilt, is that it sets up a new burden of guilt in connection with the human sacrifice itself. Who is going to take upon himself the guilt of carrying out the human sacrifice? The answer is to arrange, mythopoeically, for the sacrifice to be carried out for unworthy motives by someone who can then be regarded as evil. In this way, the devotees who benefit by the sacrifice can wash their hands of responsibility for it, and drive away with pious horror the wretch who performs the sacrifice for them. Pilate, washing his hands of responsibility for the blood of Jesus, is thus the perfect and prophetic symbol of the Christian Church, for whom the Jews took over the responsibility of performing the sacrifice which was indispensable to the salvation of all Christian believers. An exact formulation of this solution to the problem of guilt is found in the Gospels: "The Son of man goeth as it is written of him: but woe unto that man by whom the Son of man is betrayed. It had been good for that man if he had not been born." (Matt. XXVI, 24; see also Luke XXII, 22.) The man spoken of is Judas, but the text applies to the Jewish people as a whole, and to their symbol, the Wandering Jew. The human sacrifice has to be performed, but woe unto the man who performs it!

Thus the Wandering Jew was essentially an Executioner, who, like the hangman once in England, was shunned by ordinary people and banned from their homes, just because he performed for them an act which they regarded as necessary, but had not the courage to perform for themselves. If this was true of the hangman, who executed people found guilty of great crimes, how much more so was it true of the Wandering Jew, who (as representative of the Jewish people) executed an innocent man! For Jesus was not only innocent; he *had* to be innocent, or the whole sacrifice would have been inefficacious. Only a "lamb without blemish" would be a sacrifice acceptable to God. And Jesus was not just an innocent man; he was God Himself. (The apotheosis of the victim, who represented the people, is a feature of all rites of human sacrifice, since the intention is to promote unity and identity between the people and the god.)

We must not confuse Christian mythology with the historical facts. As a matter of historical fact, as far as modern scholars are able to recover it, Jesus was executed by the Romans, at the instigation of certain Jewish quislings, on a political charge of sedition against the Roman occupying power. Jesus himself was not a Christian but a Jew, who would have regarded with horror any attempt to endow him with the mystique of a pagan sacrificial cult. But this cult was superimposed upon the historical facts after Jesus's death, and it is with the mythology of this cult that we are now concerned.

The cultic role of the Jews, then, is to take upon themselves the guilt of performing the sacrifice of Jesus. The satisfaction with which Christians contemplated the sufferings of the Jews in their

exile was not a matter of simple sadism or sense of victory. Nor
did it derive merely from the thought that the Jews, in suffering
for their sin in rejecting Christ, proved the truth of Christianity.
The real satisfaction lay in the hidden thought that the suffering
of the Jews showed that they, and they only, had to pay for the
guilt of performing the indispensable sacrifice. Christians could
benefit to the full from the Crucifixion while regarding the per-
petrators of the deed with horror. Whenever the suffering of the
Jews appeared to diminish a feeling of panic would grip the Christians. If the Jews were prosperous and flourishing, someone else
would have to pay for the deed. Perhaps, moreover, the whole
sacrifice would prove inefficacious, and the huge burden of sins
which the Crucifixion had rolled away would rush back upon
them. If only the Jews would stop complaining about their sufferings as if they did not deserve them! If only they did not insist so
on enjoying their lives, whenever they were given the opportunity! If only they would say, "Yes, we crucified God, and we are
willing to pay the penalty! We embrace our sufferings!" Then the
Christians would have regarded the Jews almost with love. This
is the Christian fantasy which is embodied in the story of the
Wandering Jew.

It is interesting to compare the role of the Wandering Jew with
that of Jesus himself. In some ways, the two roles are similar.
Jesus takes upon himself all the sins of mankind: it is as if he has
actually committed all these sins. And then, by his sufferings on
the Cross, he atones for all the sins which are now on his head,
and thus he saves mankind from the necessity of paying the penalty of eternal damnation. The Wandering Jew takes upon himself
one sin only, that of being the Executioner, but this is the greatest
of all possible sins, the murder of God. By his suffering he atones
for this sin and relieves other people of all responsibility. He is, in
fact, a kind of Christ-figure himself. This observation is by no
means new. Indeed it is quite a fashionable attitude nowadays for
Christians to regard the Jews as a Christ-nation who, by God's
design rather than out of wickedness, were burdened with the
guilt of the Crucifixion. "We are all guilty of the Crucifixion, but
the Jews were elected to bear the burden."

"To live . . . not to die"

The Jews, of course, have traditionally regarded themselves as a Chosen People, but not as one chosen to be an emblem of Man's sinfulness. The Jews have even regarded themselves as a Christ-nation, who suffer for the sins of mankind. The whole passage of Isaiah (Ch. 53) about the Suffering Servant, which Christians regard as prophetic of Jesus, is regarded by Jews as descriptive of the historical role of the Jewish people. But there is a great difference between the Jewish Christ-people and the Christian Christ-hero (even the difference between the idea of a heroic community and that of a heroic individual is full of significance). The Jewish Christ-people suffers because it knows how to live, not because it knows how to die. Its sufferings are not desired; they are the inevitable consequence of its moral stance, its insistence that man's destiny is in his own hands, a message which the world rejects with horror and persecution. The Jewish people suffers not because its sufferings are essential to mankind (as Christians think); when the Jews cease to suffer the world will have grown up. And as long as the world has not grown up, the Jews will suffer. This, at any rate, has been the Jewish interpretation of the role of the Jews.

In some pagan cults, the human sacrifice was carried out without guilt. The performer of the sacrifice was a Priest who was regarded with honour (examples are the priests of Moloch, and much later the priests of the Aztecs). But as civilization progressed, people began to see human sacrifice as something shameful. In Hebrew religion, this shame led to the complete abolition of human sacrifice and the substitution of animal sacrifice. The story of Cain, as re-modelled in the Bible from earlier sources, is an allegory of this tremendous step forward in human civilization. (Another such story is that of Abraham's cancelled sacrifice of Isaac.) Abel is an animal-sacrificer, and thus gains God's favour by being free of the guilt of murder; Cain refuses to sacrifice animals, and therefore stains his hands with human blood. But in other cults, the shame felt about human sacrifice did not lead to its abolition. It was thought that human sacrifice was too necessary ever to be abolished; but expedients were found by which the newly-experienced shame could be appeased. Someone else could be blamed for the sacrifice. A bizarre example (which shows that guilt attached even to animal sacrifice) is the Buphonia sacrifice by the priests of Athens, who killed Zeus in the form of a bull. After killing the bull with an axe, they fled without looking round. Later they held a trial in which the axe was tried and condemned for the murder of Zeus. The story of the killing of the Norse god Balder by the blind Hother suggests that another expedient was the use of a blind man as Executioner, so that inadvertence could be pleaded. A parallel to this story can be found in the Midrashic legend of the killing of Cain by the blind Lamech. (In both stories the killing is performed by shooting with an arrow, i.e., a remote control execution, which further lessens the feeling of responsibility.)

The story of Cain points to another expedient that must have been common. The man who performed the sacrifice would be solemnly excommunicated. A curse would be pronounced on him, and he would be sent away to wander in the desert. However, his sacramental role as officiating Priest at the sacrifice would not be entirely forgotten. A holy mark would be put on his forehead, so that, though an outlaw, he would be immune from violence. And he would be credited with magic powers of divination and with supernatural skills (What was the "mark of Cain"? Robert Graves, adducing Ezekiel IX, 4, has conjectured plausibly that the mark was a cross in the shape of a capital T, symbolizing the name of the god who was sacrificed and resurrected, Tammuz. On a cross of this shape the human sacrifice in early times was performed. Later, sacred kings escaped being sacrificed by substituting criminals for themselves. The cross eventually degenerated, in the hands of the Romans, into a mere method of executing dangerous political prisoners. But when Jesus died as a rebel on a cross of this very same design, the ancient Tammuz Cross-cult, still alive in Adonis-worship, was included in the cult of Jesus. The Wandering Jew, in some versions, had the mark of a cross on his forehead.)

In Judaism, a remnant of this expedient of excommunicating the Sacrificer may survive in the Day of Atonement ceremony of the Scapegoat (see Leviticus XVI). On this solemn day of release from sin (probably originally a day of human sacrifice), two goats were involved in the ceremony. One was sacrificed in the Temple, but the other, the Scapegoat, was cursed and sent away alive into the desert. (This, at any rate, was the Biblical practice, though later the Scapegoat was killed in the desert by being thrown over a cliff.) The first goat represents the human sacrifice itself; the Scapegoat (how he reminds us of the Wandering Jew!) represents the Sacrificer. Actually, the word "Azazel," wrongly translated "scapegoat" on the basis of a fanciful Rabbinical etymology, is really the name of an evil spirit of the desert. Just as Satan entered Judas when he became the Betrayer of Jesus, so the evil spirit Azazel once entered the Executioner, who then became his wandering devotee. Indeed, the expedient of blaming someone for the human sacrifice may account, historically, for the creation of the figure of the Devil. The cult of Osiris, for example, originally human-sacrificial, gave rise to the dark Murderer-figure of Osiris's enemy Typhon or Set. Christianity, with its revival of the concept of human sacrifice, led to a great revival in the status of the Devil-figure Satan, who had been relegated in Judaism to a lowly position as a minor angel obeying God's orders as a kind of counsel for the prosecution.

Christianity prides itself on having abolished the Hebrew rite of animal sacrifice. Certainly, animal sacrifice (as the Hebrew prophets pointed out) was not an ideal solution to the problem of guilt. But it was a great advance on human sacrifice, which represented such an enormous need that it could not be abolished without trace. The proof of the inescapability of this need is that Christianity was forced to re-institute human sacrifice, not in the old form of a periodic literal event, but in the form of an interpretation of the death of Jesus, ritualized in the Mass. This was human-sacrifice-in-the-head, which was in some ways even worse than actual human sacrifice, since it required a permanent communal Scapegoat instead of a periodic individual one.

This Scapegoat was the Jewish people, who, however, refused to accept the role or even to understand what was required of them. So the fantasy-figure of the Wandering Jew was created to fill the Christian need for acceptance by the Jews of their role in

Christianity. In this way, in 17th century Europe, an ancient myth was revitalized. It derives from a period of pre-history when devotees were beginning to awake to the horror of human sacrifice, but were still unable to abandon it.

The legend of the Wandering Jew[1] also contributed to the Nazi anti-Semitic image, though, in some of its versions at least, this legend was the least hostile of the Christian fantasies about the Jews. The legend has roots in early Christian times, but it first became widely popular only as late as the seventeenth century. In its most amiable form the legend concerns a Jew named Ahasuerus, who was a shoemaker in Jerusalem at the time of Jesus's Crucifixion. While Jesus was carrying his cross, he stopped for a rest outside the cobbler's shop, but Ahasuerus drove him on with harsh words, or, in some versions, with a push. Jesus said, "I go, and you will wait for me until I return." Ahasuerus was thus condemned to live until the Second Coming of Christ. He is always restless and cannot stay in one place for long. He longs for death, but cannot die; even if he throws himself into a river, the waters refuse to drown him. He has long ago repented of his sin, and become a converted Christian; and by telling his story wherever he goes he witnesses to the truth of Christianity, having been an eye-witness of the Crucifixion and personally assured by Christ of the Second Coming.

In this form, the legend clearly embodies a Christian wish-fulfilment. It expresses the desire that the Jews will accept the role assigned to them in the Christian myth. The push given to Jesus by Ahasuerus symbolizes his participation in the execution and his involvement in the guilt of the Jewish people. The Wandering

Jew, therefore (as has always been realized), symbolizes the Jewish people as a whole, and his wanderings are nothing less than the weary exile of the Jews, with their constant expulsions even from places like Spain where they had made a priceless contribution to the culture and well-being of the host nation. The prolonged life of the Wandering Jew symbolizes also the miraculous survival of the Jews, ascribed by Christians not to the strength of Jewish identity and culture, but to the desire of God to prolong their agony until the time of the millennium. But these two elements—the wandering and the prolongation of life—are, as we have seen, features of the Sacred Executioner. Cain, too, was a wanderer, and was given a charmed life. For the early death of the Sacred Executioner would remove his saving power; there would be no one to bear the sins of the community, and particularly to bear the guilt arising from the continuing efficacy of the divine sacrifice.

Finally, the "waiting" of the Wandering Jew for the Second Coming of Jesus echoes the waiting of the Jews in the Christian myth, in which the millennium cannot occur without their participation. This aspect no doubt accounts for the sudden popularity of the legend in the seventeenth century, a time of millennial expectations throughout Europe (even among the Jews themselves). The proliferating stories of the appearances of the Wandering Jew in various European towns would heighten the hopes of the imminent Second Coming of Christ.

But in Christian eyes the legend of the Wandering Jew was more than merely a symbol of the sufferings of the Jews themselves: there was also the idea of the Wandering Jew's belief in Christianity. This was the expression of a fervent wish, not merely that the Jews would become converted, but that, like the Wandering Jew, they would acknowledge their guilt for the death of Jesus and accept as deserved the consequent sufferings heaped upon them in Christendom. If this were to happen, the time for the millennium would have arrived—not that the conversion of the Jews would actually bring about the millennium, but it would show that the millennium was at hand. For the millennium, as we shall see shortly, is that period in which the function of the Jews as Sacred Executioner is no longer necessary.

But before pursuing this important aspect, it must be pointed

out that the version of the Wandering Jew legend just described is
not the only one. Other versions existed (especially in Germany)
which lacked the positive hope of reconciliation. In those negative
versions, the sufferings of the Wandering Jew are seen merely as
just punishment for his depravity. He is not a convert to Christianity, but an unregenerate Jew, with evil magic powers derived
from his long experience of life and his association with the Devil.
It was this negative version that gave rise to the nineteenth-century anti-Semitic stereotype, taken up with enthusiasm by the
Nazis, of the Jew as a "rootless cosmopolitan"—an interpretation
that sometimes took the form of a theory that the Jews were
essentially nomads, who had invaded Palestine from the desert
and remained at heart creatures of the desert.[2] This was something
of a twist, since in this development the wanderings of the Wandering Jew became part of his nature rather than his punishment.
In the negative Christian stereotype (which the Nazis were giving
a would-be anthropological interpretation) the restlessness of the
Wandering Jew is a kind of neurotic affliction which impels him
from country to country, an idea partly derived from the figure
of Herod in the medieval Passion Plays, who was presented as
suffering from an inability to remain still, his whole body continually in motion. This portrayal of Jews persists as far as the nineteenth-century novel.[3]

In these negative versions, the wanderings of the Jews were held
against them as indicative of their evil nature. But the Jews did
not actually wander because they wanted to, or because they were
in the grip of a neurosis, but because they were forced to. In
Germany, in particular, the Jews were not allowed to remain in
any place for long, but were continually harried into moving on.
Yet it was particularly in Germany that the Wandering Jew was
portrayed as an inveterate nomad. The wanderings of the Jews are
the antithesis of the wanderings of a nomadic people such as the
Gypsies. The Jews regarded themselves as in exile, from their
settled home Palestine, to which they would eventually return
when they had expiated the sins for which the exile was a punishment. Their intense love of home showed itself in their love for
any place where they were allowed to settle for any length of time,
so that when the inevitable expulsion eventually came it was ex-

perienced as an exile within the great exile. The nostalgia of the
Jews for Spain, for Poland, and even for Germany, remains even
today—even in Jews who have returned to the Promised Land!
The Jews, indeed, have always been great travellers, but there is a
great distinction to be made between travellers and nomads. The
aim of a traveller is always to return home.

In the negative versions of the Wandering Jew legend, the prolonged life of the Wandering Jew was also given a hostile conno-
tation: it meant that the Jew was an eternal plague. In Germany
the immortality of the Jew was stressed, rather than his wandering, in the appellation *'der ewige Jude'*; but the question that it
posed was, 'Will this nuisance never have an end?'

In the positive version of the Wandering Jew legend, a happy
outcome of the Jewish problem is envisaged. Because he has acknowledged his guilt for the Crucifixion, the Wandering Jew can
be regarded by the Christian clientele of this legend without
hatred, even with a certain reverence. The Wandering Jew is in all
respects an example of the Sacred Executioner, but one who will-
ingly embraces his misery and thus functions as the perfect bearer
of the guilt of the Christian community. He contrasts remarkably
with the medieval picture of the Jew as a ghoulish, demonic figure
abducting Christian children, mutilating the Host or poisoning
wells. The hatred expressed in the medieval picture may arise
partly from the refusal of the Jews to accept the role assigned to
them in the Christian myth, whereas the Wandering Jew legend
gives conscious expression to the way that, in Christian eyes, the
Jews ought to behave. This kind of penitent, sad Jew, meekly
accepting his sufferings as his destined and deserved lot, could be
regarded by Christians with something approaching friendliness.
The actual Jews, however, who insisted on pursuing their own
life and religious culture in complete oblivion to Christian require-
ments, seizing with both hands any temporary respite and opportunity for happiness and prosperity, and wondering only why
Christians would not let them alone, had to be persecuted and
degraded and regarded as fiends, since they wilfully refused to
understand the part they were supposed to play. Even the positive
version of the Wandering Jew legend, therefore, does not really
offer much hope of satisfactory Jewish-Christian relations, since it

demands of the Jews a drastic change in their self-image, by which they would regard themselves as primarily actors in the Christian myth rather than as the bearers of a religious tradition and myth of their own where *they* are the principal actors and heroes, not the foil and repentant villain. Some Christians today have seized on an image not unlike that of the Wandering Jew as a means of avoiding anti-Semitism: the Jews are to be regarded with pity and awe as enacting a God-given role within the Christian myth.[4] Such an attitude, however, is only too likely to revert to the crudest hostility when it is realized that the Jews are not in the least interested in the offered role.

It was mainly the positive version of the Wandering Jew legend that was the basis for the treatment of the Wandering Jew in Romantic literature. Yet the Wandering Jew, as found in Romantic poetry from Christian Daniel Schubart to Shelley, or in the novels of Monk Lewis, Godwin, Bulwer Lytton, and Sue, has little to do with the present study. The Romantic writers were not interested in the sacrificial aspects of the Wandering Jew, seeing him as a victim rather than as a sacrificer. They saw him as one more example of the Romantic hero—a wandering hero, isolated from normal society, expiating some crime which, in the last resort, was a praiseworthy act of rebellion against a tyrannous authority. Thus Shelley sees the Wandering Jew as a kind of Prometheus and even denounces the Crucifixion as a fraud by which two divine tyrants, father and son, impose their authority on mankind.[5] Alternatively, the Romantics might see the Wandering Jew as guilty of a real crime, but one that had heroic quality, since it introduced him to a new dimension of knowledge beyond the range of ordinary mankind. This is to assimilate the Wandering Jew to Adam, or Teiresias, or Faust, heroes who buy knowledge at the expense of some degree of damnation. Thus the Romantic writers take the Wandering Jew outside his true context of the Christian myth and the conflict between Christianity and Judaism. By universalizing him they falsify him, and make him just one more peg for the concept of the anti-bourgeois hero, like the Flying Dutchman or Byron's Corsair. They turn him into an individualist who has sharpened his sense of individuality through sin, while it is the essence of the Wandering Jew in the authentic legend that he is not an individualist, however lonely his suffering, but a figure that has an expiatory role in relation to the Christian community. (Actually, the Romantic character that is nearest to the authentic Wandering Jew is Coleridge's Ancient Mariner.)

There is an interesting exception to be found in T. S. Eliot's poem "Gerontion," in which the figure of the "jew" is almost certainly modelled on the *negative* version of the Wandering Jew legend. The "jew" is a wanderer, a "rootless cosmopolitan," "spawned in some estaminet of Antwerp, /Blistered in Brussels, patched and peeled in London." The old age of the "jew" is compared to the dilapidated state of the decaying house and is regarded not as something miraculous, but negatively, as Jewish remoteness from the values of youth, symbolized in the youthful death of Christ and in other images of youthful violent death ("the hot gates," that is, Thermopylae, where the army of young Spartans died a sacrificial death). Thus, in Eliot's poem the Wandering Jew with his inability to die is not a Romantic hero, as in Shelley, but the exact opposite, a symbol of anti-Romanticism, the withering of the soul that comes from the refusal to accept the revivifying force of sacrificial death. Eliot was well aware of the connections between Christianity and pagan cults of human sacrifice, and also of the connections of both with the youth-worship of Romanticism.[6] His version of the Wandering Jew has much in common with that of a movement that must be regarded as belonging to the darker side of the history of Romanticism, namely, Nazism.

It was certainly the negative version of the Wandering Jew legend that was adopted in nineteenth-century anti-Semitism and in its successor, Nazism. The possibility of regeneration for the Jews through repentance, found in the positive version, was ruled out completely by the racialist doctrine. The Wandering Jew was a wanderer in the sense that he had no attachment to any human group, but was the common enemy and scourge of mankind in all his settled habitations. The detailed picture of the Jew was built up from medieval sources: the blood-sucking usurer, the murderer of children, the enemy of chastity, the poisoner of wells, the fiend in barely human shape. In addition there was the fantasy of the Elders of Zion, according to which the Jews had a highly organized international network, governed by a central body, the

Elders of Zion, dedicated to the overthrow of all Gentile civilization and to the domination of the whole world by the Jews, to
which end different policies were employed in different contexts,
so that the Jews could be accused of being the moving force of
both capitalism and communism.[7] Even this fantasy of a worldwide Jewish conspiracy had its medieval source in the blood-libel
stories which portrayed the Jews as meeting in international conclave to decide where the next child sacrifice would take place.

Yet in general it can be said that nineteenth-century racialist
anti-Semitism has departed from its Christian origins in providing
no safeguard or loophole for Jewish survival. It was the hope of
the millennial conversion of the Jews that preserved them in
Christendom at times when they came close to annihilation. Thus
modern anti-Semitism has all the negative aspects of Christian
anti-Semitism without any of its restraints. From Christianity it
derived the picture of the Jews as the people of the Devil; but it
jettisoned the Christian idea that the Devil too has his place in the
scheme of things. Thus, dangerous as Christianity was to the
Jews, the move from Christian to post-Christian society was even
more dangerous. For post-Christian society, while believing itself
to be secular, retains all the deepest and most irrational prejudices
of Christianity while freeing itself of the moral and mythopoeic
checks by which Christianity exerts some moderating influence
on these prejudices.

Yet is it quite true to say that Christianity provided no model
for the plan of completely exterminating the Jews? While it is true
that the scenario of the millennial conversion of the Jews rules out
such a plan, medieval and Renaissance Christianity contained an
alternative scenario that did indeed contemplate the extermination
of the Jews. This is the myth of the Antichrist. Here we have a
picture of what would happen at the time of the millennium that
contradicts the eirenic concept of the conversion of the Jews and
its attendant legend of the Wandering Jew, and substitutes a paranoiac, dualistic scheme which implements the hysterical medieval
Jew-phobia and foreshadows the mass extermination programmes
of the Nazis.

The apocalyptic fantasy of the Antichrist, in its most influential form, runs as follows.[8] In the last days, a man would appear who would lead the armies of the Devil against the armies of Christ. This man, the Antichrist, would be a Jew, and his chief supporters would be the Jews. He would be a kind of demonic parody of Christ himself, for he would be born through the impregnation of a Jewish harlot by the Devil himself. He would be born in Babylon, but would proceed to Palestine where he would be instructed in the black arts. He would achieve great success, and would rebuild the Jewish Temple and reign over a Jewish empire which would comprise the whole world. But at the point of his greatest success the Second Coming of the true Christ would occur. Christ would lead the Christian armies against the Antichrist, who would be defeated, and all his supporters including the entire Jewish people would be annihilated. Part of the demonic forces thus defeated would be the Lost Ten Tribes of Israel, who would appear from their remote retreat to take part in the triumph of the Jewish empire and be defeated in its ultimate overthrow.

This extraordinary vision of future events had its main adherents among the populace rather than among the leading thinkers of Christendom. Indeed, the belief in the coming of the Antichrist was sometimes turned against the official leadership of Christendom, for popular movements of discontent sometimes identified the pope himself as the Antichrist and the officials of the Church, rather than the Jews, as his army. But the prevailing theory was that it was indeed the Jews who would form the army of the Antichrist, and this belief became particularly strong at times of millennial excitement. The widespread massacres of Jews by a frenzied populace at the time of the Crusades, for example, were partly actuated by the identification of the Jews with the Antichrist. The Muslims too, against whom the Crusaders fought, were regarded as armies of the Antichrist, but to the Christian populace the Muslims were hardly differentiated from the Jews, and were even widely regarded as the Oriental hordes of the Lost Ten Tribes (the "Red Jews") who formed one of the nightmare images in the medieval mind. Even Christian leaders were not above such fantasies, as was shown by the almost incredible episode of the impostor David Reubeni, who in 1524 was given audience by the pope and treated with great fear and honour, on the pretense of being the ambassador of an Oriental Jewish empire—the realm of the Lost Ten Tribes.[9]

The myth of the Antichrist was thus a millennial notion based on a belief in the Jews as a powerful, dangerous political entity. The Wandering Jew legend, on the other hand, was based on the much more factual premise that the Jews were helpless and downtrodden, beaten into submission by their sufferings. Both myths were visions of the millennium, but of very different kinds: one envisaged a time of reconciliation, while the other a time of violence, worldwide battles and the final annihilation of a fearsome enemy. Both, it may be added, envisaged a time when the continued existence of the Jews would not be necessary: in the Wandering Jew legend because the Jews would be allowed to expiate their sin at last and find oblivion in the bosom of the Church, and in the Antichrist myth because the reign of the Devil would at last be over, and his allies the Jews would share his downfall and disappearance. In the Antichrist myth, the necessary role of the Devil as Sacred Executioner is lost sight of; he is regarded as merely the old power of evil, engaged in perpetual combat with the Light, but destined eventually to be defeated by it. This is essentially a Gnostic conception. The Wandering Jew legend, however, retains the idea that the existence of the Jews is necessary: the Wandering Jew is an essential witness and a harbinger of the millennium. Though his sin itself is not consciously acknowledged to be necessary, the sympathy and awe with which he is regarded give him the aura of the Sacred Executioner. Christianity, as we have seen, was formed by a combination between Gnosticism and the salvation doctrine of the mystery religions. This double strand persists throughout the history of Christianity. When the salvation doctrine of the necessary sacrifice predominates, the Jew retains some sanctity. When the sheer dualism of Gnosticism predominates, the Jew becomes a demon, and his annihilation becomes a desideratum. He is no longer in any sense a representative of the Christian community.

Even the Gnostic Christian, however, may regard the Jew as a necessary evil, like the Devil himself, in the sense that evil in this world is inevitable. But once it is believed that the millennium has already started, the last vestige of this necessity vanishes. That is why millennial movements associated with the doctrine of the Antichrist soon lead to massacres of Jews of a radical kind. The massacres at the time of the Crusades were on a scale hitherto unknown in Christendom.[10] They should be regarded as the precursors of the mass extermination programme of that modern millennial movement, Nazism.

NOTES

1. See J. Gaer, *The Legend of the Wandering Jew* (New York, 1961); Edgar Rosenberg, *From Shylock to Svengali: Jewish Stereotypes in English Fiction* (London, 1961); and G. K. Anderson, *The Legend of the Wandering Jew* (Providence, 1965).

2. For example, Werner Sombart, who argued that the alleged desert philosophy of the Jews was responsible for modern capitalism. See Werner Sombart, *The Jews and Modern Capitalism* (London, 1913), pp. 324–51, where all the ingredients of this type of anti–Semitic theory can be found.

3. See Rosenberg, pp. 320–24.

4. This attitude was initiated by Paul in Romans 11:28, "they are treated as enemies for your sake." This is called by Paul a "secret," or "mystery." Modern exponents of the view are Leon Bloy, Nicholas Berdyaev and Malcolm Muggeridge. There has been a temptation to some Jews to accept the offer of this role as awesome, wandering bearers of the guilt of mankind (e.g., Disraeli, George Steiner, Leo Abse), since such a romantic posture seems preferable to the boring, if realistic, position of being the irritated victim of paranoid fantasies.

5. See Shelley's *Queen Mab*, Canto vii, and *Hellas*; also his earlier treatment of the theme in *St. Irvyne* and "The Victim of the Eternal Avenger."

6. See Hyam Maccoby, "A Study of the 'jew' in 'Gerontion,' " *Jewish Quarterly*, 17, No. 2 (1969).

7. See Norman Cohn, *Warrant for Genocide: The Myth of the Jewish World-conspiracy and the Protocols of the Elders of Zion* (London, 1967).

8. See Wilhelm Bousset, *Der Antichrist in der Überlieferung des Judentums, des neuen Testaments und der alten Kirche* (Göttingen, 1893). Eng. tr. *The Antichrist Legend* (London, 1896); Bousset, "Antichrist," *Encyclopaedia of Religion and Ethics*, I (1908), pp. 578–81; Bousset, "Antichrist," *Encyclopaedia Britannica*, II (1947), p. 61; and H. Preuss, *Die Vorstellung von Antichrist im späteren Mittelalter* (Leipzig, 1906).

9. See Cecil Roth, "David Reubeni," *Midstream*, 9 (1963): 76–81; E. N. Adler, *Jewish Travellers* (London, 1930); and the *Encyclopaedia Judaica*, XIV, pp. 114–16.

10. See Salo W. Baron, *A Social and Religious History of the Jews*, Vol. IV (New York, 1957), chapter 21; and Léon Poliakov, *The History of Antisemitism*, Vol. I, Pt. II (London, 1974).

APPENDIX

Gustave Doré's Depictions of the Wandering Jew
Reproduced through the courtesy of the Bancroft Library,
University of California, Berkeley.

Since thou art pitiless, thy weary way
Thou'rt doom'd to wander till Judgement Day.

Too late he feels, by look, and deed, and word,
How often he has crucified his Lord.

Spell-bound, they gather far and near to scan
The weird senescence of that wondrous man.

The end releases other men from strife;
His fate is ceaseless toil and deathless life.

Now when fantastic visions fill the air,
Sorrow surrenders to a dull despair.

Transfix'd with awe, he feels his God is nigh;
And, conscience-stricken, looks on Calvary.

Secure he stands, and fearless gazes round,
Where arrows fall and corpses strew the ground.

On thro' the storm he speeds, 'midst drowning cries,
Whilst helpless vessels sink before his eyes.

Trees intertwined with snakes he walks beneath,
Safe thro' dark valleys ripe with hideous death.

The Judgement Day! He hears the trumpet's blast;
And, prostrate, owns his Saviour's love at last.

SUGGESTIONS FOR FURTHER READING
ON THE WANDERING JEW:
A SELECTED BIBLIOGRAPHY

A complete bibliography listing all known texts, oral and literary, plus all the popular and scholarly articles and monographs on the subject would probably need to include more than 3000 entries. More than 2000 may be found simply by consulting the works of Neubaur, Gielen, Anderson, and Knecht. In the following selected bibliography, we have restricted ourselves to enumerating representative major scholarly treatments of the legend beginning with the late nineteenth century. Consistent with the bias in this volume, we have tended to favor the inclusion of works which treat the oral versions of the legend (as opposed to the many discussions limited to purely literary texts).

Anderson, George K.
    1963   "The Legend of the Wandering Jew." *Books at Brown*, 19:143–59. A preliminary survey of the earliest accounts of the legend as well as some of the major literary renderings. This essay was superseded by his 1965 magnum opus.

    1965   *The Legend of the Wandering Jew*. Providence: Brown University Press. 489pp. The definitive account of the legend, its literary forms, and the history of the scholarship devoted to it. (For the latter, see especially Appendix A: Notes on the Study of the Legend, pp. 399–413.)

Ariste, Paul
    1934   "Jaan Bergmann'i 'Igavene Juut.' " *Eesti Kirjandus*, 28:271–74. A discussion of Estonian writer Jaan Bergmaan's treatment of the theme.

Auguet, Roland
    1977   *Le juif errant*. Paris: Payot. 194pp. A sensible overview of the legend and its significance, careful to distinguish between folklore produced *by* a people and literary versions produced *for* the people. Standard sources are in the bibliography, but individual citations are not footnoted.

Bataillon, Marcel
1941 "Pérégrinations espagnoles du Juif errant." *Bulletin Hispanique*, 43:81–122. A useful account of the Wandering Jew in Spain.

Bitton, Livia
1975 "The Names of the Wandering Jew." *Literary Onomastics Studies*, 2:169–80. An inventory of the various names attributed to the figure of the Wandering Jew with no formal reference to the scholarship.

Briggs, Katharine M.
1981 "The Legends of Lilith and of the Wandering Jew in Nineteenth-Century Literature." *Folklore*, 92:132–40. A brief account of several versions of the legend.

Champfleury [Jules Fleury]
1864 "D'Une Nouvelle Interprétation de la légende gothique du Juif-errant." *Revue Germanique et Française*, 30:299–325. A helpful compilation of mainly chapbook versions with a brief section on the iconography of the legend (318–25) which was precursor of his later book on the subject, *Histoire de l'imagerie populaire* (Paris: E. Dentu, 1869) [for the Wandering Jew, see pp. 1–104].

Cornioley, Hans
1949 "Der Ewige Jude." *Der Psychologe*, 1(3):89–96. After a brief review of mostly literary occurrences, the legend is interpreted from the perspective of individual psychology.

Dal, Erik
1964 "Ahasverus in Danemark: Volksbuch, Volkslieder und Verwandtes." *Jahrbuch für Volksliedforschung*, 9:144–70. An extensively documented discussion of the Danish broadside ballad and chapbook versions of the legend.
1965 "Ahasverus, Den evige jøde: Sagnet i Dansk og Tysk Folkedigtning." *Fund og Forskning i Det Kongelige Biblioteks Samlinger*, 12:31–42. An abbreviated form of his 1964 essay in which he attempts to trace the sources of Danish literary versions of the legend back to broadside and chapbook traditions including the German Volksbuch sources. Dal's article is followed by a short discussion (pp. 42–46) by R. Edelmann on the origin and background of the legend.

Danilevskij, R. Ju.
1976 " 'Moskovskij' episod v nemeckoj narodnoj knige ob Agasfere." In E. A. Smirnova, ed., *Sravnitel'noe izucenie literatur.* Leningrad: Nauka. Pp. 69–73. A consideration of reports of the appearance of the Wandering Jew in Moscow.

Dübi, Heinrich
1907   "Drei spätmittelalterliche Legenden in ihrer Wanderung aus It-
       alien durch die Schweiz nach Deutschland, 2. Vom Ewigen
       Juden." *Zeitschrift des Vereins für Volkskunde*, 17:143–60. An im-
       portant consideration of Swiss oral versions of the legend as a
       link between Italian and German traditions.

Edmunds, Albert J.
1913   "The Wandering Jew: His Probable Buddhist Origin." *Notes
       and Queries*, NS 7 (Jan. 18, 1913), 47. A short note proposing a
       Buddhist source on the basis of a suggested similarity between
       the names Buddha and Buttadeo.

Együd, Árpád
1980   "A bolygó zsidó mondája a somogyi néphagyományban." *Év-
       könyv, 1979–1980, Izraelita Magyar Irodalmi Társulat kiadványai*
       (Budapest):126–43. A survey of three Hungarian legend texts
       plus musical versions referring to a calendar custom "Rich-man
       play" known in the eighteenth century.

Gaer, Joseph
1961   *The Legend of the Wandering Jew*. New York: New American
       Library. 159pp. A popular, unscholarly account.

Gielen, Josephus Johannes
1931   *De wandelende Jood in Volkskunde en Letterkunde*. Amsterdam:
       De Spieghel. 254pp. A bibliographically comprehensive treat-
       ment of the European tradition including a consideration of the
       rarely discussed Dutch and Flemish materials.

Gillet, Joseph E.
1931   "Traces of the Wandering Jew in Spain." *Romanic Review*,
       22:16–27. The most useful gathering of Spanish materials prior
       to Bataillon's 1941 essay.

Glaesener, Henri
1931   "Le Type d'Ahasvérus aux XVIIIe and XIXe siècles." *Revue de
       Littérature Comparée*, 11:373–97. A comparison of the European
       literary characterizations of the legendary figure.

Haavio, Martti
1933   " 'Minä näin': Erään 'lappalais-suomalaisen kansanrunon' taus-
       taa." *Suomi*, 5:16:120–30. Explicates the meaning of an escha-
       tological motif in a Lappish ballad by comparing it with a
       Finnish broadside version of the Wandering Jew.

Heggenes, Eivind
  1938 "Folkesegna um Ahasverus, Den evige jøden." *Syn og Segn*, 44:321–27. An unsystematic comparison of several versions including oral Norwegian ones and a Mormon newspaper account of 1868.

Killen, Alice M.
  1925 "L'Évolution de la légende du Juif errant." *Revue de Littérature Comparée*, 5:5–36. One of the better general overall surveys including coverage of French and Italian sources.

Knecht, Edgar
  1974 "Le Mythe du Juif errant: Esquisse de bibliographie raisonée (1600–1844)." *Romantisme: Revue de la Société des Études romantiques*, 8:103–16. The first of a three part chronologically organized annotated bibliography of literary texts and scholarship, mostly from France, Germany, and England. A numerical shorthand code signals features in each entry, e.g., classic chronicle, legendary account, romanticized account, incarnation of Jews, scholarly study, etc.
  1975 "Le Juif errant. Éléments d'un mythe populaire." *Romantisme*, 9:84–96. Using a literary definition of myth, the author describes the transformation of the legend into such a myth.
  1976 "Le Mythe du Juif errant." *Romantisme*, 12:95–102. A continuation of the annotated bibliography covering the period from 1844—the year of the publication of Eugene Sue's *Le Juif errant*—to 1861.
  1977a "Le Mythe du Juif errant." *Romantisme*, 16:101–15. The final part of the annotated bibliography with coverage from 1862 to 1960. This three part bibliography constitutes an important updating of the earlier compilations by Neubaur, Gielen and Anderson.
  1977b *Le Mythe du Juif errant: Essai de mythologie litteraire et de sociologie religieuse.* Grenoble: Presses Universitaires de Grenoble. 351pp. An expansion of the argument contained in his 1975 essay with extensive discussion of mainly literary sources, especially in the French tradition, seeing the figure of the Wandering Jew on the one hand as a metaphor for the individual and on the other as a symbol for the Jewish people.

Leschnitzer, Adolf
  1962 "Der Gestaltwandel Ahasvers." In *In zwei Welten: Siegfried Moses zum 75th Geburtstag*. Tel-Aviv: Verlag Bitaon. Pp. 470–505. An earlier, longer version of the paper included in the present volume.

Lewinsky, Yom-Tov
  1926, 1927   "Ha-yehudi ha-nitshi be-aggadat ha-belgim [The Wan-
               dering Jew in Belgian Legend]." *Moznaim*, 1 (Dec. 1926):
               10–13; 2 (Jan. 1927): 17–20. Briefly mentions the Belgian
               chapbook tradition.

Morpurgo, S.
  1891   *L'Ebreo Errante in Italia*. Firenze: Libreria Dante. 54pp. Reprints
          an Italian text considerably earlier than the German chapbook
          of 1602, which is followed by a short comparative discussion.

Neubaur, Leonhard
  1893a   *Die Sage vom ewigen Juden*. Leipzig: J. C. Hinrichs. 156pp. The
           first edition of this major scholar's work appeared in 1884.
           Neubaur's bibliographical research has formed the basis for
           nearly all modern studies of the legend. He continued to pub-
           lish notes and bibliographical addenda on the subject.
  1893b   "Bibliographie der Sage vom ewigen Juden." *Zentralblatt für
           Bibliothekswesen*, 10:249–67; 297–316. The first of several im-
           portant bibliographical compilations.

  1911   "Zur Bibliographie der Sage vom ewigen Juden." *Zentralblatt
          für Bibliothekswesen*, 28:495–509. Further references on the leg-
          end.
  1912   "Zur Geschichte der Sage vom ewigen Juden." *Zeitschrift des
          Vereins für Volkskunde*, 22:33–54. Unlike the majority of his
          contemporaries, Neubaur concentrated on the chapbook and
          oral versions of the legend. In this essay, he traces the early
          development of the tradition.
  1914   "Zur Geschichte und Bibliographie des Volksbuchs von Ahas-
          verus." *Zeitschrift für Bücherfreunde*, N.F. 5(2):211–23. A further
          detailed enumeration of primarily German chapbook editions.
  1917   "Einige Bemerkungen zur Sage vom Ewigen Juden." *Zeit-
          schrift für Bücherfreunde*, N.F. 9(1):310–13. Additional data relat-
          ing to the history of the legend.

Paris, Gaston
  1903   *Légendes du Moyen Age*. Paris: Librairie Hachette. A section
          devoted to the Wandering Jew (pp. 149–221) reprints two ear-
          lier essays by this distinguished literary scholar, essays which
          were first published in 1880 and 1891. Paris is interested in
          medieval versions which antedate the German chapbook tradi-
          tion, with particular reference to the various names given to the
          figure.

Prost, Johann
  1905   *Die Sage vom ewigen Juden in der neueren deutschen Literatur*. Leipzig: Verlag von Georg Wigand. 167pp. A review of German literary texts and criticism.

Rappaport, Ernest A.
  1975   *Anti-Judaism: A Psychohistory*. Chicago: Perspective Press. 312pp. Chapter 5 (pp. 80–93), entitled "A Legend to Prove a Legend," treats the Wandering Jew narrative in terms of its verifying and authenticating "the legend of the crucified Christ" for sceptical Christians.

Rosenman, Stanley
  1979   "The American Nazi and the Wandering Jew." *American Journal of Psychoanalysis*, 39:363–68. Attempts to relate the positive and negative aspects of the Wandering Jew with ambivalent attitudes towards Jews in Nazi Germany and postwar America with special reference to the moral implications of the stereotype of the Jew passively accepting his fate.

Satrústegui, José María
  1975   El cantar de 'El Judío Errante.' *Fontes Lingvae Vasconvm: stvdia et docvmenta*, 7:339–61. A survey of the Basque song tradition of the Wandering Jew.

Scheiber, Alexander
  1954   "The Legend of the Wandering Jew in Hungary." *Midwest Folklore*, 4:221–35. Presents references and some texts of Hungarian literary and oral versions of the legend.
  1956   "Additions to the History of the Legend of the Wandering Jew in Hungary." *Midwest Folklore*, 6:155–58. Cites several more literary and oral versions.

Taylor, Archer
  1918   "Notes on the Wandering Jew." *Modern Language Notes*, 33:394–98. A brief discussion of a possible source for an illusion in an O. Henry short story, "Door of Unrest," followed by bibliographical references in many languages.

Vasconcellos, Carolina Michaelis de
  1887   "O Judeu errante em Portugal." *Revista Lusitana*, 1:34–44. A survey of oral and literary Portuguese texts.

Wesselofsky, A.
  1881   "Der ewige Jude." *Archiv für Slavische Philologie*, 5:398–401. A short discussion of early literary texts is followed by an inter-

esting suggestion of parallelism between the Wandering Jew and the phases of the moon. Both seem to be dying, but are invariably rejuvenated.

1885 "Der ewige Jude." *Archiv für Slavische Philologie*, 8:331–33. Further references to the legend.

Yarmolinsky, Avrahm

1929 "The Wandering Jew: A Contribution Toward the Slavonic Bibliography of the Legend." In *Studies in Jewish Bibliography and Related Subjects in Memory of Abraham Solomon Freidus (1867–1923)*. New York: Alexander Kohut Memorial Foundation. Pp. 319–28. A valuable, annotated listing of Czech, Polish, and Russian literary versions of the legend with a few oral texts.

Zirus, Werner

1928 *Der ewige Jude in der Dichtung, vornehmlich in der englischen und deutschen*. *Palaestra* 162. Leipzig: Mayer & Müller. 159pp. A review of English and German literary occurrences of the Wandering Jew motif.

1930 *Ahasverus, Der Ewige Jude, Stoff- und Motifgeschichte der Deutschen Literatur* 6. Berlin: Walter De Gruyter. 77pp. A systematic account of the poetic functions of the Ahasverus figure in mostly German poems, plays, and novels.